Magento 2 Developer's

Harness the power of Magento 2, the most recent version of the world's favorite e-commerce platform, for your online store

Branko Ajzele

PUBLISHING

BIRMINGHAM - MUMBAI

Magento 2 Developer's Guide

First published: December 2015

Production reference: 1171215

Published by Packt Publishing Ltd.
Livery Place
35 Livery Street
Birmingham B3 2PB, UK.

ISBN 978-1-78588-658-4

www.packtpub.com

Credits

Author
Branko Ajzele

Reviewer
Mitchell Robles, Jr

Commissioning Editor
Neil Alexander

Acquisition Editor
Vinay Argekar

Content Development Editor
Preeti Singh

Technical Editor
Gaurav Suri

Copy Editors
Vedangi Narvekar
Jonathan Todd

Project Coordinator
Shweta H. Birwatkar

Proofreader
Safis Editing

Indexer
Priya Sane

Production Coordinator
Shantanu N. Zagade

Cover Work
Shantanu N. Zagade

About the Author

Branko Ajzele is a husband, father of two, son, brother, author, and a software developer.

He has a degree in electrical engineering. A lover of all things digital, he makes a living from software development. He hopes to find enough quality time some day to seriously dive into hobby electronics; he has his eye on Arduino and Raspberry Pi.

He has years of hands-on experience with full-time software development and team management, and has specializing in e-commerce platforms. He has been working with Magento since 2008; he has been knee-deep in it since its very first beta version. Branko is regularly in touch with everything related to PHP, databases (MySQL/MongoDB), search/analytics (Solr/Elasticsearch), Node.js, and related technologies.

He has a strong technical knowledge with an ability to communicate those technicalities frequently and clearly with a strong direction. He feels comfortable proposing alternatives to demands which he feels can be improved, even when this means pulling a late shift to meet the deadlines.

He holds several respected IT certifications, such as Zend Certified Engineer (ZCE PHP), Magento Certified Developer (MCD), Magento Certified Developer Plus (MCD+), Magento Certified Solution Specialist (MCSS), and JavaScript Certified Developer.

Instant E-Commerce with Magento: Build a Shop, Packt Publishing, was his first Magento-related book that was oriented towards Magento newcomers. After writing this book, he wrote *Getting Started with Magento Extension Development* for developers.

Currently, he works as a full-time contractor for Lab Lateral Ltd, an award-winning team of innovative thinkers, artists, and developers who specialize in customer-centric websites, digital consultancy, and marketing. He is the Lead Magento Developer and Head of Lab's Croatia office.

He was awarded the *E-Commerce Developer of the Year* by Digital Entrepreneur Awards in October 2014 for his excellent knowledge and expertise in e-commerce development. His work is second to none. He is truly dedicated to helping the Lab Lateral Ltd team and his fellow developers across the world.

About the Reviewer

Mitchell Robles, Jr, is a solutions architect and applications engineer who has worked in various lead roles for several award-winning digital agencies in San Diego, CA, USA. Through his own entrepreneurial spirit, he founded Mojo Creative & Technical Solutions (for more information, visit `http://www.mojomage.com/`), which specializes in day-to-day Magento support and development for merchants, agencies, freelancers, and industry partners. As a certified Magento developer, Mitchell is the brainchild and lead in developing several must-have Magento extensions, including Mojo Creative & Technical Solutions' Bundled Mojo, a popular, full-featured Magento extension that gives administrators total control over how they display and sell their bundled products. When he is not in the digital matrix, Mitchell enjoys traveling abroad, exploring, skateboarding, scuba diving, and tinkering with random projects, from woodworking to 3D printing.

You can follow Mitchell on the Mojo Creative & Technical Solutions' blog, which can be viewed by visiting `http://b.mojomage.com/`.

www.PacktPub.com

Support files, eBooks, discount offers, and more

For support files and downloads related to your book, please visit www.PacktPub.com.

Did you know that Packt offers eBook versions of every book published, with PDF and ePub files available? You can upgrade to the eBook version at www.PacktPub.com and as a print book customer, you are entitled to a discount on the eBook copy. Get in touch with us at service@packtpub.com for more details.

At www.PacktPub.com, you can also read a collection of free technical articles, sign up for a range of free newsletters and receive exclusive discounts and offers on Packt books and eBooks.

https://www2.packtpub.com/books/subscription/packtlib

Do you need instant solutions to your IT questions? PacktLib is Packt's online digital book library. Here, you can search, access, and read Packt's entire library of books.

Why subscribe?
- Fully searchable across every book published by Packt
- Copy and paste, print, and bookmark content
- On demand and accessible via a web browser

Free access for Packt account holders

If you have an account with Packt at www.PacktPub.com, you can use this to access PacktLib today and view 9 entirely free books. Simply use your login credentials for immediate access.

Table of Contents

Preface

Building Magento-powered stores can be a challenging task. It requires a great range of technical skills that are related to the PHP/JavaScript programing language, development and production environments, and numerous Magento-specific features. This book will provide necessary insights into the building blocks of Magento.

By the end of this book, you should be familiar with configuration files, the dependency injection, models, collections, blocks, controllers, events, observers, plugins, cron jobs, shipping methods, payment methods, and a few other things. All of these should form a solid foundation for your development journey later on.

What this book covers

Chapter 1, Understanding the Platform Architecture, gives a high-level overview of the technology stack, architectural layers, top-level system structure, and individual module structure.

Chapter 2, Managing the Environment, gives an introduction to VirtualBox, Vagrant, and Amazon AWS as platforms to set up development and production environments. It further provides hands-on examples to set up/script Vagrant and Amazon EC2 boxes.

Chapter 3, Programing Concepts and Conventions, introduces readers to a few seemingly unrelated but important parts of Magento, such as composer, service contracts, code generation, the var directory, and finally, coding standards.

Chapter 4, Models and Collections, takes a look into models, resources, collections, schemas, and data scripts. It also shows the practical CRUD actions that are applied to an entity alongside filtering collections.

Chapter 5, Using the Dependency Injection, guides readers through the dependency injection mechanism. It explains the role of an object manager, how to configure class preferences, and how to use virtual types.

Chapter 6, Plugins, gives a detailed insight into the powerful new concept called plugins. It shows how easy it is to extend, or add to, an existing functionality using the before/after/around listeners.

Chapter 7, Backend Development, takes readers through a hands-on approach to what is mostly considered backend-related development bits. These involve cron jobs, notification messages, sessions, cookies, logging, profiler, events, cache, widgets, and so on.

Chapter 8, Frontend Development, uses a higher-level approach to guide the reader through what is mostly considered frontend-related development. It touches on rendering the flow, view elements, blocks, templates, layouts, themes, CSS, and JavaScript in Magento.

Chapter 9, The Web API, takes up a detailed approach to the powerful Web API provided by Magento. It gives hands-on practical examples to create and use both REST and SOAP, either through the PHP cURL library, or from the console.

Chapter 10, The Major Functional Areas, adopts a high-level approach towards introducing readers with some of the most common sections of Magento. These include CMS, catalog and customer management, and products and customer import. It even shows how to create a custom product type and a shipping and payment method.

Chapter 11, Testing, gives an overview of the types of test that are available in Magento. It further shows how to write and execute a custom test.

Chapter 12, Building a Module from Scratch, shows the entire process of developing a module, which uses most of the features introduced in the previous chapters. The final result is a module that has admin and storefront interface, an admin configuration area, e-mail templates, installed schema scripts, tests, and so on.

What you need for this book

In order to successfully run all the examples provided in this book, you will need either your own web server or a third-party web hosting solution. The high-level technology stack includes PHP, Apache/Nginx, and MySQL. The Magento 2 Community Edition platform itself comes with a detailed list of system requirements that can be found at `http://devdocs.magento.com/guides/v2.0/install-gde/system-requirements.html`. The actual environment setup is explained in *Chapter 2, Managing the Environment*.

Who this book is for

This book is intended primarily for intermediate to professional PHP developers who are interested in Magento 2 development. For backend developers, several topics are covered that will enable you to modify and extend your Magento store. Frontend developers will also find some coverage on how to customize the look of a site in the frontend.

Given the massive code and structure changes, Magento version 2.x can be described as a platform that is significantly different from its predecessor. Keeping this in mind, this book will neither assume nor require previous knowledge of Magento 1.x.

Conventions

In this book, you will find a number of text styles that distinguish between different kinds of information. Here are some examples of these styles and an explanation of their meaning.

Code words in text, database table names, folder names, filenames, file extensions, pathnames, dummy URLs, user input, and Twitter handles are shown as follows: "The `AbstractProductPlugin1` class does not have to be extended from another class for the plugin to work."

A block of code is set as follows:

```
<config xmlns:xsi="http://www.w3.org/2001/XMLSchema-instance"
  xsi:noNamespaceSchemaLocation="urn:magento:framework:
  ObjectManager/etc/config.xsd">
    <type name="Magento\Catalog\Block\Product\AbstractProduct">
        <plugin name="foggyPlugin1"
          type="Foggyline\Plugged\Block\Catalog\Product\
          AbstractProductPlugin1"
          disabled="false" sortOrder="100"/>
        <plugin name="foggyPlugin2"
          type="Foggyline\Plugged\Block\Catalog\Product\
          AbstractProductPlugin2"
          disabled="false" sortOrder="200"/>
        <plugin name="foggyPlugin3"
          type="Foggyline\Plugged\Block\Catalog\Product\
          AbstractProductPlugin3"
          disabled="false" sortOrder="300"/>
    </type>
</config>
```

Any command-line input or output is written as follows:

```
php bin/magento setup:upgrade
```

New terms and **important words** are shown in bold. Words that you see on the screen, for example, in menus or dialog boxes, appear in the text like this: "In the **Store View** drop-down field, we select the store view where we want to apply the theme."

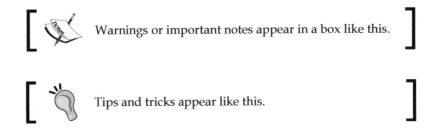

Warnings or important notes appear in a box like this.

Tips and tricks appear like this.

Reader feedback

Feedback from our readers is always welcome. Let us know what you think about this book—what you liked or disliked. Reader feedback is important for us as it helps us develop titles that you will really get the most out of.

To send us general feedback, simply e-mail feedback@packtpub.com, and mention the book's title in the subject of your message.

If there is a topic that you have expertise in and you are interested in either writing or contributing to a book, see our author guide at www.packtpub.com/authors.

Customer support

Now that you are the proud owner of a Packt book, we have a number of things to help you to get the most from your purchase.

Downloading the example code

You can download the example code files from your account at http://www.packtpub.com for all the Packt Publishing books you have purchased. If you purchased this book elsewhere, you can visit http://www.packtpub.com/support and register to have the files e-mailed directly to you.

Errata

Although we have taken every care to ensure the accuracy of our content, mistakes do happen. If you find a mistake in one of our books—maybe a mistake in the text or the code—we would be grateful if you could report this to us. By doing so, you can save other readers from frustration and help us improve subsequent versions of this book. If you find any errata, please report them by visiting http://www.packtpub.com/submit-errata, selecting your book, clicking on the **Errata Submission Form** link, and entering the details of your errata. Once your errata are verified, your submission will be accepted and the errata will be uploaded to our website or added to any list of existing errata under the Errata section of that title.

To view the previously submitted errata, go to https://www.packtpub.com/books/content/support and enter the name of the book in the search field. The required information will appear under the **Errata** section.

Piracy

Piracy of copyrighted material on the Internet is an ongoing problem across all media. At Packt, we take the protection of our copyright and licenses very seriously. If you come across any illegal copies of our works in any form on the Internet, please provide us with the location address or website name immediately so that we can pursue a remedy.

Please contact us at copyright@packtpub.com with a link to the suspected pirated material.

We appreciate your help in protecting our authors and our ability to bring you valuable content.

Questions

If you have a problem with any aspect of this book, you can contact us at questions@packtpub.com, and we will do our best to address the problem.

Understanding the Platform Architecture

1

Magento is a powerful, highly scalable, and highly customizable e-commerce platform that can be used to build web shops and, if needed, some non-e-commerce sites. It provides a large number of e-commerce features out of the box.

Features such as product inventory, shopping cart, support for numerous payment and shipment methods, promotion rules, content management, multiple currencies, multiple languages, multiple websites, and so on make it a great choice for merchants. On the other hand, developers enjoy the full set of merchant-relevant features plus all the things related to actual development. This chapter will touch upon the topic of robust Web API support, extensible administration interface, modules, theming, embedded testing frameworks, and much more.

In this chapter, a high-level overview of Magento is provided in the following sections:

- The technology stack
- The architectural layers
- The top-level filesystem structure
- The module filesystem structure

The technology stack

Magento's highly modular structure is a result of several open source technologies embedded into a stack. These open source technologies are composed of the following components:

- **PHP**: PHP is a server-side scripting language. This book assumes that you have advanced knowledge of the object-oriented aspects of PHP, which is often referred to as **PHP OOP**.

- **Coding standards**: Magento puts a lot of emphasis on coding standards. These include **PSR-0** (the autoloading standard), **PSR-1** (the basic coding standards), **PSR-2** (the coding style guide), **PSR-3**, and **PSR-4**.

- **Composer**: Composer is a dependency management package for PHP. It is used to pull in all the vendor library requirements.

- **HTML**: HTML5 is supported out of the box.

- **CSS**: Magento supports CSS3 via its in-built **LESS CSS** preprocessor.

- **jQuery**: jQuery is a mature cross-platform JavaScript library that was designed to simplify the DOM manipulation. It is one of the most popular JavaScript frameworks today.

- **RequireJS**: RequireJS is a JavaScript file and module loader. Using a modular script loader such as RequireJS helps improve the speed and quality of code.

- **Third-party libraries**: Magento comes packed with lot of third-party libraries, with the most notable ones being **Zend Framework** and **Symfony**. It is worth noting that Zend Framework comes in two different major versions, namely version 1.x and version 2.x. Magento uses both of these versions internally.

- **Apache or Nginx**: Both Apache and Nginx are HTTP servers. Each has its distinct advantages and disadvantages. It would be unfair to say one is better than another, as their performance widely depends on the entire system's setup and usage. Magento works with Apache 2.2 and 2.4 and Nginx 1.7.

- **MySQL**: MySQL is a mature and widely used **relational database management system (RDBMS)** that uses **structured query language (SQL)**. There are both free community versions and commercial versions of MySQL. Magento requires at least the of **MySQL Community Edition** version 5.6.

- **MTF**: **Magento Testing Framework (MTF)** delivers an automated testing suite. It covers various types of tests, such as performance, functional, and unit testing. The entire MTF is available on GitHub, which can be viewed by visiting `https://github.com/magento/mtf` as an isolated project.

Different pieces of technology can be glued into various architectures. There are different ways to look at the Magento architecture—from the perspective of a module developer, system integrator, or a merchant, or from some other angle.

The architectural layers

From top to bottom, Magento can be divided into four architectural layers, namely *presentation, service, domain*, and *persistence*.

The *presentation* layer is the one that we directly interact with through the browser. It contains layouts, blocks, templates, and even controllers, which process commands to and from the user interface. Client-side technologies such as jQuery, RequireJS, CSS, and LESS are also a part of this layer. Usually, three types of users interact with this layer, namely web users, system administrators, and those making the Web API calls. Since the Web API calls can be made via HTTP in a manner that is the same as how a user uses a browser, there's a thin line between the two. While web users and Web API calls consume the presentation layer as it is, the system administrators have the power to change it. This change manifests in the form of setting the active theme and changing the content of the **CMS** (short for **content management system**) pages, blocks, and the products themselves.

When the components of a presentation layer are being interacted with, they usually make calls to the underlying service layer.

The *service* layer is the bridge between the presentation and domain layer. It contains the service contracts, which define the implementation behavior. A **service contract** is basically a fancy name for a PHP interface. This layer is where we can find the REST/SOAP APIs. Most user interaction on the storefront is routed through the service layer. Similarly, the external applications that make the REST/SOAP API calls also interact with this layer.

When the components of a service layer are being interacted with, they usually make calls to the underlying domain layer.

The *domain* layer is really the business logic of Magento. This layer is all about generic data objects and models that compose the business logic. The domain layer models themselves do not contribute to data persistence, but they do contain a reference to a resource model that is used to retrieve and persist the data to a MySQL database. A domain layer code from one module can interact with a domain module code from another module via the use of *event observers, plugins*, and the *di.xml* definitions. We will look into the details of these later on in other chapters. Given the power of plugins and di.xml, its important to note that this interaction is best established using service contracts (the PHP interface).

When the components of the domain layer are being interacted with, they usually make calls to the underlying persistence layer.

The *persistence* layer is where the data gets persisted. This layer is in charge of all the **CRUD** (short for **create, read, update, and delete**) requests. Magento uses an active record pattern strategy for the persistence layer. The model object contains a resource model that maps an object to one or more database rows. Here, it is important to differentiate the cases of simple resource model and the **Entity-Attribute-Value (EAV)** resource models. A simple resource model maps to a single table, while the EAV resource models have their attributes spread out over a number of MySQL tables. As an example, the `Customer` and `Catalog` resource models use EAV resource models, while the newsletter's `Subscriber` resource model uses a simple resource model.

The top-level filesystem structure

The following list depicts the root Magento filesystem structure:

- `.htaccess`
- `.htaccess.sample`
- `.php_cs`
- `.travis.yml`
- `CHANGELOG.md`
- `CONTRIBUTING.md`
- `CONTRIBUTOR_LICENSE_AGREEMENT.html`
- `COPYING.txt`
- `Gruntfile.js`
- `LICENSE.txt`
- `LICENSE_AFL.txt`
- `app`
- `bin`
- `composer.json`
- `composer.lock`
- `dev`
- `index.php`

- lib
- nginx.conf.sample
- package.json
- php.ini.sample
- phpserver
- pub
- setup
- update
- var
- vendor

The app/etc/di.xml file is one of the most important files that we might often look into during development. It contains various class mappings or preferences for individual interfaces.

The var/magento/language-* directories is where the registered languages reside. Though each module can declare its own translations under app/code/{VendorName}/{ModuleName}/i18n/, Magento will eventually fall back to its own individual module named i18n in case translations are not found in the custom module or within the theme directory.

The bin directory is where we can find the magento file. The magento file is a script that is intended to be run from a console. Once triggered via the php bin/magento command, it runs an instance of the Magento\Framework\Console\Cli application, presenting us with quite a number of console options. We can use the magento script to enable/disable cache, enable/disable modules, run an indexer, and do many other things.

The dev directory is where we can find the Magento test scripts. We will have a look at more of those in later chapters.

The lib directory comprises two major subdirectories, namely the server-side PHP library code and fonts found under lib/internal and the client-side JavaScript libraries found in lib/web.

The pub directory is where the publicly exposed files are located. This is the directory that we should set as root when setting up Apache or Nginx. The pub/index.php file is what gets triggered when the storefront is opened in a browser.

The `var` directory is where the dynamically generated group type of files such as cache, log, and a few others get created in. We should be able to delete the content of this folder at any time and have Magento automatically recreate it.

The `vendor` directory is where most of the code is located. This is where we can find various third-party vendor code, Magento modules, themes, and language packs. Looking further into the `vendor` directory, you will see the following structure:

- `.htaccess`
- `autoload.php`
- `bin`
- `braintree`
- `composer`
- `doctrine`
- `fabpot`
- `justinrainbow`
- `league`
- `lusitanian`
- `magento`
- `monolog`
- `oyejorge`
- `pdepend`
- `pelago`
- `phpmd`
- `phpseclib`
- `phpunit`
- `psr`
- `sebastian`
- `seld`
- `sjparkinson`
- `squizlabs`
- `symfony`
- `tedivm`
- `tubalmartin`
- `zendframework`

Within the vendor directory, we can find code from various vendors, such as `phpunit`, `phpseclib`, `monolog`, `symfony`, and so on. Magento itself can be found here. The Magento code is located under `vendor/magento` directory, listed (partially) as follows:

- `composer`
- `framework`
- `language-en_us`
- `magento-composer-installer`
- `magento2-base`
- `module-authorization`
- `module-backend`
- `module-catalog`
- `module-customer`
- `module-theme`
- `module-translation`
- `module-ui`
- `module-url-rewrite`
- `module-user`
- `module-version`
- `module-webapi`
- `module-widget`
- `theme-adminhtml-backend`
- `theme-frontend-blank`
- `theme-frontend-luma`

You will see that the further structuring of directories follows a certain naming schema, whereas the `theme-*` directory stores themes, the `module-*` directory stores modules, and the `language-*` directory stores registered languages.

The module filesystem structure

Magento identifies itself as a highly modular platform. What this means is that there is literally a directory location where modules are placed. Let's take a peak at the individual module structure now. The following structure belongs to one of the simpler core Magento modules—the Contact module that can be found in vendor/magento/module-contact:

- Block
- composer.json
- Controller
- etc
    - acl.xml
    - adminhtml
        - system.xml
    - config.xml
    - email_templates.xml
    - frontend
        - di.xml
        - page_types.xml
        - routes.xml
    - module.xml
- Helper
- i18n
- LICENSE_AFL.txt
- LICENSE.txt
- Model
- README.md
- registration.php
- Test
    - Unit
        - Block
        - Controller
        - Helper
        - Model
- view
    - adminhtml
    - frontend
        - layout

- ○ contact_index_index.xml
- ○ default.xml
- ○ templates
  - ○ form.phtml

Even though the preceding structure is for one of the simpler modules, you can see that it is still quite extensive.

The Block directory is where the view-related block PHP classes are located.

The Controller directory is where the controller-related PHP classes are stored. This is the code that responds to the storefront POST and GET HTTP actions.

The etc directory is where the module configuration files are present. Here, we can see files such as module.xml, di.xml, acl.xml, system.xml, config.xml, email_templates.xml, page_types.xml, routes.xml, and so on. The module.xml file is an actual module declaration file. We will look into the contents of some of these files in the later chapters.

The Helper directory is where various helper classes are located. These classes are usually used to abstract various store configuration values into the getter methods.

The i18n directory is where the module translation package CSV files are stored.

The Module directory is where the entities, resource entities, collections, and various other business classes can be found.

The Test directory stores the module unit tests.

The view directory contains all the module administrator and storefront template files (.phtml and .html) and static files (.js and .css).

Finally, the registration.php is a module registration file.

Summary

In this chapter, we took a quick look at the technology stack used in Magento. We discussed how Magento, being an open source product, takes extensive use of other open source projects and libraries such as MySQL, Apache, Nginx, Zend Framework, Symfony, jQuery, and so on. We then learned how these libraries are arranged into directories. Finally, we explored one of the existing core modules and briefly took a look at an example of a module's structure.

In the next chapter, we are going to tackle the environment setup so that we can get Magento installed and ready for development.

Managing the Environment

Throughout this chapter, we will look into setting up our development and production environments. The idea is to have a fully automated development environment, which can be initiated with a single console command. For a production environment, we will turn our focus to one of the available cloud services, and see how easy it is to set up Magento for simpler production projects. We will not be covering any robust environment setups like auto-scaling, caching servers, content delivery networks, and similar. These are really jobs for *System Administrator or DevOps* roles. Our attention here is the bare minimum needed to get our Magento store up and running; a milestone we will achieve throughout the following sections would be:

- Setting up a development environment
    - VirtualBox
    - Vagrant
    - Vagrant project
        - Provisioning PHP
        - Provisioning MySQL
        - Provisioning Apache
        - Provisioning Magento installation
- Setting up a production environment
    - Introduction to **Amazon Web Services (AWS)**
    - Setting up access for S3 usage
        - Creating IAM users
        - Creating IAM groups

- ° Setting up S3 for database and media files backup
- ° Bash script for automated EC2 setup
    - ° Setting up EC2
    - ° Setting up Elastic IP and DNS

Setting up a development environment

In this section, we will build a development environment using **VirtualBox** and **Vagrant**.

 Magento official requirements call for Apache 2.2 or 2.4, PHP 5.6.x or 5.5.x (PHP 5.4 is not supported), and MySQL 5.6.x. We need to keep this in mind during the environment setup.

VirtualBox

VirtualBox is powerful and feature-rich x86 and AMD64/Intel64 virtualization software. It is free, runs on a large number of platforms, and supports a large number of guest operating systems. If we are using Windows, Linux, or OS X in our daily development, we can use VirtualBox to spin up a virtual machine with an isolated guest operating system in which we can install our server software needed to run Magento. This means using MySQL, Apache, and a few other things.

Vagrant

Vagrant is a high-level software wrapper used for virtualization software management. We can use it to create and configure development environments. Vagrant supports several types of virtualization software such as VirtualBox, **VMware, Kernel-based Virtual Machine (KVM)**, **Linux Containers (LXC)**, and others. It even supports server environments like Amazon EC2.

 Before we start, we need to make sure we have VirtualBox and Vagrant installed already. We can download them and install the following instructions from their official websites: `https://www.virtualbox.org` and `https://www.vagrantup.com`.

Vagrant project

We start by manually creating an empty directory somewhere within our host operating system, let's say `/Users/branko/www/B05032-Magento-Box/`. This is the directory we will pull in Magento code. We want Magento source code to be external to Vagrant box, so we can easily work with it in our favorite IDE.

We then create a Vagrant project directory, let's say `/Users/branko/www/magento-box/`.

Within the `magento-box` directory, we run the console command `vagrant init`. This results in an output as follows:

```
A 'Vagrantfile' has been placed in this directory. You are now ready
to 'vagrant up' your first virtual environment! Please read the
comments in the Vagrantfile as well as documentation on 'vagrantup.
com' for more information on using Vagrant.
```

The `Vagrantfile` is actually a Ruby language source file. If we strip away the comments, its original content looks like the following:

```
# -*- mode: ruby -*-
# vi: set ft=ruby :

Vagrant.configure(2) do |config|
  config.vm.box = "base"
end
```

If we were to run `vagrant up` now within the `magento-box` directory, this would start the VirtualBox in headless (no GUI) mode and run the base operating system. However, let's hold off running that command just now.

The idea is to create a more robust `Vagrantfile` that covers everything required for running Magento, from Apache, MySQL, PHP, PHPUnit, composer, and full Magento installation with performance fixture data.

Though Vagrant does not have a separate configuration file on its own, we will create one, as we want to store configuration data like a MySQL user and password in it.

Let's go ahead and create the `Vagrantfile.config.yml` file, alongside a `Vagrantfile` in the same directory, with content as follows:

```
ip: 192.168.10.10
s3:
  access_key: "AKIAIPRNHSWEQNWHLCDQ"
  secret_key: "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"
```

```
    bucket: "foggy-project-dhj6"
synced_folder:
    host_path: "/Users/branko/www/B05032-Magento-Box/"
    guest_path: "/vagrant-B05032-Magento-Box/"
mysql:
    host: "127.0.0.1"
    username: root
    password: user123
http_basic:
    repo_magento_com:
        username: a8adc3ac98245f519ua0d2v2c8770ec8
        password: a38488dc908c6d6923754c268vc41bc4
github_oauth:
    github_com: "d79fb920d4m4c2fb9d8798b6ce3a043f0b7c2af6"
magento:
    db_name: "magento"
    admin_firstname: "John"
    admin_lastname: "Doe"
    admin_password: "admin123"
    admin_user: "admin"
    admin_email: "email@change.me"
    backend_frontname: "admin"
    language: "en_US"
    currency: "USD"
    timezone: "Europe/London"
    base_url: "http://magento.box"
    fixture: "small"
```

There is no Vagrant-imposed structure here. This can be any valid YAML file. The values presented are merely examples of what we can put in.

Magento enables us to generate a pair of 32-character authentication tokens that can use to access the Git repository. This is done by logging in to Magento Connect with a user name and password, then going to **My Account | Developers | Secure Keys**. The Public Key and Private Key then become our username and password for accessing Magento GitHub repository.

Having a separate configuration file means we can commit Vagrantfile to version control with our project, while leaving the Vagrantfile.config.yml out of version control.

We now edit the Vagrantfile by replacing its content with the following:

```
# -*- mode: ruby -*-
# vi: set ft=ruby :

require 'yaml'

vagrantConfig = YAML.load_file 'Vagrantfile.config.yml'
```

```
Vagrant.configure(2) do |config|

  config.vm.box = "ubuntu/vivid64"

  config.vm.network "private_network", ip: vagrantConfig['ip']

  # Mount local "~/www/B05032-Magento-Box/" path into box's "/vagrant-
B05032-Magento-Box/" path
  config.vm.synced_folder
    vagrantConfig['synced_folder']['host_path'],
    vagrantConfig['synced_folder']['guest_path'], owner:"vagrant",
    group: "www-data", mount_options:["dmode=775, fmode=664"]

  # VirtualBox specific settings
  config.vm.provider "virtualbox" do |vb|
    vb.gui = false
    vb.memory = "2048"
    vb.cpus = 2
  end

  # <provisioner here>

end
```

The preceding code first includes the yaml library, and then reads the content of the Vagrantfile.config.yml file into a vagrantConfig variable. Then we have a config block, within which we define the box type, fixed IP address, shared folder between our host and guest operating system, and a few VirtualBox specific details such as CPU and memory allocated.

We are using the ubuntu/vivid64 box that stands for the server edition of Ubuntu 15.04 (Vivid Vervet). The reason is that this Ubuntu version gives us the MySQL 5.6.x and PHP 5.6.x, which stand as requirements for Magento installation, among other things.

We further have a configuration entry assigning a fixed IP to our virtual machine. Let's go ahead and add an entry in the *hosts* file of our host operating system as follows:

```
192.168.10.10 magento.box
```

> The reason why we are assigning the fixed IP address to our box is that we can directly open a URL like http://magento.box within our host operating system, and then access Apache served page within our guest operating system.

Another important part of the preceding code is the one where we defined `synced_folder`. Besides source and destination paths, the crucial parts here are `owner`, group, and `mount_options`. We set those to the vagrant user the `www-data` user group, and `774` and `664` for directory and file permissions that play nicely with Magento.

Let's continue editing our `Vagrantfile` adding several provisioners to it, one below the other. We do so by replacing the `# <provisioner here>` from the preceding example, with content as follows:

```
config.vm.provision "file", source: "~/.gitconfig", destination:
  ".gitconfig"
config.vm.provision "shell", inline: "sudo apt-get update"
```

Here we are instructing Vagrant to pass our `.gitconfig` file from the host to the guest operating system. This is so we inherit the host operating system Git setup to the guest operating system Git. We then call for `apt-get update` in order to update the guest operating system.

Provisioning PHP

Further adding to `Vagrantfile`, we run several provisioners that will install PHP, required PHP modules, and PHPUnit, as follows:

```
config.vm.provision "shell", inline: "sudo apt-get -y install php5
  php5-dev php5-curl php5-imagick php5-gd php5-mcrypt php5-mhash
  php5-mysql php5-xdebug php5-intl php5-xsl"
config.vm.provision "shell", inline: "sudo php5enmod mcrypt"
config.vm.provision "shell", inline: "echo
  \"xdebug.max_nesting_level=200\" >> /etc/php5/apache2/php.ini"
config.vm.provision "shell", inline: "sudo apt-get -y install
  phpunit"
```

There is one thing worth pointing out here – the line where we are writing `xdebug.max_nesting_level=200` into the `php.ini` file. This is done to exclude the possibility that Magento would not start throwing a **Maximum Functions Nesting Level of '100' reached...** error.

Provisioning MySQL

Further adding to `Vagrantfile`, we run provisioners that will install the MySQL server, as follows:

```
config.vm.provision "shell", inline: "sudo debconf-set-selections
  <<< 'mysql-server mysql-server/root_password password
  #{vagrantConfig['mysql']['password']}'"
config.vm.provision "shell", inline: "sudo debconf-set-selections
  <<< 'mysql-server mysql-server/root_password_again password
  #{vagrantConfig['mysql']['password']}'"
config.vm.provision "shell", inline: "sudo apt-get -y install
  mysql-server"
config.vm.provision "shell", inline: "sudo service mysql start"
config.vm.provision "shell", inline: "sudo update-rc.d mysql
  defaults"
```

What is interesting with the MySQL installation is that it requires a password and a password confirmation to be provided during installation. This makes it a troubling part of the provisioning process that expects shell commands to simply execute without asking for input. To bypass this, we use `debconf-set-selections` to store the parameters for input. We read the password from the `Vagrantfile.config.yml` file and pass it onto `debconf-set-selections`.

Once installed, `update-rc.d mysql` defaults will add MySQL to the operating system boot process, thus making sure MySQL is running when we reboot the box.

Provisioning Apache

Further adding to `Vagrantfile`, we run the Apache provisioner as follows:

```
config.vm.provision "shell", inline: "sudo apt-get -y install
  apache2"
config.vm.provision "shell", inline: "sudo update-rc.d apache2
  defaults"
config.vm.provision "shell", inline: "sudo service apache2 start"
config.vm.provision "shell", inline: "sudo a2enmod rewrite"
config.vm.provision "shell", inline: "sudo awk '/<Directory
  \\/>/,/AllowOverride None/{sub(\"None\", \"All\",$0)}{print}'
  /etc/apache2/apache2.conf > /tmp/tmp.apache2.conf"
config.vm.provision "shell", inline: "sudo mv
  /tmp/tmp.apache2.conf /etc/apache2/apache2.conf"
config.vm.provision "shell", inline: "sudo awk '/<Directory
  \\/var\\/www\\/>/,/AllowOverride None/{sub(\"None\",
  \"All\",$0)}{print}' /etc/apache2/apache2.conf >
  /tmp/tmp.apache2.conf"
```

```
config.vm.provision "shell", inline: "sudo mv
    /tmp/tmp.apache2.conf /etc/apache2/apache2.conf"
config.vm.provision "shell", inline: "sudo service apache2 stop"
```

The preceding code installs Apache, adds it to the boot sequence, starts it, and turns on the rewrite module. We then have an update to the Apache configuration file, as we want to replace AllowOverride None with AllowOverride All, or else our Magento won't work. Once the changes are done, we stop Apache due to the later processes.

Provisioning Magento installation

Further adding to Vagrantfile, we now turn our attention to Magento installation, which we split into several steps. First, we link our host folder, /vagrant-B05032-Magento-Box/, with the guest, /var/www/html, using Vagrant's synced folder feature:

```
config.vm.provision "shell", inline: "sudo rm -Rf /var/www/html"
config.vm.provision "shell", inline: "sudo ln -s
    #{vagrantConfig['synced_folder']['guest_path']} /var/www/html"
```

We then use the composer create-project command to pull the Magento 2 files from the official repo.magento.com source into the /var/www/html/ director:

```
config.vm.provision "shell", inline: "curl -sS
    https://getcomposer.org/installer | php"
config.vm.provision "shell", inline: "mv composer.phar
    /usr/local/bin/composer"
config.vm.provision "shell", inline: "composer clearcache"
config.vm.provision "shell", inline: "echo '{\"http-basic\":
    {\"repo.magento.com\": {\"username\": \"#{vagrantConfig
    ['http_basic']['repo_magento_com']['username']}\",\"password\":
    \"#{vagrantConfig['http_basic']['repo_magento_com']['password']}
    \"}}, \"github-oauth\": {\"github.com\":
    \"#{vagrantConfig['github_oauth']['github_com']}\"}}' >>
    /root/.composer/auth.json"
config.vm.provision "shell", inline: "composer create-project --
    repository-url=https://repo.magento.com/ magento/project-
    community-edition /var/www/html/"
```

We then create a database in which Magento will be installed later on:

```
config.vm.provision "shell", inline: "sudo mysql --
    user=#{vagrantConfig['mysql']['username']} --
    password=#{vagrantConfig['mysql']['password']} -e \"CREATE
    DATABASE #{vagrantConfig['magento']['db_name']};\""
```

We then run the Magento installation from the command line:

```
config.vm.provision "shell", inline: "sudo php
  /var/www/html/bin/magento setup:install --base-
  url=\"#{vagrantConfig['magento']['base_url']}\" --db-
  host=\"#{vagrantConfig['mysql']['host']}\" --db-
  user=\"#{vagrantConfig['mysql']['username']}\" --db-
  password=\"#{vagrantConfig['mysql']['password']}\" --db-
  name=\"#{vagrantConfig['magento']['db_name']}\" --admin-
  firstname=\"#{vagrantConfig['magento']['admin_firstname']}\" --
  admin-lastname=\"#{vagrantConfig['magento']['admin_lastname']}\"
  --admin-email=\"#{vagrantConfig['magento']['admin_email']}\" --
  admin-user=\"#{vagrantConfig['magento']['admin_user']}\" --
  admin-password=\"#{vagrantConfig['magento']['admin_password']}\"
  --backend-
  frontname=\"#{vagrantConfig['magento']['backend_frontname']}\" -
  -language=\"#{vagrantConfig['magento']['language']}\" --
  currency=\"#{vagrantConfig['magento']['currency']}\" --
  timezone=\"#{vagrantConfig['magento']['timezone']}\""
config.vm.provision "shell", inline: "sudo php
  /var/www/html/bin/magento deploy:mode:set developer"
config.vm.provision "shell", inline: "sudo php
  /var/www/html/bin/magento cache:disable"
config.vm.provision "shell", inline: "sudo php
  /var/www/html/bin/magento cache:flush"
config.vm.provision "shell", inline: "sudo php
  /var/www/html/bin/magento setup:performance:generate-fixtures
  /var/www/html/setup/performance-toolkit/profiles/ce/small.xml"
```

The preceding code shows we are installing the fixtures data as well.

We need to be careful during the `Vagrantfile.config.yml` file configuration.
Magento installation is quite sensible around provided data. We need to make sure
we provide valid data for fields like mail and password or else the installation will
fail showing errors similar to the following:

```
SQLSTATE[28000] [1045] Access denied for user 'root'@'localhost'
  (using password: NO)
User Name is a required field.
First Name is a required field.
Last Name is a required field.
'magento.box' is not a valid hostname for email address
  'john.doe@magento.box'
'magento.box' appears to be a DNS hostname but cannot match TLD
  against known list
'magento.box' appears to be a local network name but local network
  names are not allowed
Password is required field.
Your password must be at least 7 characters.
Your password must include both numeric and alphabetic characters.
```

With this, we conclude our `Vagrantfile` content.

Running the `vagrant up` command now within the same directory as `Vagrantfile` triggers the box creation process. During this process, all of the previously listed commands will get executed. The process alone takes up to an hour or so.

Once vagrant up is complete, we can issue another console command, `vagrant ssh`, to log in to the box.

At the same time, if we open a URL like `http://magento.box` in our browser, we should see the Magento storefront loading.

The preceding `Vagrantfile` simply pulls from the official Magento Git repository and installs Magento from the ground up. `Vagrantfile` and `Vagrantfile.config.yml` can be further extended and tailored to suit our individual project needs, like pulling the code from the private Git repository, restoring the database from the shared drive, and so on.

This makes for a simple yet powerful scripting process by which we can prepare fully ready per-project machines for other developers in a team to be able to quickly spin up.

Setting up a production environment

A production environment is the client-facing environment that focuses on good performance and availability. Setting up production environments is not really something we developers tend to do, especially if there are robust requirements around scaling, load balancing, high availability, and similar. Sometimes, however, we need to set up a simple production environment. There are various cloud providers that offer quick and simple solutions to this. For the purpose of this section, we will turn to Amazon Web Services.

Introduction to Amazon Web Services

Amazon Web Services (AWS) is a collection of remote computing services frequently referred to as web services. AWS provides on-demand computing resources and services in the cloud, with *pay-as-you-go* pricing. Amazon gives a nice comparison of its AWS resources, saying that using AWS resources instead of your own is like purchasing electricity from a power company instead of running your own generator.

If we stop and think about it for a minute, this makes it interesting to not only system operation roles but also for developers like us. We (developers) are now able to spin various databases, web application servers, and even complex infrastructures in a matter of minutes and a few mouse clicks. We can run these services for a few minutes, hours, or days then shut them down. Meanwhile, we only pay for the actual usage, not the full monthly or yearly price as we do with most of the hosting services. Although the overall AWS pricing for certain services might not be the cheapest out there, it certainly provides a level of commodity and usability unlike many other services. Commodity comes from things like auto-scaling resources, a feature that often offers significant cost savings compared to the equivalent on-premises infrastructure.

Quality training and a certification program is another important aspect of the AWS ecosystem. Certifications are available for **Solutions Architect**, **Developer**, and **SysOps Administrator**, across associate and professional levels. Though the certification is not mandatory, if we deal with AWS on a regular basis, we are encouraged to take one. Earning the certification puts the seal on our expertise to design, deploy, and operate highly available, cost-effective, and secure applications on the AWS platform.

We can manage our AWS through a simple and intuitive web-based user interface called AWS management console, which is available at `https://aws.amazon.com/console`. Signing into AWS, we should be able to see a screen similar to the following one:

The preceding image shows how the AWS management console groups the AWS services visually into several major groups, as follows:

- **Compute**
- **Developer Tools**
- **Mobile Services**
- **Storage & Content Delivery**
- **Management Tools**
- **Application Services**
- **Database**
- **Security & Identity**
- **Networking**
- **Analytics**
- **Enterprise Applications**

As part of this chapter, we will be taking a look at the **EC2** service found under the **Compute** group and the **S3** service found under the **Storage & Content Delivery** group.

Amazon Elastic Compute Cloud (Amazon EC2) is a web service that provides a re-sizable compute capacity in the cloud. We can think of it as a virtual computer machine in the cloud that we can turn on and off at any time, within minutes. We can further commission one, hundreds, or even thousands of these machine instances simultaneously. This makes for the *re-sizable* compute capacity.

S3 provides secure, durable, and highly scalable object storage. It is designed to provide durability of 99.99% of objects. The service provides a web service interface to store and retrieve any amount of data from anywhere on the web. S3 is charged only per storage that is actually used. S3 can be used alone or together with other AWS services such as EC2.

Setting up access for S3 usage

As part of our production environment, it is good to have reliable storage where we can archive database and media files. Amazon S3 stands out as a possible solution.

In order to properly set access to the S3 scalable storage service, we need to take a quick look into AWS **Identity and Access Management (IAM** for short). IAM is a web service that helps us securely control access to AWS resources for our users. We can use IAM to control authentication (who can use our AWS resources) and authorization (what resources they can use and in what ways). More specifically, as we will soon see, we are interested in **Users** and **Groups**.

Creating IAM users

This section describes how to create IAM users. An IAM user is an entity that we create in AWS to represent the person or service using it when interacting with AWS.

Log in to the AWS console.

Under the user menu, click on **Security Credentials** as shown in the following screenshot:

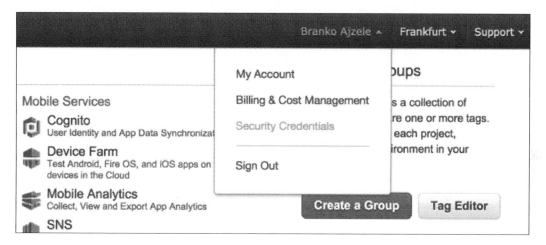

This opens up the security dashboard page.

Clicking on the **Users** menu should open a screen like the following one:

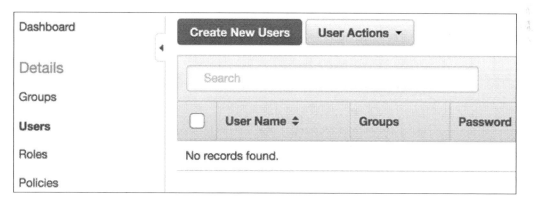

On the **Users** menu, we click on **Create New User**, which opens a page like
the following:

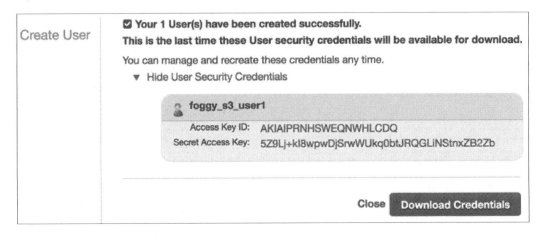

Here, we fill in the desired username for one or more users, something like
foggy_s3_user1, and then click on the **Create** button.

We should now see a screen like the following one:

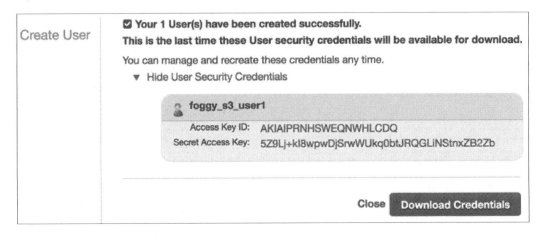

Here, we can click on **Download Credentials** to initiate the CSV format file
download or copy and paste our credentials manually.

Access Key ID and **Secret Access Key** are the two pieces of information we will be using to access S3 storage.

Clicking the close link takes us back to the **Users** menu, showing our newly created user listed as shown in the following screenshot:

Creating IAM groups

This section describes how to create IAM groups. Groups are collections of IAM users that we can manage as a single unit. So let's begin:

1. Log in to the AWS console.

2. Under the user menu, click on **Security Credentials** as shown in the following screenshot:

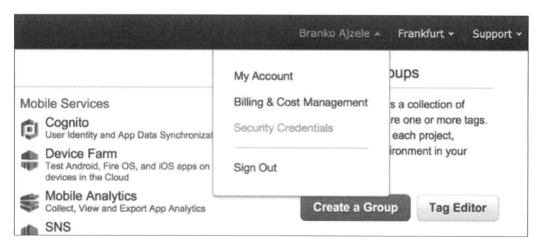

3. This opens up the security dashboard page. Clicking on the **Groups** menu should open a screen like the following one:

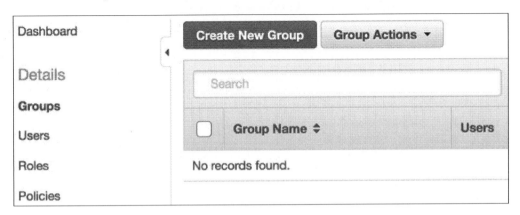

4. On the **Groups** menu, we click on **Create New Group**, which opens a page like the following:

5. Here, we fill in the desired group name, something like FoggyS3Test.

6. We should now see a screen like the following one, where we need to select the group **Policy Type** and click the **Next Step** button:

7. We select the **AmazonS3FullAccess** policy type and click the **Next Step** button. The **Review** screen is now shown, asking us to review the provided information:

8. If the provided information is correct, we confirm it by clicking the **Create Group** button. We should now be able to see our group under the **Groups** menu as shown in the following screenshot:

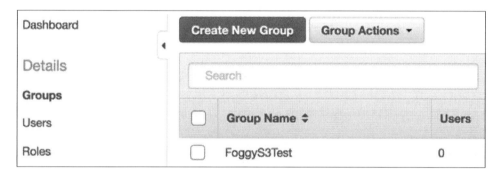

9. Mark the checkbox to the left of **Group Name**, click the **Group Actions** dropdown, and then select **Add Users to Group** as shown in the following screenshot:

10. This opens the **Add Users to Group** page as shown in the following screenshot:

11. Mark the checkbox to the left of **User Name** and click on the **Add Users** button. This should add the selected user to the group and throw us back to the **Groups** listing.

The result of this user and group creation process is a user with **Access Key Id**, **Secret Access Key**, and assigned user group with the **AmazonS3FullAccess** policy. We will use this information later on when we demonstrate backing up the database to S3.

Setting up S3 for database and media files backup

S3 consists of buckets. We can think of a bucket as the first level directory within our S3 account. We then set the permissions and other options on that directory (bucket). In this section, we are going to create our own bucket, with two empty folders called `database` and `media`. We will use these folders later on during our environment setup in order to back up our MySQL database and our media files.

We start by logging in to the AWS management console.

Under the **Storage & Content Delivery** group, we click on **S3**. This opens a screen similar to the following:

Click on the **Create Bucket** button. This opens a popup like the one shown in the following screenshot:

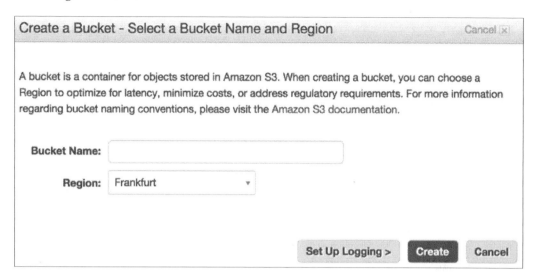

Let's provide a unique **Bucket Name**, preferably something identifying the project for which we will be backing up the `database` and `media` file, and click the **Create** button. For the purpose of this chapter, let's imagine we selected something like `foggy-project-dhj6`.

Our bucket should now be visible under the **All Buckets** list. If we click on it, a new screen opens like the one shown in the following screenshot:

Here, we click on the **Create Folder** button and add the necessary `database` and `media` folders.

While still within the root bucket directory, click on the **Properties** button and fill in the **Permissions** section as shown in the following screenshot:

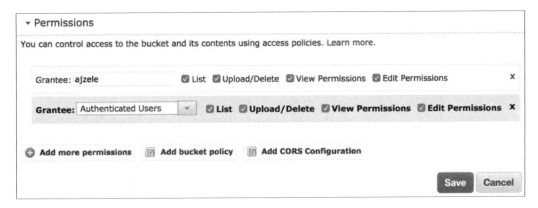

Here, we are basically assigning all permissions to **Authenticated Users**.

We should now have an S3 bucket to which we can potentially store our database and media backups using the s3cmd console tool that we will soon reference.

Bash script for automated EC2 setup

Similar to the Vagrantfile shell provisioners, let's go ahead and create a sequence of bash shell commands we can use for a production setup.

The first block of commands goes as follows:

```
#!/bin/bash
apt-get update
apt-get -y install s3cmd
```

Here, start with the #!/bin/bash expression. This specifies the type of script we are executing. Then we have a system update and s3cmd tool installation. The s3cmd is a free command-line tool and client for uploading, retrieving, and managing data in Amazon S3. We can use it later on for database and media file backups and restores.

We then install the postfix mail server, using the following commands. Since the postfix installation triggers a graphical interface in the console, asking for mailname and main_mailer_type, we bypass those using sudo debconf-set-selections. Once installed, we reload postfix.

```
sudo debconf-set-selections <<< "postfix postfix/mailname string
magentize.me"
sudo debconf-set-selections <<< "postfix postfix/main_mailer_type
string 'Internet Site'"
sudo apt-get install -y postfix
sudo /etc/init.d/postfix reload
```

Using mail server directly on the EC2 box is fine for smaller production sites, where we do not expect high traffic or a large number of customers. For more intensive production sites, we need to pay attention to Amazon, possibly putting a throttle on port 25, thus resulting in outgoing e-mail timeouts. In which case we can either ask Amazon to remove the limitation on our account, or move on to more robust services like **Amazon Simple Email Service**.

We then install all things related to PHP. Notice how we even install xdebug, though immediately turning it off. This might come in handy for those very rare moments when we really need to debug the live site, then we can turn it off and play with remote debugging. We further download and set composer to the user path:

```
apt-get -y install php5 php5-dev php5-curl php5-imagick php5-gd php5-
mcrypt php5-mhash php5-mysql php5-xdebug php5-intl php5-xsl
php5enmod mcrypt
php5dismod xdebug
service php5-fpm restart
apt-get -y install phpunit
echo "Starting Composer stuff" >> /var/tmp/box-progress.txt
curl -sS https://getcomposer.org/installer | php
mv composer.phar /usr/local/bin/composer
```

We then move on to MySQL installation. Here, we are also using debconf-set-selections to automate the console part of providing input parameters to the installation. Once installed, MySQL is started and added to the boot process.

```
debconf-set-selections <<< 'mysql-server mysql-server/root_password
password RrkSBi6VDg6C'
debconf-set-selections <<< 'mysql-server mysql-server/root_password_again
password RrkSBi6VDg6C'
apt-get -y install mysql-server
service mysql start
update-rc.d mysql defaults
```

Alongside MySQL, another major component is Apache. We install it using the following commands. With Apache, we need to pay attention to its `apache2.conf` file. We need to change `AllowOverride None` to `AllowOverride All` for the Magento directory:

```
apt-get -y install apache2

update-rc.d apache2 defaults

service apache2 start

a2enmod rewrite

awk '/<Directory \/>/,/AllowOverride None/{sub("None",
"All",$0)}{print}' /etc/apache2/apache2.conf > /tmp/tmp.apache2.conf

mv /tmp/tmp.apache2.conf /etc/apache2/apache2.conf

awk '/<Directory \/var\/www\/>/,/AllowOverride None/{sub("None",
"All",$0)}{print}' /etc/apache2/apache2.conf > /tmp/tmp.apache2.conf

mv /tmp/tmp.apache2.conf /etc/apache2/apache2.conf

service apache2 restart
```

Now that we have MySQL and Apache installed, we move on to getting the source code files in place. Next, we are pulling from the official Magento Git repository. This is not the same as `repo.magento.com` we used when setting up the vagrant. Though in this case the Magento Git repository is public, the idea is to be able to pull the code from the private GitHub repository. Based on the production environment we tend to set up, we can easily replace the next part with pulling from any other private Git repository.

```
sudo rm -Rf /var/www/html/*

git clone https://github.com/magento/magento2.git /var/www/html/.

sudo composer config --global github-oauth.github.com
7d6da6b1d50dub454edc27db70db78b1f8997e6

sudo composer install --working-dir="/var/www/html/"

mysql -uroot -pRrkSBi6VDg6C -e "CREATE DATABASE magento;"

PUBLIC_HOSTNAME="'wget -q -O - http://instance-data/latest/meta-
data/public-hostname'"
```

 To pull the code from a private git repository, we can use a command of the following form, Git clone: `https://<user>:<OAuthToken>@github.com/<user>/<repo>.git`.

The PUBLIC_HOSTNAME variable stores the response of the wget command that calls the http://instance-data/latest/meta-data/public-hostname URL. This URL is a feature of AWS that allows us to get the current EC2 instance metadata. We then use the PUBLIC_HOSTNAME variable during Magento installation, passing it as the --base-url parameter:

```
php /var/www/html/bin/magento setup:install --base-
   url="http://$PUBLIC_HOSTNAME" --db-host="127.0.0.1" --db-
   user="root" --db-password="RrkSBi6VDg6C" --db-name="magento" --
   admin-firstname="John" --admin-lastname="Doe" --admin-
   email="john.doe@change.me" --admin-user="admin" --admin-
   password="pass123" --backend-frontname="admin" --
   language="en_US" --currency="USD" --timezone="Europe/London"
```

The preceding command takes a lot of *per project* specific configuration values, so we need to be sure to paste in our own information here appropriately before simply copying and pasting it.

Now we make sure the Magento mode is set to production, and cache is turned on and flushed, so it regenerates fresh:

```
php /var/www/html/bin/magento deploy:mode:set production
```

```
php /var/www/html/bin/magento cache:enable
```

```
php /var/www/html/bin/magento cache:flush
```

Finally, we reset the permissions on the /var/www/html directory in order for our Magento to function properly:

```
chown -R ubuntu:www-data /var/www/html
```

```
find /var/www/html -type f -print0 | xargs -r0 chmod 640
```

```
find /var/www/html -type d -print0 | xargs -r0 chmod 750
```

```
chmod -R g+w /var/www/html/pub
```

```
chmod -R g+w /var/www/html/var
```

```
chmod -R g+w /var/www/html/app
```

```
chmod -R g+w /var/www/html/vendor
```

We need to take caution with the preceding Git and Magento installation example. The idea here was to show how we could automatically set Git pull from the public or private repository. The Magento installation part is a little bonus for this specific case, not something we would actually do on our production machine. The whole purpose of this script would be to serve as a blueprint for powering up new AMI images. So ideally what we would usually do once the code is pulled, is to restore the database from some private storage like S3 and then attach it to our installation. Thus making for a complete restore of files, database, and media once the script is finished.

Putting that thought aside, let's get back to our script, further adding the daily database backup using the set of command as follows:

```
CRON_CMD="mysql --user=root --password=RrkSBi6VDg6C magento | gzip -9
> ~/database.sql.gz"
CRON_JOB="30 2 * * * $CRON_CMD"
( crontab -l | grep -v "$CRON_CMD" ; echo "$CRON_JOB" ) | crontab -


CRON_CMD="s3cmd  --access_key="AKIAINLIM7M6WGJKMMCQ" --
secret_key="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" put
~/database.sql.gz s3://foggy-project-ghj7/database/database_'date
+"%Y-%m-%d_%H-%M"'.sql.gz"
CRON_JOB="30 3 * * * $CRON_CMD"
( crontab -l | grep -v "$CRON_CMD" ; echo "$CRON_JOB" ) | crontab -
```

Here, we are adding the 2:30 AM **cron job** for backing up the database into the home directory file named `database.sql.gz`. Then we are adding another cron job that executes at 3:30 AM, which pushes the database backup to S3 storage.

Similar to the database backup, we can add media backup instructions to our script using the set of command as follows:

```
CRON_CMD="tar -cvvzf ~/media.tar.gz /var/www/html/pub/media/"
CRON_JOB="30 2 * * * $CRON_CMD"
( crontab -l | grep -v "$CRON_CMD" ; echo "$CRON_JOB" ) | crontab -


CRON_CMD="s3cmd --access_key="AKIAINLIM7M6WGJKMMCQ" --
secret_key="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" put
~/media.tar.gz s3://foggy-project-ghj7/media/media_'date +"%Y-%m-
%d_%H-%M"'.tar.gz"
CRON_JOB="30 3 * * * $CRON_CMD"
( crontab -l | grep -v "$CRON_CMD" ; echo "$CRON_JOB" ) | crontab -
```

The preceding commands have several pieces of information coded in them. We need to make sure to paste in our access key, secret key, and S3 bucket name accordingly. For simplicity sake, we are not addressing security implications such as hardcoding the access tokens into the cron jobs. Amazon provides an extensive *AWS Security Best Practices* guide that can be downloaded via the official AWS website.

Now that we have some understanding of what the bash script for automated EC2 setup could look like, let's proceed to setting up the EC2 instance.

Setting up EC2

Follow these steps to get the setting done:

1. Log in to the AWS console

2. Under the **Compute** group, click on **EC2**, which should open a screen like the following:

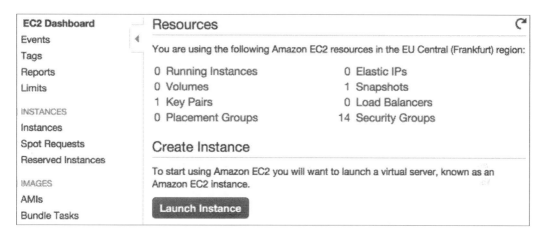

3. Click on the **Launch Instance** button, which should open a screen like the following:

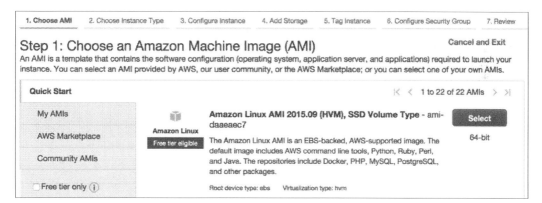

4. Click on the **Community AMIs** tab to the left, and type in Ubuntu Vivid into the search field, as shown in the following screenshot:

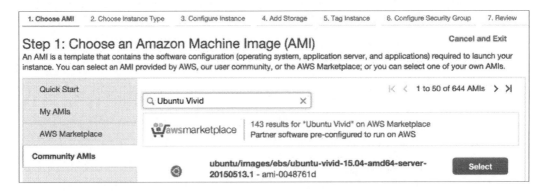

 The Ubuntu 15.x (Vivid Vervet) server by default supports MySQL 5.6.x and PHP 5.6.x, which makes it a good candidate for Magento installation.

We should now see a screen like the following:

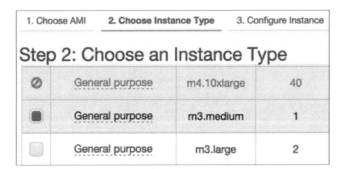

5. Choose an instance type and click the **Next: Configure Instance Details** button. We should now see a screen like the following:

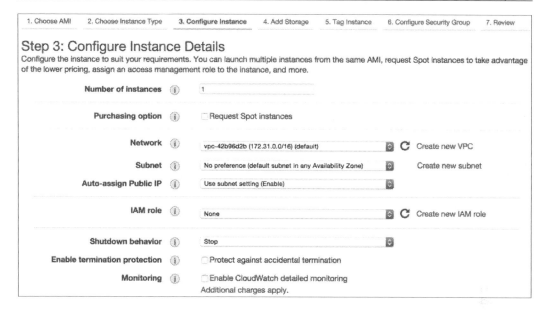

 We won't be getting into the details of each of these options. Suffice to say that if we are working on smaller production sites, chances are we can leave most of these options with their default values.

6. Make sure **Shutdown behavior** is set to **Stop**.

7. While still on the **Step 3: Configure Instance Details** screen, scroll down to the bottom **Advanced Details** area and expand it. We should see a screen like the following:

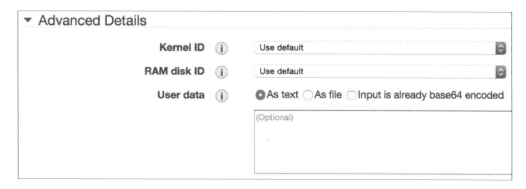

8. The **User Data** input is where we will copy and paste the `auto-setup` `bash` script described in the previous section, as shown in the following screenshot:

9. Once we copy and paste in the **User Data**, click on the **Next: Add Storage** button. This should bring up the screen as shown in the following screenshot:

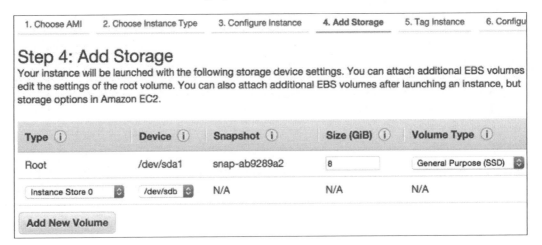

10. Within **Step 4: Add Storage**, we can select one or more volumes to attach to our EC2 instance. Preferably, we should select the SSD type of storage for faster performance. Once the volume is set, click on **Next: Tag Instance**. We should now see a screen like the following:

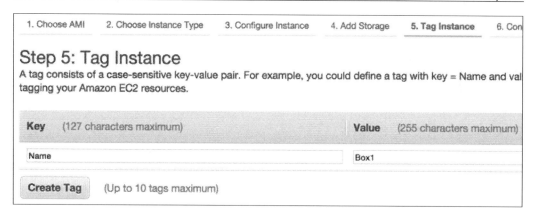

11. The **Tag Instance** screen allows us to assign tags. Tags enable us to categorize our AWS resource by purpose, owner, environment, or some other way. Once we have assigned one or more tags, we click on the **Next: Configure Security Group** button. We should now see a screen like the following:

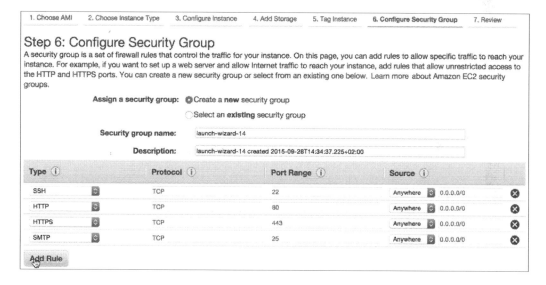

12. The **Configure Security Group** screen allows us to set rules for inbound and outbound traffic. We want to be able to access SSH, HTTP, HTTPs, and SMTP services on the box. Once we add the rules we want, click on the **Review and Launch** button. This opens a screen like the following:

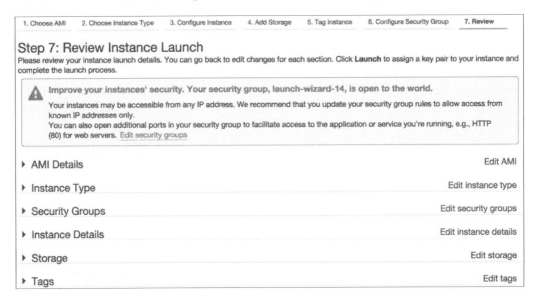

13. The **Review Instance Launch** screen is where we can view the summary of the box we configured up to this point. If needed, we can go back and edit individual settings. Once we are satisfied with the summary, we click on the **Launch** button. This opens a popup like the following:

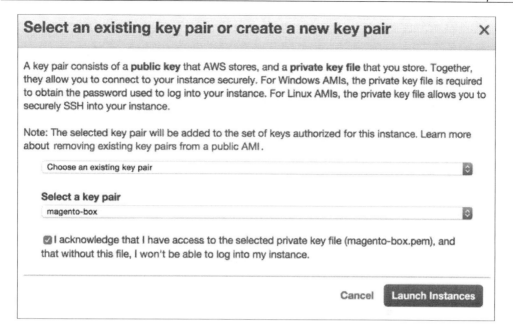

Select an existing key pair or create a new key pair   ✕

A key pair consists of a **public key** that AWS stores, and a **private key file** that you store. Together, they allow you to connect to your instance securely. For Windows AMIs, the private key file is required to obtain the password used to log into your instance. For Linux AMIs, the private key file allows you to securely SSH into your instance.

Note: The selected key pair will be added to the set of keys authorized for this instance. Learn more about removing existing key pairs from a public AMI.

Choose an existing key pair

Select a key pair

magento-box

☑ I acknowledge that I have access to the selected private key file (magento-box.pem), and that without this file, I won't be able to log into my instance.

Cancel   **Launch Instances**

14. Here, we get to choose an existing security key, or create a new one. Keys are provided in PEM format. Once we select the key, we click on the **Launch Instance** button.

    We should now see the **Launch Status** screen like the following:

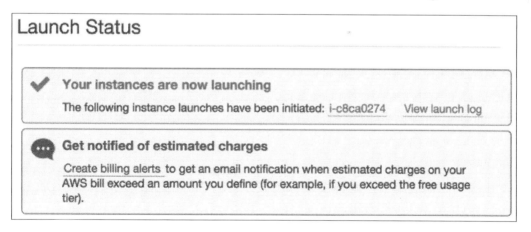

Launch Status

✔ **Your instances are now launching**

The following instance launches have been initiated: i-c8ca0274   View launch log

💬 **Get notified of estimated charges**

Create billing alerts to get an email notification when estimated charges on your AWS bill exceed an amount you define (for example, if you exceed the free usage tier).

15. Clicking on the instance name link should throw us back at the **EC2 Dashboard** like shown in the following screenshot:

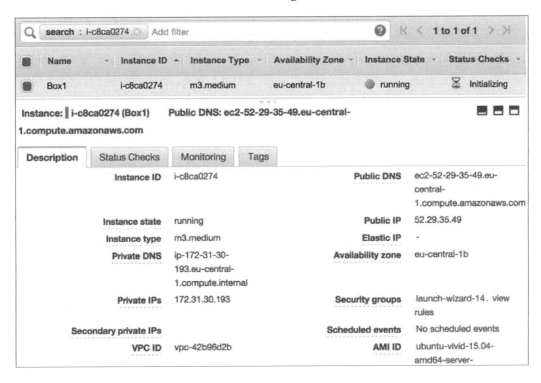

With regard to the preceding image, we should now be able to connect to our EC2 box with either one of the following console commands:

```
ssh -i /path/to/magento-box.pem ubuntu@ec2-52-29-35-49.eu-central-1.
compute.amazonaws.com
```

```
ssh -i /path/to/magento-box.pem ubuntu@52.29.35.49
```

It might take some time for our EC2 box to execute all of the shell commands passed to it. We can conveniently SSH into the box and then execute the following command to get an overview of current progress:

```
sudo tail -f /var/tmp/box-progress.txt
```

With this, we conclude our instance launch process.

Setting up Elastic IP and DNS

Now that we have an EC2 box in place, let's go ahead and create the so-called Elastic IP for it. The **Elastic IP address** is a static IP address designed for dynamic cloud computing. It is tied to the AWS account, and not some specific instance. This makes it convenient to easily re-map it from one instance to another.

Let's go ahead and create an Elastic IP as follows:

1. Log in to the AWS console.

2. Under the **Compute** group, click on **EC2**, which should get us to the **EC2 Dashboard**.

3. Under the **EC2 Dashboard**, in the left area under Network and Security grouping, click on Elastic IPs. This should open a screen like the following:

4. Click on the **Allocate New Address** button, which should open a popup like the following:

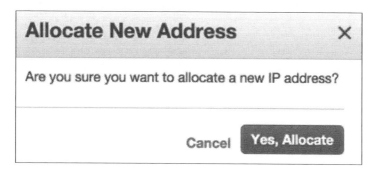

5. Click on the **Yes, Allocate** button, which should open another popup like the following:

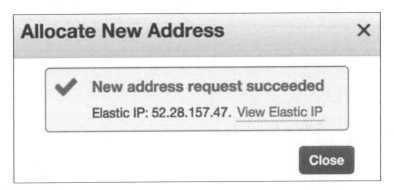

6. Now that the Elastic IP address is created, right-clicking on it within the table listing should bring up the options menu as shown in the following screenshot:

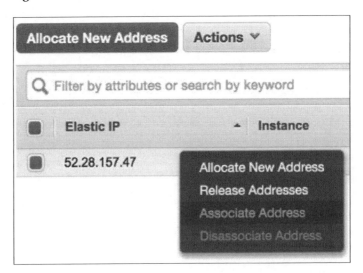

7. Click on the **Associate Address** link. This should open a popup like the following:

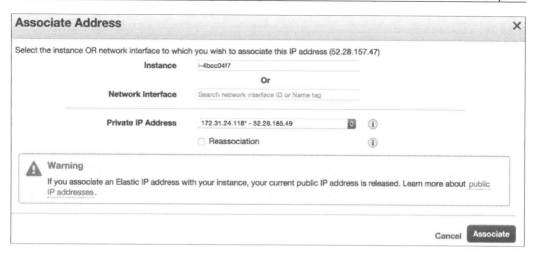

8. On the **Associate Address** popup, we select the **Instance** to which we want to assign the Elastic IP address and click on the **Associate** button.

At this point, our EC2 box has a static (Elastic IP) address assigned. We can now log in to our domain registrar and point the A-record of our DNS to the Elastic IP we just created.

Until we wait for the DNS change to kick in, there is one more thing we need to address. We need to SSH into our box and execute the following set of commands:

```
mysql -uroot -pRrkSBi6VDg6C -e "USE magento; UPDATE core_config_data
SET value = 'http://our-domain.something/' WHERE path LIKE
"%web/unsecure/base_url%";"

php /var/www/html/bin/magento cache:flush
```

This will update the Magento URL, so we can access it via a web browser once the DNS change kicks in. With a little bit of upfront planning, we could have easily made this bit a part of the user data for our EC2 instance, simply by providing the right `--base-url` parameter value in the first place.

Summary

Throughout this chapter, we focused on two main things: setting up development and production environments.

As part of the development environment, we embraced free software such as VirtualBox and Vagrant to manage our environment setup. The setup alone came down to a single `Vagrantfile` script that contained the necessary set of commands to install everything from the Ubuntu server, PHP, Apache, MySQL, and even Magento itself. We should by no means look at this script as final and only as a valid script to set up our development environment. Investing time in making the development environment closer to the project-specific requirements pays off in terms of team productivity.

We then moved on to the production environment. Here, we looked into Amazon Web Services, utilizing S3 and EC2 along the way. The production environment also came with its own scripted installation process that sets most of the things. Similarly, this script is by no means final and is only a valid way to set things up; it's more of a base example of how to do it.

In the next chapter, we will take a closer look at some of programming concepts and conventions.

3
Programming Concepts and Conventions

With years of experience, the Magento platform grew up to implement a lot of industry concepts, standards, and conventions. Throughout this chapter, we will look into several of these independent sections that stand out in day-to-day interactions with Magento development.

We will go through the following sections in this chapter:

- Composer
- Service contracts
- Code generation
- The var directory
- Coding standards

Composer

Composer is a tool that handles dependency management in PHP. It is not a package manager like **Yum** and **Apt** on Linux systems are. Though it deals with libraries (packages), it does so on a per-project level. It does not install anything globally. Composer is a multiplatform tool. Therefore, it runs equally well on Windows, Linux, and OS X.

Installing Composer on a machine is as simple as running the installer in the project directory by using the following command:

```
curl -sS https://getcomposer.org/installer | php
```

More information about the installation of Composer can be found on its official website, which can be viewed by visiting `https://getcomposer.org`.

Composer is used to fetch Magento and the third-party components that it uses. As seen in the previous chapter, the following `composer` command is what pulls everything into the specified directory:

```
composer create-project --repository-url=https://repo.magento.com/
magento/project-enterprise-edition <installation directory name>
```

Once Magento is downloaded and installed, there are numerous `composer.json` files that can be found in its directory. Assuming `<installation directory name>` is `magento2`, if we were to do a quick search executing command such as find `magento2/ -name 'composer.json'`, that would yield over 100 `composer.json` files. Some of these files are (partially) listed here:

```
/vendor/magento/module-catalog/composer.json
/vendor/magento/module-cms/composer.json
/vendor/magento/module-contact/composer.json
/vendor/magento/module-customer/composer.json
/vendor/magento/module-sales/composer.json
/...
/vendor/magento/theme-adminhtml-backend/composer.json
/vendor/magento/theme-frontend-blank/composer.json
/vendor/magento/theme-frontend-luma/composer.json
/vendor/magento/language-de_de/composer.json
/vendor/magento/language-en_us/composer.json
/...
/composer.json
/dev/tests/...
/vendor/magento/framework/composer.json
```

The most relevant file is probably the `composer.json` file in the root of the `magento` directory. Its content appears like this:

```
{
    "name": "magento/project-community-edition",
    "description": "eCommerce Platform for Growth (Community
      Edition)",
    "type": "project",
    "version": "2.0.0",
    "license": [
        "OSL-3.0",
        "AFL-3.0"
    ],
    "repositories": [
```

```json
        {
            "type": "composer",
            "url": "https://repo.magento.com/"
        }
    ],
    "require": {
        "magento/product-community-edition": "2.0.0",
        "composer/composer": "@alpha",
        "magento/module-bundle-sample-data": "100.0.*",
        "magento/module-widget-sample-data": "100.0.*",
        "magento/module-theme-sample-data": "100.0.*",
        "magento/module-catalog-sample-data": "100.0.*",
        "magento/module-customer-sample-data": "100.0.*",
        "magento/module-cms-sample-data": "100.0.*",
        "magento/module-catalog-rule-sample-data": "100.0.*",
        "magento/module-sales-rule-sample-data": "100.0.*",
        "magento/module-review-sample-data": "100.0.*",
        "magento/module-tax-sample-data": "100.0.*",
        "magento/module-sales-sample-data": "100.0.*",
        "magento/module-grouped-product-sample-data": "100.0.*",
        "magento/module-downloadable-sample-data": "100.0.*",
        "magento/module-msrp-sample-data": "100.0.*",
        "magento/module-configurable-sample-data": "100.0.*",
        "magento/module-product-links-sample-data": "100.0.*",
        "magento/module-wishlist-sample-data": "100.0.*",
        "magento/module-swatches-sample-data": "100.0.*",
        "magento/sample-data-media": "100.0.*",
        "magento/module-offline-shipping-sample-data": "100.0.*"
    },
    "require-dev": {
        "phpunit/phpunit": "4.1.0",
        "squizlabs/php_codesniffer": "1.5.3",
        "phpmd/phpmd": "@stable",
        "pdepend/pdepend": "2.0.6",
        "sjparkinson/static-review": "~4.1",
        "fabpot/php-cs-fixer": "~1.2",
        "lusitanian/oauth": "~0.3 <=0.7.0"
    },
    "config": {
        "use-include-path": true
    },
    "autoload": {
        "psr-4": {
```

```
            "Magento\\Framework\\":
              "lib/internal/Magento/Framework/",
            "Magento\\Setup\\": "setup/src/Magento/Setup/",
            "Magento\\": "app/code/Magento/"
        },
        "psr-0": {
            "": "app/code/"
        },
        "files": [
            "app/etc/NonComposerComponentRegistration.php"
        ]
    },
    "autoload-dev": {
        "psr-4": {
            "Magento\\Sniffs\\":
              "dev/tests/static/framework/Magento/Sniffs/",
            "Magento\\Tools\\": "dev/tools/Magento/Tools/",
            "Magento\\Tools\\Sanity\\":
              "dev/build/publication/sanity/
              Magento/Tools/Sanity/",
            "Magento\\TestFramework\\Inspection\\":
              "dev/tests/static/framework/Magento/
               TestFramework/Inspection/",
            "Magento\\TestFramework\\Utility\\":
              "dev/tests/static/framework/Magento/
               TestFramework/Utility/"
        }
    },
    "minimum-stability": "alpha",
    "prefer-stable": true,
    "extra": {
        "magento-force": "override"
    }
}
```

Composer's JSON file follows a certain schema. You will find a detailed documentation of this schema at `https://getcomposer.org/doc/04-schema.md`. Applying to the schema ensures validity of the composer file. We can see that all the listed keys such as `name`, `description`, `require`, `config`, and so on, are defined by the schema.

Let's take a look at the individual module's `composer.json` file. One of the simpler modules with the least amount of dependencies is the `Contact` module with its `vendor/magento/module-contact/composer.json` content, which looks like this:

```
{
    "name": "magento/module-contact",
    "description": "N/A",
    "require": {
        "php": "~5.5.0|~5.6.0|~7.0.0",
        "magento/module-config": "100.0.*",
        "magento/module-store": "100.0.*",
        "magento/module-backend": "100.0.*",
        "magento/module-customer": "100.0.*",
        "magento/module-cms": "100.0.*",
        "magento/framework": "100.0.*"
    },
    "type": "magento2-module",
    "version": "100.0.2",
    "license": [
        "OSL-3.0",
        "AFL-3.0"
    ],
    "autoload": {
        "files": [
            "registration.php"
        ],
        "psr-4": {
            "Magento\\Contact\\": ""
        }
    }
}
```

You will see that the modules define dependencies on the PHP version and other modules. Furthermore, you will see the use of PSR-4 for autoloading and the direct loading of the `registration.php` file.

Next, let's take a look at the contents of `vendor/magento/language-en_us/composer.json` from the `en_us` language module:

```
{
    "name": "magento/language-en_us",
    "description": "English (United States) language",
    "version": "100.0.2",
    "license": [
        "OSL-3.0",
```

```
        "AFL-3.0"
    ],
    "require": {
        "magento/framework": "100.0.*"
    },
    "type": "magento2-language",
    "autoload": {
        "files": [
            "registration.php"
        ]
    }
}
```

Finally, let's take a look at the contents of vendor/magento/theme-frontend-luma/ composer.json from the luma theme:

```
{
    "name": "magento/theme-frontend-luma",
    "description": "N/A",
    "require": {
        "php": "~5.5.0|~5.6.0|~7.0.0",
        "magento/theme-frontend-blank": "100.0.*",
        "magento/framework": "100.0.*"
    },
    "type": "magento2-theme",
    "version": "100.0.2",
    "license": [
        "OSL-3.0",
        "AFL-3.0"
    ],
    "autoload": {
        "files": [
            "registration.php"
        ]
    }
}
```

As mentioned previously, there are a lot more composer files scattered around Magento.

Service contracts

A **service contract** is a set of PHP interfaces that is defined by a module. This contract comprises data interfaces and service interfaces.

The role of the data interface is to preserve data integrity, while the role of the service interface is to hide the business logic details from service consumers.

Data interfaces define various functions, such as validation, entity information, search related functions, and so on. They are defined within the Api/Data directory of an individual module. To better understand the actual meaning of it, let's take a look at the data interfaces for the Magento_Cms module. In the vendor/magento/module-cms/Api/Data/ directory, there are four interfaces defined, as follows:

```
BlockInterface.php
BlockSearchResultsInterface.php
PageInterface.php
PageSearchResultsInterface.php
```

The CMS module actually deals with two entities, one being Block and the other one being Page. Looking at the interfaces defined in the preceding code, we can see that we have separate data interface for the entity itself and separate data interface for search results.

Let's take a closer look at the (stripped) contents of the BlockInterface.php file, which is defined as follows:

```php
namespace Magento\Cms\Api\Data;

interface BlockInterface
{
    const BLOCK_ID       = 'block_id';
    const IDENTIFIER     = 'identifier';
    const TITLE          = 'title';
    const CONTENT        = 'content';
    const CREATION_TIME  = 'creation_time';
    const UPDATE_TIME    = 'update_time';
    const IS_ACTIVE      = 'is_active';

    public function getId();
    public function getIdentifier();
    public function getTitle();
    public function getContent();
    public function getCreationTime();
    public function getUpdateTime();
    public function isActive();
    public function setId($id);
    public function setIdentifier($identifier);
    public function setTitle($title);
    public function setContent($content);
```

```
        public function setCreationTime($creationTime);
        public function setUpdateTime($updateTime);
        public function setIsActive($isActive);
}
```

The preceding interface defines all the getter and setter methods for the entity at hand along with the constant values that denote entity field names. These data interfaces do not include management actions, such as delete. The implementation of this specific interface can be seen in the vendor/magento/module-cms/Model/ Block.php file, where these constants come to use, as follows (partially):

```
public function getTitle()
{
    return $this->getData(self::TITLE);
}

public function setTitle($title)
{
    return $this->setData(self::TITLE, $title);
}
```

Service interfaces are the ones that include management, repository, and metadata interfaces. These interfaces are defined directly within the module's Api directory. Looking back at the Magento Cms module, its vendor/magento/module-cms/Api/ directory has two service interfaces, which are defined as follows:

```
BlockRepositoryInterface.php
PageRepositoryInterface.php
```

A quick look into the contents of BlockRepositoryInterface.php reveals the following (partial) content:

```
namespace Magento\Cms\Api;

use Magento\Framework\Api\SearchCriteriaInterface;

interface BlockRepositoryInterface
{
    public function save(Data\BlockInterface $block);
    public function getById($blockId);
    public function getList(SearchCriteriaInterface
        $searchCriteria);
    public function delete(Data\BlockInterface $block);
    public function deleteById($blockId);
}
```

Here, we see methods that are used to save, fetch, search, and delete the entity.

These interfaces are then implemented via the Web API definitions, as we will see later in *Chapter 9, The Web API*. The result is well-defined and durable API's that other modules and third-party integrators can consume.

Code generation

One of the neat features of the Magento application is code generation. **Code generation**, as implied by its name, generates nonexistent classes. These classes are generated in Magento's `var/generation` directory.

The directory structure within `var/generation` is somewhat similar to that of the core `vendor/magento/module-*` and `app/code` directories. To be more precise, it follows the module structure. The code is generated for something that is called **Factory**, **Proxy**, and **Interceptor** classes.

The Factory class creates an instance of a type. For example, a `var/generation/Magento/Catalog/Model/ProductFactory.php` file with a `Magento\Catalog\Model\ProductFactory` class has been created because somewhere within the `vendor/magento` directory and its code, there is a call to the `Magento\Catalog\Model\ProductFactory` class, which originally does not exist in Magento. During runtime, when `{someClassName}Factory` is called in the code, Magento creates a Factory class under the `var/generation` directory if it does not exist. The following code is an example of the (partial) `ProductFactory` class:

```
namespace Magento\Catalog\Model;

/**
 * Factory class for @see \Magento\Catalog\Model\Product
 */
class ProductFactory
{
    //...

    /**
     * Create class instance with specified parameters
     *
     * @param array $data
     * @return \Magento\Catalog\Model\Product
     */
    public function create(array $data = array())
    {
```

```
        return $this->_objectManager->create($this->_instanceName,
            $data);
    }
}
```

Note the `create` method that creates and returns the `Product` type instance. Also, note how the generated code is *type safe* providing `@return` annotation for **integrated development environments (IDEs)** to support the autocomplete functionality.

Factories are used to isolate an object manager from the business code. Factories can be dependent on the object manager, unlike business objects.

The Proxy class is a wrapper for some **base class**. Proxy classes provide better performance than the base classes because they can be instantiated without instantiating a base class. A base class is instantiated only when one of its methods is called. This is highly convenient for cases where the base class is used as a dependency, but it takes a lot of time to instantiate, and its methods are used only during some paths of execution.

Like Factory, the Proxy classes are also generated under the `var/generation` directory.

If we were to take a look at the `var/generation/Magento/Catalog/Model/Session/Proxy.php` file that contains the `Magento\Catalog\Model\Session\Proxy` class, we would see that it actually extends `\Magento\Catalog\Model\Session`. The wrapping Proxy class implements several magical methods along the way, such as `__sleep`, `__wakeup`, `__clone`, and `__call`.

Interceptor is yet another class type that gets autogenerated by Magento. It is related to the plugins feature, which will be discussed in detail later in *Chapter 6, Plugins*.

In order to trigger code regeneration, we can use the code compiler that is available on the console. We can run either the *single-tenant* compiler or the *multi-tenant* compiler.

The *single-tenant* implies one website and store, and it is executed by using the following command:

```
magento setup:di:compile
```

The *multi-tenant* implies more than one independent Magento application, and it is executed by using following command.

```
magento setup:di:compile-multi-tenant
```

Code compilation generates factories, proxies, interceptors, and several other classes, as listed in the `setup/src/Magento/Setup/Module/Di/App/Task/Operation/` directory.

The var directory

Magento does a lot of caching and autogeneration of certain class types. These caches and generated classes are all located in Magento's root `var` directory. The usual contents of the `var` directory is as follows:

```
cache
composer_home
generation
log
di
view_preprocessed
page_cache
```

During development, we will most likely need to periodically clear these so that our changes can kick in.

We can issue the console command as follows to clear individual directories:

rm -rf {Magento root dir}/var/generation/*

Alternatively, we can use the built-in `bin/magento` console tool to trigger commands that will delete the proper directories for us, as follows:

- `bin/magento setup:upgrade`: This updates the Magento database schema and data. While doing this, it truncates the `var/di` and `var/generation` directories.

- `bin/magento setup:di:compile`: This clears the `var/generation` directory. After doing this, it compiles the code in it again.

- `bin/magento deploy:mode:set {mode}`: This changes the mode from the developer mode to the production mode and vice versa. While doing this, it truncates the `var/di`, `var/generation`, and `var/view_preprocessed` directories.

- `bin/magento cache:clean {type}`: This cleans the `var/cache` and `var/page_cache` directories.

It is important to keep the `var` directory in mind at all times during development. Otherwise, the code might encounter exceptions and function improperly.

Coding standards

Coding standards are a result of conventions designed to produce high-quality code. Adopting certain standards yields better code quality, reduces the time taken to develop, and minimizes maintenance cost. Following coding standards requires knowing the standards in question and meticulously applying it to every aspect of the code that we write.

There are several coding standards that Magento abides by, such as the following ones:

- The code demarcation standard
- The PHP coding standard
- The JavaScript coding standard
- The jQuery widget coding standard
- The DocBlock standard
- JavaScript DocBlock standard
- The LESS coding standard

The **code demarcation** standard speaks of decoupling HTML, CSS, and JS from PHP classes. By doing so, the backend-related development stays unaffected by frontend development and vice versa. This means that we can make business logic changes without fearing a broken frontend.

The **PHP** coding standard refers to **PSR-1: Basic Coding Standard** and **PSR-2: Coding Style Guide** that are described at `http://www.php-fig.org`. PSR-1 touches on PHP filenames, class names, namespaces, class constant, properties, and methods. PSR-2 extends the PSR-1 by touching upon the actual inners of a class, such as spaces, braces, method and properties visibility, control structures, and so on.

The **JavaScript** coding standard is based on the *Google JavaScript Style Guide* found at `https://google.github.io/styleguide/javascriptguide.xml`. This coding standard touches on the JavaScript language and coding style rules. It is a lot like PSR-1 and PSR-2 for PHP.

The **jQuery widget** coding standard is flagged as mandatory for Magento core developers and recommended for third-party developers. It goes without saying how important jQuery UI widgets are in Magento. The standard describes several things, such as widget naming, instantiation, extension, DOM event bubbling, and so on.

The **DocBlock** standard touches on the requirements and conventions for the addition of inline code documentation. The idea is to unify the usage of code DocBlocks for all files regardless of the programming language in use. However, a DocBlock standard for that particular language may override it.

The **JavaScript DocBlock** standard relates to the JavaScript code files and their inline documentation. It is a subset of Google JavaScript Style Guide and JSDoc, which can be found at `http://usejsdoc.org`.

The **LESS** coding standard defines the formatting and coding style when working with LESS and CSS files.

> You can read more about the actual details of each standard at `http://devdocs.magento.com`, as they are too extensive to be covered in this book.

Summary

In this chapter, we took a look at Composer, which is one of the first things that we will interact with when installing Magento. We then moved on to service contracts as one of the strongest Magento architectural parts, which turned out to be good old PHP interfaces in use. Further, we covered some bits about the Magento code generation feature. Thus, we have a basic knowledge of the Factory and Proxy classes. We then had a look at the `var` directory and explored its role, especially during development. Finally, we touched upon the coding standards used in Magento.

In the next chapter, we will discuss the dependency injection, which is one of the most important architectural parts of Magento.

4
Models and Collections

Like most modern frameworks and platforms, these days Magento embraces an **Object Relational Mapping (ORM)** approach over raw SQL queries. Though the underlying mechanism still comes down to SQL, we are now dealing strictly with objects. This makes our application code more readable, manageable, and isolated from vendor-specific SQL differences. Model, resource, and collection are three types of classes working together to allow us full entity data management, from loading, saving, deleting, and listing entities. The majority of our data access and management will be done via PHP classes called Magento models. Models themselves don't contain any code for communicating with the database.

The database communication part is decoupled into its own PHP class called resource class. Each model is then assigned a resource class. Calling load, save, or delete methods on models get delegated to resource classes, as they are the ones to actually read, write, and delete data from the database. Theoretically, with enough knowledge, it is possible to write new resource classes for various database vendors.

Next to the model and resource classes, we have collection classes. We can think of a collection as an array of individual model instances. On a base level, collections extend from the \Magento\Framework\Data\Collection class, which implements \IteratorAggregate and \Countable from **Standard PHP Library (SPL)** and a few other Magento-specific classes.

More often than not, we look at model and resource as a single unified thing, thus simply calling it a model. Magento deals with two types of models, which we might categorize as simple and EAV models.

In this chapter, we will cover the following topics:

- Creating a miniature module
- Creating a simple model
- The EAV model
- Understanding the flow of schema and data scripts
- Creating an install schema script (`InstallSchema.php`)
- Creating an upgrade schema script (`UpgradeSchema.php`)
- Creating an install data script (`InstallData.php`)
- Creating an upgrade data script (`UpgradeData.php`)
- Entity CRUD actions
- Managing collections

Creating a miniature module

For the purpose of this chapter, we will create a miniature module called `Foggyline_Office`.

The module will have two entities defined as follows:

- `Department`: a simple model with the following fields:
    - `entity_id`: primary key
    - `name`: name of department, string value

- `Employee`: an EAV model with the following fields and attributes:
    - **Fields:**
        - `entity_id`: primary key
        - `department_id`: foreign key, pointing to `Department.entity_id`
        - `email`: unique e-mail of an employee, string value
        - `first_name`: first name of an employee, string value
        - `last_name`: last name of an employee, string value

- ° **Attributes:**
  - ° `service_years`: employee's years of service, integer value
  - ° `dob`: employee's date of birth, date-time value
  - ° `salary` – monthly salary, decimal value
  - ° `vat_number`: VAT number, (short) string value
  - ° `note`: possible note on employee, (long) string value

Every module starts with the `registration.php` and `module.xml` files. For the purpose of our chapter module, let's create the `app/code/Foggyline/Office/registration.php` file with content as follows:

```php
<?php
\Magento\Framework\Component\ComponentRegistrar::register(
    \Magento\Framework\Component\ComponentRegistrar::MODULE,
    'Foggyline_Office',
    __DIR__
);
```

The `registration.php` file is sort of an entry point to our module.

Now let's create the `app/code/Foggyline/Office/etc/module.xml` file with the following content:

```xml
<config xmlns:xsi="http://www.w3.org/2001/XMLSchema-instance"
  xsi:noNamespaceSchemaLocation="urn:magento:framework:Module/
  etc/module.xsd">
    <module name="Foggyline_Office" setup_version="1.0.0">
        <sequence>
            <module name="Magento_Eav"/>
        </sequence>
    </module>
</config>
```

We will get into more details about the structure of the `module.xml` file in later chapters. Right now, we will only focus on the `setup_version` attribute and `module` element within `sequence`.

The value of `setup_version` is important because we might use it within our schema install script (`InstallSchema.php`) files, effectively turning the install script into an update script, as we will show soon.

The `sequence` element is Magento's way of setting dependencies for our module. Given that our module will make use of EAV entities, we list `Magento_Eav` as a dependency.

Creating a simple model

The `Department` entity, as per requirements, is modeled as a simple model. We previously mentioned that whenever we talk about models, we implicitly think of `model` class, `resource` class, and `collection` class forming one unit.

Let's start by first creating a `model` class, (partially) defined under the `app/code/Foggyline/Office/Model/Department.php` file as follows:

```
namespace Foggyline\Office\Model;

class Department extends \Magento\Framework\Model\AbstractModel
{
    protected function _construct()
    {
        $this->_init('Foggyline\Office\Model
            \ResourceModel\Department');
    }
}
```

All that is happening here is that we are extending from the `\Magento\Framework\Model\AbstractModel` class, and triggering the `$this->_init` method within `_construct` passing it our `resource` class.

The `AbstractModel` further extends `\Magento\Framework\Object`. The fact that our `model` class ultimately extends from `Object` means that we do not have to define a property name on our `model` class. What `Object` does for us is that it enables us to get, set, unset, and check for a value existence on properties magically. To give a more robust example than `name`, imagine our entity has a property called `employee_average_salary` in the following code:

```
$department->getData('employee_average_salary');
$department->getEmployeeAverageSalary();

$department->setData('employee_average_salary', 'theValue');
$department->setEmployeeAverageSalary('theValue');

$department->unsetData('employee_average_salary');
$department->unsEmployeeAverageSalary();

$department->hasData('employee_average_salary');
$department->hasEmployeeAverageSalary();
```

The reason why this works is due to `Object` implementing the `setData`, `unsetData`, `getData`, and magic `__call` methods. The beauty of the magic `__call` method implementation is that it understands method calls like `getEmployeeAverageSalary`, `setEmployeeAverageSalary`, `unsEmployeeAverageSalary`, and `hasEmployeeAverageSalary` even if they do not exist on the `Model` class. However, if we choose to implement some of these methods within our `Model` class, we are free to do so and Magento will pick it up when we call it.

This is an important aspect of Magento, sometimes confusing to newcomers.

Once we have a `model` class in place, we create a model `resource` class, (partially) defined under the `app/code/Foggyline/Office/Model/ResourceModel/Department.php` file as follows:

```
namespace Foggyline\Office\Model\ResourceModel;

class Department extends \Magento\Framework\Model\ResourceModel\Db\
AbstractDb
{
    protected function _construct()
    {
        $this->_init('foggyline_office_department', 'entity_id');
    }
}
```

Our resource class that extends from `\Magento\Framework\Model\ResourceModel\Db\AbstractDb` triggers the `$this->_init` method call within `_construct`. `$this->_init` accepts two parameters. The first parameter is the table name `foggyline_office_department`, where our model will persist its data. The second parameter is the primary column name `entity_id` within that table.

`AbstractDb` further extends `Magento\Framework\Model\ResourceModel\AbstractResource`.

 The resource class is the key to communicating to the database. All it takes is for us to name the table and its primary key and our models can save, delete, and update entities.

Finally, we create our `collection` class, (partially) defined under the `app/code/`
`Foggyline/Office/Model/ResourceModel/Department/Collection.php` file
as follows:

```
namespace Foggyline\Office\Model\ResourceModel\Department;

class Collection extends \Magento\Framework\Model\ResourceModel
  \Db\Collection\AbstractCollection
{
    protected function _construct()
    {
        $this->_init(
            'Foggyline\Office\Model\Department',
            'Foggyline\Office\Model\ResourceModel\Department'
        );
    }
}
```

The `collection` class extends from `\Magento\Framework\Model\ResourceModel\`
`Db\Collection\AbstractCollection` and, similar to the `model` and `resource`
classes, does a `$this->_init` method call within `_construct`. This time, `_init`
accepts two parameters. The first parameter is the full `model` class name `Foggyline\`
`Office\Model\Department`, and the second parameter is the full resource class
name `Foggyline\Office\Model\ResourceModel\Department`.

`AbstractCollection` implements `Magento\Framework\App\ResourceConnection\`
`SourceProviderInterface`, and extends `\Magento\Framework\Data\Collection\`
`AbstractDb`. `AbstractDb` further extends `\Magento\Framework\Data\Collection`.

It is worth taking some time to study the inners of these `collection` classes, as this
is our go-to place for whenever we need to deal with fetching a list of entities that
match certain search criteria.

Creating an EAV model

The `Employee` entity, as per requirements, is modeled as an EAV model.

Let's start by first creating an EAV `model` class, (partially) defined under the `app/`
`code/Foggyline/Office/Model/Employee.php` file as follows:

```
namespace Foggyline\Office\Model;

class Employee extends \Magento\Framework\Model\AbstractModel
{
```

```
    const ENTITY = 'foggyline_office_employee';

    public function _construct()
    {
        $this->_init('Foggyline\Office \Model
          \ResourceModel\Employee');
    }
}
```

Here, we are extending from the `\Magento\Framework\Model\AbstractModel` class, which is the same as with the simple model previously described. The only difference here is that we have an `ENTITY` constant defined, but this is merely syntactical sugar for later on; it bears no meaning for the actual `model` class.

Next, we create an EAV model `resource` class, (partially) defined under the app/ `code/Foggyline/Office/Model/ResourceModel/Employee.php` file as follows:

```
namespace Foggyline\Office\Model\ResourceModel;

class Employee extends \Magento\Eav\Model\Entity\AbstractEntity
{

    protected function _construct()
    {
        $this->_read = 'foggyline_office_employee_read';
        $this->_write = 'foggyline_office_employee_write';
    }

    public function getEntityType()
    {
        if (empty($this->_type)) {
            $this->setType(\Foggyline\Office\Model
              \Employee::ENTITY);
        }
        return parent::getEntityType();
    }
}
```

Our `resource` class extends from `\Magento\Eav\Model\Entity\AbstractEntity`, and sets the `$this->_read`, `$this->_write` class properties through `_construct`. These are freely assigned to whatever value we want, preferably following the naming pattern of our module. The read and write connections need to be named or else Magento produces an error when using our entities.

The `getEntityType` method internally sets the `_type` value to `\Foggyline\Office\`
`Model\Employee::ENTITY`, which is the string `foggyline_office_employee`.
This same value is what's stored in the `entity_type_code` column within the `eav_`
`entity_type` table. At this point, there is no such entry in the `eav_entity_type`
table. This is because the install schema script will be creating one, as we will be
demonstrating soon.

Finally, we create our `collection` class, (partially) defined under the `app/code/`
`Foggyline/Office/Model/ResourceModel/Employee/Collection.php` file
as follows:

```
namespace Foggyline\Office\Model\ResourceModel\Employee;

class Collection extends \Magento\Eav\Model\Entity\Collection\
AbstractCollection
{
    protected function _construct()
    {
        $this->_init('Foggyline\Office\Model\Employee',
            'Foggyline\Office\Model\ResourceModel\Employee');
    }
}
```

The `collection` class extends from `\Magento\Eav\Model\Entity\Collection\`
`AbstractCollection` and, similar to the model class, does a `$this->_init` method
call within `_construct`. `_init` accepts two parameters: the full model class name
`Foggyline\Office\Model\Employee`, and the full resource class name `Foggyline\`
`Office\Model\ResourceModel\Employee`.

`AbstractCollection` has the same parent tree as the simple model collection
class, but on its own it implements a lot of EAV collection-specific methods like
`addAttributeToFilter`, `addAttributeToSelect`, `addAttributeToSort`, and so on.

As we can see, EAV models look a lot like simple models. The
difference lies mostly in the `resource` class and `collection` class
implementations and their first level parent classes. However, we need
to keep in mind that the example given here is the simplest one possible.
If we look at the `eav_entity_type` table in the database, we can
see that other entity types make use of `attribute_model`, `entity_`
`attribute_collection`, `increment_model`, and so on. These are
all advanced properties we can define alongside our EAV model making
it closer to the implementation of the `catalog_product` entity type,
which is probably the most robust one in Magento. This type of advanced
EAV usage is out of the scope of this book as it is probably worth a book
on its own.

Now that we have simple and EAV models in place, it is time to look into installing the necessary database schema and possibly pre-fill it with some data. This is done through schema and data scripts.

Understanding the flow of schema and data scripts

Simply put, the role of the schema scripts is to create a database structure supporting your module logic. For example, creating a table where our entities would persist their data. The role of the data scripts is to manage the data within existing tables, usually in the form of adding some sample data during module installation.

If we look a few steps back, we can notice how `schema_version` and `data_version` from the database match the `setup_version` number from our `module.xml` file. They all imply the same thing. If we were to now change the `setup_version` number in our `module.xml` file and run the `php bin/magento setup:upgrade` console command again, our database `schema_version` and `data_version` would get updated to this new version number.

This is done through module's `install` and `upgrade` scripts. If we take a quick look at the `setup/src/Magento/Setup/Model/Installer.php` file, we can see a function, `getSchemaDataHandler`, with content as follows:

```
private function getSchemaDataHandler($moduleName, $type)
{
    $className = str_replace('_', '\\', $moduleName) . '\Setup';
    switch ($type) {
        case 'schema-install':
            $className .= '\InstallSchema';
            $interface = self::SCHEMA_INSTALL;
            break;
        case 'schema-upgrade':
            $className .= '\UpgradeSchema';
            $interface = self::SCHEMA_UPGRADE;
            break;
        case 'schema-recurring':
            $className .= '\Recurring';
            $interface = self::SCHEMA_INSTALL;
            break;
        case 'data-install':
            $className .= '\InstallData';
            $interface = self::DATA_INSTALL;
            break;
```

```
        case 'data-upgrade':
            $className .= '\UpgradeData';
            $interface = self::DATA_UPGRADE;
            break;
        default:
            throw new \Magento\Setup\Exception("$className does
                not exist");
    }

        return $this->createSchemaDataHandler($className, $interface);
}
```

This is what tells Magento which classes to pick up and run from the individual module Setup directory. We will ignore the Recurring case for the moment, as only the Magento_Indexer module uses it.

For the first time, we run php bin/magento setup:upgrade against our module; while it still has no entries under the setup_module table, Magento will execute the files within the module Setup folder in following order:

- InstallSchema.php
- UpgradeSchema.php
- InstallData.php
- UpgradeData.php

Notice that this is the same order, top to bottom, as in the getSchemaDataHandler method.

Every subsequent upper module version number change, followed by the console php bin/magento setup:upgrade command, would result in the following files being run in the order as listed:

- UpgradeSchema.php
- UpgradeData.php

Additionally, Magento would record the upped version number under the setup_module database. Magento will only trigger install or upgrade scripts when the version number in the database is less than the version number in the module.xml file.

 We are not required to always provide these install or upgrade scripts, if ever. They are only needed when we need to add or edit existing tables or entries in a database.

If we look carefully at the implementation of the install and update methods within the appropriate scripts, we can see they both accept ModuleContextInterface $context as a second parameter. Since upgrade scripts are the ones triggering on every upped version number, we can use $context->getVersion() to target changes specific to the module version.

Creating an install schema script (InstallSchema.php)

Now that we understand the flow of schema and data scripts and their relation to the module version number, let us go ahead and start assembling our InstallSchema. We start by defining the app/code/Foggyline/Office/Setup/InstallSchema.php file with (partial) content as follows:

```php
namespace Foggyline\Office\Setup;

use Magento\Framework\Setup\InstallSchemaInterface;
use Magento\Framework\Setup\ModuleContextInterface;
use Magento\Framework\Setup\SchemaSetupInterface;

class InstallSchema implements InstallSchemaInterface
{
    public function install(SchemaSetupInterface $setup,
      ModuleContextInterface $context)
    {
        $setup->startSetup();
        /* #snippet1 */
        $setup->endSetup();
    }
}
```

InstallSchema conforms to InstallSchemaInterface, which requires the implementation of the install method that accepts two parameters of type SchemaSetupInterface and ModuleContextInterface.

The install method is all that is required here. Within this method, we would add any relevant code we might have to create the tables and columns we need.

Looking through the code base, we can see that Magento\Setup\Module\Setup is the one extending \Magento\Framework\Module\Setup and implementing SchemaSetupInterface. The two methods seen in the preceding code, startSetup and endSetup, are used to run additional environment setup before and after our code.

Going further, let's replace the /* #snippet1 */ bit with code that will create our Department model entity table as follows:

```
$table = $setup->getConnection()
    ->newTable($setup->getTable('foggyline_office_department'))
    ->addColumn(
        'entity_id',
        \Magento\Framework\DB\Ddl\Table::TYPE_INTEGER,
        null,
        ['identity' => true, 'unsigned' => true, 'nullable' =>
          false, 'primary' => true],
        'Entity ID'
    )
    ->addColumn(
        'name',
        \Magento\Framework\DB\Ddl\Table::TYPE_TEXT,
        64,
        [],
        'Name'
    )
    ->setComment('Foggyline Office Department Table');
$setup->getConnection()->createTable($table);
/* #snippet2 */
```

Here, we are instructing Magento to create a table named foggyline_office_department, add entity_id and name columns to it, and set the comment on the table. Assuming we are using the MySQL server, when code executes, the following SQL gets executed in the database:

```
CREATE TABLE 'foggyline_office_department' (
  'entity_id' int(10) unsigned NOT NULL AUTO_INCREMENT COMMENT 'Entity
ID',
  'name' varchar(64) DEFAULT NULL COMMENT 'Name',
  PRIMARY KEY ('entity_id')
) ENGINE=InnoDB AUTO_INCREMENT=3 DEFAULT CHARSET=utf8
COMMENT='Foggyline Office Department Table';
```

The addColumn method is the most interesting one here. It takes five parameters, from column name, column data type, column length, array of additional options, and column description. However, only column name and column data type are mandatory! Accepted column data types can be found under the Magento\Framework\DB\Ddl\Table class, and go as follows:

boolean	smallint	integer	bigint
float	numeric	decimal	date
timestamp	datetime	text	blob
varbinary			

An additional options array might contain some of the following keys: unsigned, precision, scale, unsigned, default, nullable, primary, identity, auto_increment.

Having gained insight into the addColumn method, let's go ahead and create the foggyline_office_employee_entity table for the Employee entity as well. We do so by replacing the /* #snippet2 */ bit from the preceding code with the following code:

```
$employeeEntity = \Foggyline\Office\Model\Employee::ENTITY;
$table = $setup->getConnection()
    ->newTable($setup->getTable($employeeEntity . '_entity'))
    ->addColumn(
        'entity_id',
        \Magento\Framework\DB\Ddl\Table::TYPE_INTEGER,
        null,
        ['identity' => true, 'unsigned' => true, 'nullable' =>
          false, 'primary' => true],
        'Entity ID'
    )
    ->addColumn(
        'department_id',
        \Magento\Framework\DB\Ddl\Table::TYPE_INTEGER,
        null,
        ['unsigned' => true, 'nullable' => false],
        'Department Id'
    )
    ->addColumn(
        'email',
        \Magento\Framework\DB\Ddl\Table::TYPE_TEXT,
        64,
        [],
        'Email'
    )
    ->addColumn(
        'first_name',
        \Magento\Framework\DB\Ddl\Table::TYPE_TEXT,
        64,
        [],
        'First Name'
    )
    ->addColumn(
        'last_name',
        \Magento\Framework\DB\Ddl\Table::TYPE_TEXT,
        64,
```

```
        [],
        'Last Name'
    )
    ->setComment('Foggyline Office Employee Table');
$setup->getConnection()->createTable($table);
/* #snippet3 */
```

Following good database design practices, we might notice one thing here. If we agree that every employee can be assigned a single department, we should add a foreign key to this table's `department_id` column. For the moment, we will purposely skip this bit, as we want to demonstrate this through the update schema script later on.

EAV models scatter their data across several tables, three at a minimum. The table `foggyline_office_employee_entity` that we just created is one of them. The other one is the core Magento `eav_attribute` table. The third table is not a single table, rather a list of multiple tables; one for each EAV type. These tables are the result of our install script.

Information stored within the core Magento `eav_attribute` table is not the value of an attribute or anything like it; information stored there is an attribute's metadata. So how does Magento know about our `Employee` attributes (`service_years`, `dob`, `salary`, `vat_number`, `note`)? It does not; not yet. We need to add the attributes into that table ourselves. We will do so later on, as we demonstrate the `InstallData`.

Depending on the EAV attribute data type, we need to create the following tables:

- `foggyline_office_employee_entity_datetime`
- `foggyline_office_employee_entity_decimal`
- `foggyline_office_employee_entity_int`
- `foggyline_office_employee_entity_text`
- `foggyline_office_employee_entity_varchar`

The names of these attribute value tables come from a simple formula, which says *{name of the entity table}+{_}+{eav_attribute.backend_type value}*. If we look at the salary attribute, we need it to be a decimal value, thus it will get stored in `foggyline_office_employee_entity_decimal`.

Given the chunkiness of code behind defining attribute value tables, we will focus only on a single, decimal type table. We define it by replacing /* #snippet3 */ from the preceding code with the following bit:

```
$table = $setup->getConnection()
    ->newTable($setup->getTable($employeeEntity .
      '_entity_decimal'))
    ->addColumn(
        'value_id',
        \Magento\Framework\DB\Ddl\Table::TYPE_INTEGER,
        null,
        ['identity' => true, 'nullable' => false, 'primary' =>
          true],
        'Value ID'
    )
    ->addColumn(
        'attribute_id',
        \Magento\Framework\DB\Ddl\Table::TYPE_SMALLINT,
        null,
        ['unsigned' => true, 'nullable' => false, 'default' =>
          '0'],
        'Attribute ID'
    )
    ->addColumn(
        'store_id',
        \Magento\Framework\DB\Ddl\Table::TYPE_SMALLINT,
        null,
        ['unsigned' => true, 'nullable' => false, 'default' =>
          '0'],
        'Store ID'
    )
    ->addColumn(
        'entity_id',
        \Magento\Framework\DB\Ddl\Table::TYPE_INTEGER,
        null,
        ['unsigned' => true, 'nullable' => false, 'default' =>
          '0'],
        'Entity ID'
    )
```

```
    ->addColumn(
        'value',
        \Magento\Framework\DB\Ddl\Table::TYPE_DECIMAL,
        '12,4',
        [],
        'Value'
    )
    //->addIndex
    //->addForeignKey
    ->setComment('Employee Decimal Attribute Backend Table');
$setup->getConnection()->createTable($table);
```

Notice the `//->addIndex` part within code above. Lets replace it with the following bit.

```
->addIndex(
    $setup->getIdxName(
        $employeeEntity . '_entity_decimal',
        ['entity_id', 'attribute_id', 'store_id'],
        \Magento\Framework\DB\Adapter\AdapterInterface::INDEX_TYPE_
UNIQUE
    ),
    ['entity_id', 'attribute_id', 'store_id'],
    ['type' => \Magento\Framework\DB\Adapter\AdapterInterface::INDEX_
TYPE_UNIQUE]
)
->addIndex(
    $setup->getIdxName($employeeEntity . '_entity_decimal',
        ['store_id']),
    ['store_id']
)
->addIndex(
    $setup->getIdxName($employeeEntity . '_entity_decimal',
        ['attribute_id']),
    ['attribute_id']
)
```

The preceding code adds three indexes on the `foggyline_office_employee_entity_decimal` table, resulting in a SQL as follows:

- UNIQUE KEY 'FOGGYLINE_OFFICE_EMPLOYEE_ENTT_DEC_ENTT_ID_ATTR_ID_
  STORE_ID' ('entity_id','attribute_id','store_id')

- KEY 'FOGGYLINE_OFFICE_EMPLOYEE_ENTITY_DECIMAL_STORE_ID'
  ('store_id')

- KEY 'FOGGYLINE_OFFICE_EMPLOYEE_ENTITY_DECIMAL_ATTRIBUTE_ID'
  ('attribute_id')

Similarly, we replace the //->addForeignKey part from the preceding code with the following bit:

```
->addForeignKey(
    $setup->getFkName(
        $employeeEntity . '_entity_decimal',
        'attribute_id',
        'eav_attribute',
        'attribute_id'
    ),
    'attribute_id',
    $setup->getTable('eav_attribute'),
    'attribute_id',
    \Magento\Framework\DB\Ddl\Table::ACTION_CASCADE
)
->addForeignKey(
    $setup->getFkName(
        $employeeEntity . '_entity_decimal',
        'entity_id',
        $employeeEntity . '_entity',
        'entity_id'
    ),
    'entity_id',
    $setup->getTable($employeeEntity . '_entity'),
    'entity_id',
    \Magento\Framework\DB\Ddl\Table::ACTION_CASCADE
)
->addForeignKey(
    $setup->getFkName($employeeEntity . '_entity_decimal',
      'store_id', 'store', 'store_id'),
    'store_id',
    $setup->getTable('store'),
    'store_id',
    \Magento\Framework\DB\Ddl\Table::ACTION_CASCADE
)
```

The preceding code adds foreign key relations into the foggyline_office_employee_entity_decimal table, resulting in a SQL as follows:

- CONSTRAINT 'FK_D17982EDA1846BAA1F40E30694993801' FOREIGN KEY ('entity_id') REFERENCES 'foggyline_office_employee_entity' ('entity_id') ON DELETE CASCADE,

- CONSTRAINT 'FOGGYLINE_OFFICE_EMPLOYEE_ENTITY_DECIMAL_STORE_ ID_STORE_STORE_ID' FOREIGN KEY ('store_id') REFERENCES 'store' ('store_id') ON DELETE CASCADE,

- CONSTRAINT 'FOGGYLINE_OFFICE_EMPLOYEE_ENTT_DEC_ATTR_ID_EAV_ ATTR_ATTR_ID' FOREIGN KEY ('attribute_id') REFERENCES 'eav_ attribute' ('attribute_id') ON DELETE CASCADE

Notice how we added the store_id column to our EAV attribute value tables. Though our examples won't find use of it, it is a good practice to use store_id with your EAV entities to scope the data for a possible multi-store setup. To clarify further, imagine we had a multi-store setup, and with EAV attribute tables set up like the preceding one, we would be able to store a different attribute value for each store, since the unique entry in the table is defined as a combination of entity_id, attribute_id, and store_id columns.

> For the reasons of performance and data integrity, it is important to define indexes and foreign key as per good database design practice. We can do so within InstallSchema when defining new tables.

Creating an upgrade schema script (UpgradeSchema.php)

During the first-time module install, an upgrade schema is what gets run immediately after an install schema. We define upgrade schema within the app/code/Foggyline/Office/Setup/UpgradeSchema.php file with (partial) content as follows:

```php
namespace Foggyline\Office\Setup;

use Magento\Framework\Setup\UpgradeSchemaInterface;
use Magento\Framework\Setup\ModuleContextInterface;
use Magento\Framework\Setup\SchemaSetupInterface;

class UpgradeSchema implements UpgradeSchemaInterface
{
    public function upgrade(SchemaSetupInterface $setup,
      ModuleContextInterface $context)
    {
        $setup->startSetup();
          /* #snippet1 */
        $setup->endSetup();
    }
}
```

UpgradeSchema conforms to UpgradeSchemaInterface, which requires the implementation of the upgrade method that accepts two parameters of type SchemaSetupInterface and ModuleContextInterface.

This is quite similar to InstallSchemaInterface, except the method name. The update method is run when this schema gets triggered. Within this method, we would add any relevant code we might want to execute.

Going further, let's replace the /* #snippet1 */ part from the preceding code with the following code:

```
$employeeEntityTable = \Foggyline\Office\Model\Employee::ENTITY. '_
entity';
$departmentEntityTable = 'foggyline_office_department';

$setup->getConnection()
    ->addForeignKey(
        $setup->getFkName($employeeEntityTable, 'department_id',
          $departmentEntityTable, 'entity_id'),
        $setup->getTable($employeeEntityTable),
        'department_id',
        $setup->getTable($departmentEntityTable),
        'entity_id',
        \Magento\Framework\DB\Ddl\Table::ACTION_CASCADE
    );
```

Here, we are instructing Magento to create a foreign key on the foggyline_office_employee_entity table, more precisely on its department_id column, pointing to the foggyline_office_department table and its entity_id column.

Creating an install data script (InstallData.php)

An install data script is what gets run immediately after upgrade schema. We define install data schema within the app/code/Foggyline/Office/Setup/InstallData.php file with (partial) content as follows:

```
namespace Foggyline\Office\Setup;

use Magento\Framework\Setup\InstallDataInterface;
use Magento\Framework\Setup\ModuleContextInterface;
use Magento\Framework\Setup\ModuleDataSetupInterface;
```

```
class InstallData implements InstallDataInterface
{
    private $employeeSetupFactory;

    public function __construct(
        \Foggyline\Office\Setup\EmployeeSetupFactory
          $employeeSetupFactory
    )
    {
        $this->employeeSetupFactory = $employeeSetupFactory;
    }

    public function install(ModuleDataSetupInterface $setup,
      ModuleContextInterface $context)
    {
        $setup->startSetup();
        /* #snippet1 */
        $setup->endSetup();
    }
}
```

InstallData conforms to InstallDataInterface, which requires the implementation of the install method that accepts two parameters of type ModuleDataSetupInterface and ModuleContextInterface.

The install method is run when this script gets triggered. Within this method, we would add any relevant code we might want to execute.

Going further, let's replace the /* #snippet1 */ part from the preceding code with the following code:

```
$employeeEntity = \Foggyline\Office\Model\Employee::ENTITY;

$employeeSetup = $this->employeeSetupFactory->create(['setup' =>
  $setup]);

$employeeSetup->installEntities();

$employeeSetup->addAttribute(
    $employeeEntity, 'service_years', ['type' => 'int']
);

$employeeSetup->addAttribute(
    $employeeEntity, 'dob', ['type' => 'datetime']
);
```

```
$employeeSetup->addAttribute(
    $employeeEntity, 'salary', ['type' => 'decimal']
);


$employeeSetup->addAttribute(
    $employeeEntity, 'vat_number', ['type' => 'varchar']
);


$employeeSetup->addAttribute(
    $employeeEntity, 'note', ['type' => 'text']
);
```

Using the addAttribute method on the instance of \Foggyline\Office\Setup\
EmployeeSetupFactory, we are instructing Magento to add a number of attributes
(service_years, dob, salary, vat_number, note) to its entity.

We will soon get to the inners of EmployeeSetupFactory, but right now notice the
call to the addAttribute method. Within this method, there is a call to the $this-
>attributeMapper->map($attr, $entityTypeId) method. attributeMapper
conforms to Magento\Eav\Model\Entity\Setup\PropertyMapperInterface,
which looking at vendor/magento/module-eav/etc/di.xml has a preference for
the Magento\Eav\Model\Entity\Setup\PropertyMapper\Composite class, which
further initializes the following mapper classes:

- Magento\Eav\Model\Entity\Setup\PropertyMapper
- Magento\Customer\Model\ResourceModel\Setup\PropertyMapper
- Magento\Catalog\Model\ResourceModel\Setup\PropertyMapper
- Magento\ConfigurableProduct\Model\ResourceModel\Setup\
  PropertyMapper

Since we are defining our own entity types, the mapper class we are mostly
interested in is Magento\Eav\Model\Entity\Setup\PropertyMapper. A quick
look inside of it reveals the following mapping array in the map method:

```
[
    'backend_model' => 'backend',
    'backend_type' => 'type',
    'backend_table' => 'table',
    'frontend_model' => 'frontend',
    'frontend_input' => 'input',
    'frontend_label' => 'label',
    'frontend_class' => 'frontend_class',
    'source_model' => 'source',
    'is_required' => 'required',
```

```
    'is_user_defined' => 'user_defined',
    'default_value' => 'default',
    'is_unique' => 'unique',
    'note' => 'note'
    'is_global' => 'global'
]
```

Looking at the preceding array keys and value strings gives us a clue as to what is happening. The key strings match the column names in the `eav_attribute` table, while the value strings match the keys of our array passed to the `addAttribute` method within `InstallData.php`.

Let's take a look at the `EmployeeSetupFactory` class within the `app/code/Foggyline/Office/Setup/EmployeeSetup.php` file, (partially) defined as follows:

```
namespace Foggyline\Office\Setup;
use Magento\Eav\Setup\EavSetup;

class EmployeeSetup extends EavSetup
{
    public function getDefaultEntities()
    {
        /* #snippet1 */
    }
}
```

What's happening here is that we are extending from the Magento\Eav\Setup\ EavSetup class, thus effectively telling Magento we are about to create our own entity. We do so by overriding `getDefaultEntities`, replacing `/* #snippet1 */` with content as follows:

```
$employeeEntity = \Foggyline\Office\Model\Employee::ENTITY;
$entities = [
    $employeeEntity => [
        'entity_model' => 'Foggyline\Office\Model\ResourceModel\
Employee',
        'table' => $employeeEntity . '_entity',
        'attributes' => [
            'department_id' => [
                'type' => 'static',
            ],
            'email' => [
                'type' => 'static',
            ],
```

```
            'first_name' => [
                'type' => 'static',
            ],
            'last_name' => [
                'type' => 'static',
            ],
        ],
    ],
];
return $entities;
```

The `getDefaultEntities` method returns an array of entities we want to register with Magento. Within our `$entities` array, the key `$employeeEntity` becomes an entry in the `eav_entity_type` table. Given that our `$employeeEntity` has a value of `foggyline_office_employee`, running the following SQL query should yield a result:

```
SELECT * FROM eav_entity_type WHERE entity_type_code =
    "foggyline_office_employee";
```

Only a handful of metadata values are required to make our new entity type functional. The `entity_model` value should point to our EAV model `resource` class, not the `model` class. The table value should equal the name of our EAV entity table in the database. Finally, the attributes array should list any attribute we want created on this entity. Attributes and their metadata get created in the `eav_attribute` table.

If we look back at all those `foggyline_office_employee_entity_*` attribute value tables we created, they are not the ones that actually create attributes or register a new entity type in Magento. What creates attributes and a new entity type is the array we just defined under the `getDefaultEntities` method. Once Magento creates the attributes and registers a new entity type, it simply routes the entity save process to proper attribute value tables depending on the type of attribute.

Creating an upgrade data script (UpgradeData.php)

The upgrade data script is the last one to execute. We will use it to demonstrate the example of creating the sample entries for our `Department` and `Employee` entities.

We start by creating the app/code/Foggyline/Office/Setup/UpgradeData.php file with (partial) content as follows:

```php
namespace Foggyline\Office\Setup;

use Magento\Framework\Setup\UpgradeDataInterface;
use Magento\Framework\Setup\ModuleContextInterface;
use Magento\Framework\Setup\ModuleDataSetupInterface;

class UpgradeData implements UpgradeDataInterface
{
    protected $departmentFactory;
    protected $employeeFactory;

    public function __construct(
        \Foggyline\Office\Model\DepartmentFactory
          $departmentFactory,
        \Foggyline\Office\Model\EmployeeFactory $employeeFactory
    )
    {
        $this->departmentFactory = $departmentFactory;
        $this->employeeFactory = $employeeFactory;
    }

    public function upgrade(ModuleDataSetupInterface $setup,
      ModuleContextInterface $context)
    {
        $setup->startSetup();
        /* #snippet1 */
        $setup->endSetup();
    }
}
```

UpgradeData conforms to UpgradeDataInterface, which requires the implementation of the upgrade method that accepts two parameters of type ModuleDataSetupInterface and ModuleContextInterface. We are further adding our own __construct method to which we are passing DepartmentFactory and EmployeeFactory, as we will be using them within the upgrade method as shown next, by replacing /* #snippet1 */ with the following code:

```php
$salesDepartment = $this->departmentFactory->create();
$salesDepartment->setName('Sales');
$salesDepartment->save();
```

```
$employee = $this->employeeFactory->create();
$employee->setDepartmentId($salesDepartment->getId());
$employee->setEmail('john@sales.loc');
$employee->setFirstName('John');
$employee->setLastName('Doe');
$employee->setServiceYears(3);
$employee->setDob('1983-03-28');
$employee->setSalary(3800.00);
$employee->setVatNumber('GB123456789');
$employee->setNote('Just some notes about John');
$employee->save();
```

The preceding code creates an instance of the department entity and then saves it. An instance of employee is then created and saved, passing it the newly created department ID and other attributes.

> A more convenient and professional-looking approach for saving an entity could be given as follows:
>
> ```
> $employee->setDob('1983-03-28')
>     ->setSalary(3800.00)
>     ->setVatNumber('GB123456789')
>     ->save();
> ```
>
> Here, we are utilizing the fact that each of the entity setter methods returns $this (an instance of the entity object itself), so we can chain the method calls.

Entity CRUD actions

Up to this point, we have learned how to create a simple model, an EAV model, and install and upgrade types of schema and data script. Now, let us see how we can create, read, update and delete our entities, operations that are commonly referred to as CRUD.

Though this chapter is about models, collections, and related things, for the purpose of demonstration, let's make a tiny detour into routes and controllers. The idea is to create a simple Test controller with the Crud action we can trigger in the browser via a URL. Within this Crud action, we will then dump our CRUD-related code.

To make Magento respond to the URL we punch into the browser, we need to define the route. We do so by creating the `app/code/Foggyline/Office/etc/frontend/routes.xml` file with the following content:

```xml
<config xmlns:xsi="http://www.w3.org/2001/XMLSchema-instance"
  xsi:noNamespaceSchemaLocation="urn:magento:framework:App/
  etc/routes.xsd">
    <router id="standard">
        <route id="foggyline_office" frontName="foggyline_office">
            <module name="Foggyline_Office"/>
        </route>
    </router>
</config>
```

Route definition requires a unique ID and `frontName` attribute values, which in our case both equal `foggyline_office`. The `frontName` attribute value becomes the part of our URL structure. Simply put, the URL formula for hitting the `Crud` action goes like *{magento-base-url}/index.php/{route frontName}/{controller name}/{action name}*.

> For example, if our base URL were `http://shop.loc/`, the full URL would be `http://shop.loc/index.php/foggyline_office/test/crud/`. If we have URL rewrites turned on, we could omit the `index.php` part.

Once the route has been defined, we can go ahead and create the `Test` controller, defined in the `app/code/Foggyline/Office/Controller/Test.php` file with (partial) code as follows:

```php
namespace Foggyline\Office\Controller;

abstract class Test extends \Magento\Framework\App\Action\Action
{
}
```

This really is the simplest controller we could have defined. The only thing worth noting here is that the controller class needs to be defined as abstract and extend the \Magento\Framework\App\Action\Action class. Controller actions live outside of the controller itself and can be found under the subdirectory on the same level and named as controller. Since our controller is called Test, we place our Crud action under the app/code/Foggyline/Office/Controller/Test/Crud.php file with content as follows:

```
namespace Foggyline\Office\Controller\Test;

class Crud extends \Foggyline\Office\Controller\Test
{
    protected $employeeFactory;
    protected $departmentFactory;

    public function __construct(
        \Magento\Framework\App\Action\Context $context,
        \Foggyline\Office\Model\EmployeeFactory $employeeFactory,
        \Foggyline\Office\Model\DepartmentFactory
          $departmentFactory
    )
    {

        $this->employeeFactory = $employeeFactory;
        $this->departmentFactory = $departmentFactory;
        return parent::__construct($context);
    }

    public function execute()
    {
        /* CRUD Code Here */
    }
}
```

The Controller action class is basically just an extension of the controller defining the execute method. Code within the execute method is what gets run when we hit the URL in the browser. Additionally, we have a __construct method to which we are passing the EmployeeFactory and DepartmentFactory classes, which we will soon use for our CRUD examples. Note that EmployeeFactory and DepartmentFactory are not classes created by us. Magento will autogenerate them under the DepartmentFactory.php and EmployeeFactory.php files within the var/generation/Foggyline/Office/Model folder. These are factory classes for our Employee and Department model classes, generated when requested.

With this, we finish our little detour and focus back on our entities.

Creating new entities

There are three different flavors, if we might call them that, by which we can set property (field and attribute) values on our entity. They all lead to the same result. The following few code snippets can be copied and pasted into our Crud class execute method for testing, simply by replacing /* CRUD Code Here */ with one of the following code snippets:

```
//Simple model, creating new entities, flavour #1
$department1 = $this->departmentFactory->create();
$department1->setName('Finance');
$department1->save();
//Simple model, creating new entities, flavour #2
$department2 = $this->departmentFactory->create();
$department2->setData('name', 'Research');
$department2->save();
//Simple model, creating new entities, flavour #3
$department3 = $this->departmentFactory->create();
$department3->setData(['name' => 'Support']);
$department3->save();
```

The flavour #1 approach from the preceding code is probably the preferred way of setting properties, as it is using the magic method approach we mentioned previously. Both flavour #2 and flavour #3 use the setData method, just in a slightly different manner. All three examples should yield the same result once the save method is called on an object instance.

Now that we know how to save the simple model, let's take a quick look at doing the same with the EAV model. The following are analogous code snippets:

```
//EAV model, creating new entities, flavour #1
$employee1 = $this->employeeFactory->create();
$employee1->setDepartment_id($department1->getId());
$employee1->setEmail('goran@mail.loc');
$employee1->setFirstName('Goran');
$employee1->setLastName('Gorvat');
$employee1->setServiceYears(3);
$employee1->setDob('1984-04-18');
$employee1->setSalary(3800.00);
$employee1->setVatNumber('GB123451234');
$employee1->setNote('Note #1');
$employee1->save();
```

```
//EAV model, creating new entities, flavour #2
$employee2 = $this->employeeFactory->create();
$employee2->setData('department_id', $department2->getId());
$employee2->setData('email', 'marko@mail.loc');
$employee2->setData('first_name', 'Marko');
$employee2->setData('last_name', 'Tunukovic');
$employee2->setData('service_years', 3);
$employee2->setData('dob', '1984-04-18');
$employee2->setData('salary', 3800.00);
$employee2->setData('vat_number', 'GB123451234');
$employee2->setData('note', 'Note #2');
$employee2->save();

//EAV model, creating new entities, flavour #3
$employee3 = $this->employeeFactory->create();
$employee3->setData([
    'department_id' => $department3->getId(),
    'email' => 'ivan@mail.loc',
    'first_name' => 'Ivan',
    'last_name' => 'Telebar',
    'service_years' => 2,
    'dob' => '1986-08-22',
    'salary' => 2400.00,
    'vat_number' => 'GB123454321',
    'note' => 'Note #3'
]);
$employee3->save();
```

As we can see, the EAV code for persisting the data is identical to the simple model. There is one thing here worth noting. The Employee entity has a relation defined toward department. Forgetting to specify department_id on a new employee entity save would result in an error message similar to the following:

```
SQLSTATE[23000]: Integrity constraint violation: 1452 Cannot add
  or update a child row: a foreign key constraint fails
  ('magento'.'foggyline_office_employee_entity', CONSTRAINT
  'FK_E2AEE8BF21518DFA8F02B4E95DC9F5AD' FOREIGN KEY
  ('department_id') REFERENCES 'foggyline_office_department'
  ('entity_id') ON), query was: INSERT INTO
  'foggyline_office_employee_entity' ('email', 'first_name',
  'last_name', 'entity_id') VALUES (?, ?, ?, ?)
```

Magento saves these types of errors under its var/report directory.

Reading existing entities

Reading an entity based on a provided entity ID value comes down to instantiating the entity and using the load method to which we pass the entity ID as shown next:

```
//Simple model, reading existing entities
$department = $this->departmentFactory->create();
$department->load(28);

/*
    \Zend_Debug::dump($department->toArray());

    array(2) {
      ["entity_id"] => string(2) "28"
      ["name"] => string(8) "Research"
    }
*/
```

There is no real difference between loading the simple model or EAV model, as shown in the following EAV model example:

```
//EAV model, reading existing entities
$employee = $this->employeeFactory->create();
$employee->load(25);

/*
    \Zend_Debug::dump($employee->toArray());

    array(10) {
      ["entity_id"] => string(2) "25"
      ["department_id"] => string(2) "28"
      ["email"] => string(14) "marko@mail.loc"
      ["first_name"] => string(5) "Marko"
      ["last_name"] => string(9) "Tunukovic"
      ["dob"] => string(19) "1984-04-18 00:00:00"
      ["note"] => string(7) "Note #2"
      ["salary"] => string(9) "3800.0000"
      ["service_years"] => string(1) "3"
      ["vat_number"] => string(11) "GB123451234"
    }
*/
```

Notice how the EAV entity loads all of its field and attribute values, which is not always the case when we obtain the entity through EAV collection, as we will show later on.

Updating existing entities

Updating entities comes down to using the `load` method to read an existing entity, reset its value, and calling the `save` method in the end, like shown in the following example:

```
$department = $this->departmentFactory->create();
$department->load(28);
$department->setName('Finance #2');
$department->save();
```

Regardless of the entity being the simple model or an EAV, the code is the same.

Deleting existing entities

Calling the `delete` method on a loaded entity will delete the entity from the database or throw `Exception` if it fails. Code to delete the entity looks as follows:

```
$employee = $this->employeeFactory->create();
$employee->load(25);
$employee->delete();
```

There is no difference in deleting the simple and EAV entities. We should always use try/catch blocks when deleting or saving our entities.

Managing collections

Let's start with EAV model collections. We can instantiate the collection either through the entity `factory` class like follows:

```
$collection = $this->employeeFactory->create()
                    ->getCollection();
```

Or we can use object manager to instantiate the collection as shown next:

```
$collection = $this->_objectManager->create(
    'Foggyline\Office\Model\ResourceModel\Employee\Collection's
);
```

There is also a third way, which might be the preferred one, but it requires us to define APIs so we will skip that one for the moment.

Once we instantiate the collection object, we can loop through it and do some variable dumps to see the content on individual $employee entities, like shown next:

```
foreach ($collection as $employee) {
    \Zend_Debug::dump($employee->toArray(), '$employee');
}
```

The preceding would yield results like the following:

```
$employee array(5) {
  ["entity_id"] => string(2) "24"
  ["department_id"] => string(2) "27"
  ["email"] => string(14) "goran@mail.loc"
  ["first_name"] => string(5) "Goran"
  ["last_name"] => string(6) "Gorvat"
}
```

Notice how the individual $employee only has fields on it, not the attributes. Let's see what happens when we want to extend our collection by using addAttributeToSelect to specify the individual attributes to add to it, like shown next:

```
$collection->addAttributeToSelect('salary')
          ->addAttributeToSelect('vat_number');
```

The preceding would yield results like the following:

```
$employee array(7) {
  ["entity_id"] => string(2) "24"
  ["department_id"] => string(2) "27"
  ["email"] => string(14) "goran@mail.loc"
  ["first_name"] => string(5) "Goran"
  ["last_name"] => string(6) "Gorvat"
  ["salary"] => string(9) "3800.0000"
  ["vat_number"] => string(11) "GB123451234"
}
```

Though we are making progress, imagine if we had tens of attributes, and we want each and every one to be included into collection. Using addAttributeToSelect numerous times would make for cluttered code. What we can do is pass '*' as a parameter to addAttributeToSelect and have collection pick up every attribute, as shown next:

```
$collection->addAttributeToSelect('*');
```

This would yield results like the following:

```
$employee array(10) {
    ["entity_id"] => string(2) "24"
    ["department_id"] => string(2) "27"
    ["email"] => string(14) "goran@mail.loc"
    ["first_name"] => string(5) "Goran"
    ["last_name"] => string(6) "Gorvat"
    ["dob"] => string(19) "1984-04-18 00:00:00"
    ["note"] => string(7) "Note #1"
    ["salary"] => string(9) "3800.0000"
    ["service_years"] => string(1) "3"
    ["vat_number"] => string(11) "GB123451234"
}
```

Though the PHP part of the code looks seemingly simple, what's happening in the background on the SQL layer is relatively complex. Though Magento executes several SQL queries prior to fetching the final collection result, let's focus on the last three queries as shown next:

```
SELECT COUNT(*) FROM 'foggyline_office_employee_entity' AS 'e'

SELECT 'e'.* FROM 'foggyline_office_employee_entity' AS 'e'

SELECT
  'foggyline_office_employee_entity_datetime'.'entity_id',
  'foggyline_office_employee_entity_datetime'.'attribute_id',
  'foggyline_office_employee_entity_datetime'.'value'
FROM 'foggyline_office_employee_entity_datetime'
WHERE (entity_id IN (24, 25, 26)) AND (attribute_id IN ('349'))
UNION ALL SELECT
            'foggyline_office_employee_entity_text'.'entity_id',
            'foggyline_office_employee_entity_text'.'
              attribute_id',
            'foggyline_office_employee_entity_text'.'value'
          FROM 'foggyline_office_employee_entity_text'
          WHERE (entity_id IN (24, 25, 26)) AND (attribute_id IN
          ('352'))
UNION ALL SELECT
            'foggyline_office_employee_entity_decimal'.'
              entity_id',
            'foggyline_office_employee_entity_decimal'.'
              attribute_id',
            'foggyline_office_employee_entity_decimal'.'value'
          FROM 'foggyline_office_employee_entity_decimal'
```

```
            WHERE (entity_id IN (24, 25, 26)) AND (attribute_id IN
              ('350'))
UNION ALL SELECT
            'foggyline_office_employee_entity_int'.'entity_id',
            'foggyline_office_employee_entity_int'.'attribute_id',
            'foggyline_office_employee_entity_int'.'value'
        FROM 'foggyline_office_employee_entity_int'
        WHERE (entity_id IN (24, 25, 26)) AND (attribute_id IN
              ('348'))
UNION ALL SELECT
            'foggyline_office_employee_entity_varchar'.'
              entity_id',
            'foggyline_office_employee_entity_varchar'.'
              attribute_id',
            'foggyline_office_employee_entity_varchar'.'value'
        FROM 'foggyline_office_employee_entity_varchar'
        WHERE (entity_id IN (24, 25, 26)) AND (attribute_id IN
              ('351'))
```

> Before we proceed any further, it is important to know that these queries are not copy and paste applicable. The reason is that the attribute_id values will for sure differ from installation to installation. Queries given here are for us to gain a high-level understanding of what is happening in the backend on the SQL layer when we use Magento collections on the PHP application level.

The first query select simply counts the number of entries in the entity table, and then passes that info to the application layer. The second select fetches all entries from foggyline_office_employee_entity, then passes that info to the application layer to use it to pass entity IDs in the third query as part of entity_id IN (24, 25, 26). Second and third queries here can be pretty resource intense if we have a large amount of entries in our entity and EAV tables. To prevent possible performance bottlenecks, we should always use the setPageSize and setCurPage methods on collection, like shown next:

```
$collection->addAttributeToSelect('*')
        ->setPageSize(25)
        ->setCurPage(5);
```

This would result in the first COUNT query still being the same, but the second query would now look like the following:

```
SELECT 'e'.* FROM 'foggyline_office_employee_entity' AS 'e' LIMIT
  25 OFFSET 4
```

This makes for a much smaller, thus performance-lighter dataset if we have thousands or tens of thousands of entries. The point here is to always use setPageSize and setCurPage. If we need to work with a really large set, then we need to page through it, or walk through it.

Now we know how to limit the size of the result set and fetch the proper page, let's see how we can further filter the set to avoid overusing PHP loops for the same purpose. Thus effectively passing the filtering to the database and not the application layer. To filter the EAV collection, we use its addAttributeToFilter method.

Let's instantiate a clean new collection like shown next:

```
$collection = $this->_objectManager->create(
    'Foggyline\Office\Model\ResourceModel\Employee\Collection'
);

$collection->addAttributeToSelect('*')
            ->setPageSize(25)
            ->setCurPage(1);

$collection->addAttributeToFilter('email',
            array('like'=>'%mail.loc%'))
        ->addAttributeToFilter('vat_number',
          array('like'=>'GB%'))
        ->addAttributeToFilter('salary', array('gt'=>2400))
        ->addAttributeToFilter('service_years',
          array('lt'=>10));
```

Notice that we are now using the addAttributeToSelect and addAttributeToFilter methods on collection. We have already seen the database impact of addAttributeToSelect on a SQL query. What addAttributeToFilter does is something completely different.

With the addAttributeToFilter method, the count query now gets transformed into the following SQL query:

```
SELECT COUNT(*)
FROM 'foggyline_office_employee_entity' AS 'e'
  INNER JOIN 'foggyline_office_employee_entity_varchar' AS
    'at_vat_number'
    ON ('at_vat_number'.'entity_id' = 'e'.'entity_id') AND
      ('at_vat_number'.'attribute_id' = '351')
  INNER JOIN 'foggyline_office_employee_entity_decimal' AS
    'at_salary'
    ON ('at_salary'.'entity_id' = 'e'.'entity_id') AND
      ('at_salary'.'attribute_id' = '350')
```

```
    INNER JOIN 'foggyline_office_employee_entity_int' AS
        'at_service_years'
        ON ('at_service_years'.'entity_id' = 'e'.'entity_id') AND
            ('at_service_years'.'attribute_id' = '348')
    WHERE ('e'.'email' LIKE '%mail.loc%') AND (at_vat_number.value
        LIKE 'GB%') AND (at_salary.value > 2400) AND
            (at_service_years.value < 10)
```

We can see that this is much more complex than the previous count query, now we have INNER JOIN stepping in. Notice how we have four addAttributeToFilter method calls but only three INNER JOIN. This is because one of those four calls is for e-mail, which is not an attribute but a field within the foggyline_office_employee_entity table. That is why there is no need for INNER JOIN as the field is already there. The three INNER JOIN then simply merge the required info into the query in order to get the select.

The second query also becomes more robust, as shown next:

```
SELECT
    'e'.*,
    'at_vat_number'.'value'    AS 'vat_number',
    'at_salary'.'value'        AS 'salary',
    'at_service_years'.'value' AS 'service_years'
FROM 'foggyline_office_employee_entity' AS 'e'
    INNER JOIN 'foggyline_office_employee_entity_varchar' AS
        'at_vat_number'
        ON ('at_vat_number'.'entity_id' = 'e'.'entity_id') AND
            ('at_vat_number'.'attribute_id' = '351')
    INNER JOIN 'foggyline_office_employee_entity_decimal' AS
        'at_salary'
        ON ('at_salary'.'entity_id' = 'e'.'entity_id') AND
            ('at_salary'.'attribute_id' = '350')
    INNER JOIN 'foggyline_office_employee_entity_int' AS
        'at_service_years'
        ON ('at_service_years'.'entity_id' = 'e'.'entity_id') AND
            ('at_service_years'.'attribute_id' = '348')
    WHERE ('e'.'email' LIKE '%mail.loc%') AND (at_vat_number.value
        LIKE 'GB%') AND (at_salary.value > 2400) AND
            (at_service_years.value < 10)
    LIMIT 25
```

Here, we also see the usage of INNER JOIN. We also have three and not four INNER JOIN, because one of the conditions is done against email, which is a field. The result of the query is a flattened piece of rows where the attributes vat_number, salary, and service_years are present. We can imagine the performance impact if we haven't used setPageSize to limit the result set.

Finally, the third query is also affected and now looks similar to the following:

```
SELECT
  'foggyline_office_employee_entity_datetime'.'entity_id',
  'foggyline_office_employee_entity_datetime'.'attribute_id',
  'foggyline_office_employee_entity_datetime'.'value'
FROM 'foggyline_office_employee_entity_datetime'
WHERE (entity_id IN (24, 25)) AND (attribute_id IN ('349'))
UNION ALL SELECT
          'foggyline_office_employee_entity_text'.'entity_id',
          'foggyline_office_employee_entity_text'.'
            attribute_id',
          'foggyline_office_employee_entity_text'.'value'
        FROM 'foggyline_office_employee_entity_text'
        WHERE (entity_id IN (24, 25)) AND (attribute_id IN
          ('352'))
```

Notice here how `UNION ALL` has been reduced to a single occurrence now, thus effectively making for two selects. This is because we have a total of five attributes (`service_years`, `dob`, `salary`, `vat_number`, `note`), and three of them have been pulled in through second query. Out of the preceding three queries demonstrated, Magento basically pulls the collection data from second and third query. This seems like a pretty optimized and scalable solution, though we should really give it some thought on the proper use of `setPageSize`, `addAttributeToSelect`, and `addAttributeToFilter` methods when creating collection.

During development, if working with collections that have lot of attributes, filters, and possibly a future large dataset, we might want to use SQL logging to record actual SQL queries hitting the database server. This might help us spot possible performance bottlenecks and react on time, either by adding more limiting values to `setPageSize` or `addAttributeToSelect`, or both.

In the preceding examples, the use of `addAttributeToSelect` results in AND conditions on the SQL layer. What if we want to filter collection using OR conditions? `addAttributeToSelect` can also result in SQL OR conditions if the `$attribute` parameter is used in the following way:

```
$collection->addAttributeToFilter([
    ['attribute'=>'salary', 'gt'=>2400],
    ['attribute'=>'vat_number', 'like'=>'GB%']
]);
```

Without going into the details of actual SQL queries this time, it is suffice to say that they are near identical to the previous example with the AND condition use of `addAttributeToFilter`.

Using collection methods like addExpressionAttributeToSelect, groupByAttribute, and addAttributeToSort, collections offer further gradient filtering and even shift some calculations from the PHP application layer to the SQL layer. Getting into the ins and outs of those and other collection methods is beyond the scope of this chapter, and would probably require a book on its own.

Collection filters

Looking back at the preceding addAttributeToFilter method call examples, questions pop out as to where can we see the list of all available collection filters. If we take a quick look inside the vendor/magento/framework/DB/Adapter/Pdo/ Mysql.php file, we can see the method called prepareSqlCondition (partially) defined as follows:

```php
public function prepareSqlCondition($fieldName, $condition)
{
    $conditionKeyMap = [
        'eq'        => "{{fieldName}} = ?",
        'neq'       => "{{fieldName}} != ?",
        'like'      => "{{fieldName}} LIKE ?",
        'nlike'     => "{{fieldName}} NOT LIKE ?",
        'in'        => "{{fieldName}} IN(?)",
        'nin'       => "{{fieldName}} NOT IN(?)",
        'is'        => "{{fieldName}} IS ?",
        'notnull'   => "{{fieldName}} IS NOT NULL",
        'null'      => "{{fieldName}} IS NULL",
        'gt'        => "{{fieldName}} > ?",
        'lt'        => "{{fieldName}} /* AJZELE */ < ?",
        'gteq'      => "{{fieldName}} >= ?",
        'lteq'      => "{{fieldName}} <= ?",
        'finset'    => "FIND_IN_SET(?, {{fieldName}})",
        'regexp'    => "{{fieldName}} REGEXP ?",
        'from'      => "{{fieldName}} >= ?",
        'to'        => "{{fieldName}} <= ?",
        'seq'       => null,
        'sneq'      => null,
        'ntoa'      => "INET_NTOA({{fieldName}}) LIKE ?",
    ];

    $query = '';
    if (is_array($condition)) {
        $key = key(array_intersect_key($condition,
            $conditionKeyMap));

    ...
}
```

This method is what eventually gets called at some point during SQL query construction. The $condition parameter is expected to have one of the following (partially listed) forms:

- `array("from" => $fromValue, "to" => $toValue)`
- `array("eq" => $equalValue)`
- `array("neq" => $notEqualValue)`
- `array("like" => $likeValue)`
- `array("in" => array($inValues))`
- `array("nin" => array($notInValues))`
- `array("notnull" => $valueIsNotNull)`
- `array("null" => $valueIsNull)`
- `array("gt" => $greaterValue)`
- `array("lt" => $lessValue)`
- `array("gteq" => $greaterOrEqualValue)`
- `array("lteq" => $lessOrEqualValue)`
- `array("finset" => $valueInSet)`
- `array("regexp" => $regularExpression)`
- `array("seq" => $stringValue)`
- `array("sneq" => $stringValue)`

If $condition is passed as an integer or string, then the exact value will be filtered (`'eq'` condition). If none of the conditions is matched, then a sequential array is expected as a parameter and OR conditions will be built using the preceding structure.

The preceding examples covered EAV model collections, as they are slightly more complex. Though the approach to filtering more or less applies to simple model collections as well, the most notable difference is that there are no `addAttributeToFilter`, `addAttributeToSelect`, and `addExpressionAttributeToSelect` methods. The simple model collections make use of `addFieldToFilter`, `addFieldToSelect`, and `addExpressionFieldToSelect`, among other subtle differences.

Summary

In this chapter, we first learned how to create simple model, its resource, and collection class. Then we did the same for an EAV model. Once we had the required model, resource, and collection classes in place, we took a detailed look at the type and flow of schema and data scripts. Going hands-on, we covered `InstallSchema`, `UpgradeSchema`, `InstallData`, and `UpgradeData` scripts. Once the scripts were run, the database ended up having the required tables and sample data upon which we based our entity CRUD examples. Finally, we took a quick but focused look at collection management, mostly comprising filtering collection to get the desired result set.

The full module code can be downloaded from `https://github.com/ajzele/B05032-Foggyline_Office`.

5
Using the Dependency Injection

Dependency injection is a software design pattern via which one or more dependencies are injected or passed by reference into an object. What this exactly means on a practical level is shown in the following two simple examples:

```php
public function getTotalCustomers()
{
    $database = new \PDO( … );
    $statement = $database->query('SELECT …');
    return $statement->fetchColumn();
}
```

Here, you will see a simplified PHP example, where the `$database` object is created in the `getTotalCustomers` method. This means that the dependency on the database object is being locked in an object instance method. This makes for tight coupling, which has several disadvantages such as reduced reusability and a possible system-wide effect caused by changes made to some parts of the code.

A solution to this problem is to avoid methods with these sorts of dependencies by injecting a dependency into a method, as follows:

```php
public function getTotalCustomers($database)
{
    $statement = $database->query('SELECT ...');
    return $statement->fetchColumn();
}
```

Here, a `$database` object is passed (injected) into a method. That's all that dependency injection is—a simple concept that makes code loosely coupled. While the concept is simple, it may not be easy to implement it across large platforms such as Magento.

Magento has its own object manager and dependency injection mechanism that we will soon look at in detail in the following sections:

- The object manager
- Dependency injection
- Configuring class preferences
- Using virtual types

To follow and test the code examples given in the following sections, we can use the code available at https://github.com/ajzele/B05032-Foggyline_Di. To install it, we simply need to download it and put it in the app/code/Foggyline/Di directory. Then, run the following set of commands on the console within Magento's root directory:

```
php bin/magento module:enable Foggyline_Di
php bin/magento setup:upgrade
php bin/magento foggy:di
```

The last command can be used repeatedly when testing the snippets presented in the following section. When php bin/magento foggy:di is run, it will run the code within the execute method in the DiTestCommand class. Therefore, we can use the __construct and execute methods from within the DiTestCommand class and the di.xml file itself as a playground for **DI**.

The object manager

The initializing of objects in Magento is done via what is called the **object manager**. The object manager itself is an instance of the Magento\Framework\ObjectManager\ObjectManager class that implements the Magento\Framework\ObjectManagerInterface class. The ObjectManager class defines the following three methods:

- create($type, array $arguments = []): This creates a new object instance
- get($type): This retrieves a cached object instance
- configure(array $configuration): This configures the di instance

The object manager can instantiate a PHP class, which can be a model, helper, or block object. Unless the class that we are working with has already received an instance of the object manager, we can receive it by passing `ObjectManagerInterface` into the class constructor, as follows:

```
public function __construct(
    \Magento\Framework\ObjectManagerInterface $objectManager
)
{

    $this->_objectManager = $objectManager;
}
```

Usually, we don't have to take care of the constructor parameter's order in Magento. The following example will also enable us to fetch an instance of the object manager:

```
public function __construct(
    $var1,
    \Magento\Framework\ObjectManagerInterface $objectManager,
    $var2 = []
)
{

    $this->_objectManager = $objectManager;
}
```

Though we can still use plain old PHP to instantiate an object such as `$object = new \Foggyline\Di\Model\Object()`, by using the object manager, we can take advantage of Magento's advanced object features such as automatic constructor dependency injection and object proxying.

Here are a few examples of using object manager's `create` method to create new objects:

```
$this->_objectManager->create('Magento\Sales\Model\Order')
$this->_objectManager->create('Magento\Catalog\Model\Product\Image')
$this->_objectManager->create('Magento\Framework\UrlInterface')
$this->_objectManager->create('SoapServer', ['wsdl' => $url, 'options'
    => $options])
```

The following are a few examples of using object manager's `get` method to create new objects:

```
$this->_objectManager->get('Magento\Checkout\Model\Session')
$this->_objectManager->get('Psr\Log\LoggerInterface')->critical($e)
$this->_objectManager->get('Magento\Framework\Escaper')
$this->_objectManager->get('Magento\Sitemap\Helper\Data')
```

The object manager's `create` method always returns a new object instance, while the `get` method returns a singleton.

Note how some of the string parameters passed to `create` and `get` are actually interface names and not strictly class names. We will soon see why this works with both class names and interface names. For now, it suffices to say that it works because of Magento's dependency injection implementation.

Dependency injection

Until now, we have seen how the object manager has control over the instantiation of dependencies. However, by convention, the object manager isn't supposed to be used directly in Magento. Rather, it should be used for system-level things that bootstrap Magento. We are encouraged to use the module's `etc/di.xml` file to instantiate objects.

Let's dissect one of the existing `di.xml` entries, such as the one found under the `vendor/magento/module-admin-notification/etc/adminhtml/di.xml` file for the `Magento\Framework\Notification\MessageList` type:

```xml
<type name="Magento\Framework\Notification\MessageList">
    <arguments>
        <argument name="messages" xsi:type="array">
            <item name="baseurl" xsi:type="string">
              Magento\AdminNotification\Model\System
              \Message\Baseurl</item>
            <item name="security" xsi:type="string">
              Magento\AdminNotification\Model\System\
              Message\Security</item>
            <item name="cacheOutdated" xsi:type="string">
              Magento\AdminNotification\Model\System\
              Message\CacheOutdated</item>
            <item name="media_synchronization_error"
              xsi:type="string">Magento\AdminNotification\Model\
              System\Message\Media\Synchronization\Error</item>
            <item name="media_synchronization_success"
              xsi:type="string">Magento\AdminNotification\Model\
              System\Message\Media\Synchronization\Success</item>
        </argument>
    </arguments>
</type>
```

Basically, what this means is that whenever an instance of Magento\Framework\ Notification\MessageList is being created, the messages parameter is passed on to the constructor. The messages parameter is being defined as an array, which further consists of other string type items. In this case, values of these string type attributes are class names, as follows:

- Magento\Framework\ObjectManager\ObjectManager
- Magento\AdminNotification\Model\System\Message\Baseurl
- Magento\AdminNotification\Model\System\Message\Security
- Magento\AdminNotification\Model\System\Message\CacheOutdated
- Magento\AdminNotification\Model\System\Message\Media\ Synchronization\Error
- Magento\AdminNotification\Model\System\Message\Media\ Synchronization\Success

If you now take a look at the constructor of MessageList, you will see that it is defined in the following way:

```
public function __construct(
    \Magento\Framework\ObjectManagerInterface $objectManager,
    $messages = []
)
{
    //Method body here...
}
```

If we modify the MessageList constructor as follows, the code will work:

```
public function __construct(
    \Magento\Framework\ObjectManagerInterface $objectManager,
    $someVarX = 'someDefaultValueX',
    $messages = []
)
{
    //Method body here...
}
```

After modification:

```
public function __construct(
    \Magento\Framework\ObjectManagerInterface $objectManager,
    $someVarX = 'someDefaultValueX',
    $messages = [],
```

```
        $someVarY = 'someDefaultValueY'
    )
    {
        //Method body here...
    }
```

However, if we change the MessageList constructor to one of the following variations, the code will fail to work:

```
public function __construct(
    \Magento\Framework\ObjectManagerInterface $objectManager,
    $Messages = []
)
{
    //Method body here...
}
```

Another variation is as follows:

```
public function __construct(
    \Magento\Framework\ObjectManagerInterface $objectManager,
    $_messages = []
)
{
    //Method body here...
}
```

The name of the $messages parameter in the constructor of the PHP class has to exactly match the name of the argument within the arguments' list of di.xml. The order of parameters in the constructor does not really matter as much as their naming.

Looking further in the MessageList constructor, if we execute func_get_args somewhere within it, the list of items within the $messages parameter will match and exceed the one shown in vendor/magento/module-admin-notification/etc/adminhtml/di.xml. This is so because the list is not final, as Magento collects the DI definitions from across entire the platform and merges them. So, if another module is modifying the MessageList type, the modifications will be reflected.

If we perform a string search within all the di.xml files across the entire Magento code base for <type name="Magento\Framework\Notification\MessageList">, this will yield some additional di.xml files that have their own additions to the MessageList type, as follows:

```
//vendor/magento/module-indexer/etc/adminhtml/di.xml
<type name="Magento\Framework\Notification\MessageList">
```

```
<arguments>
    <argument name="messages" xsi:type="array">
        <item name="indexer_invalid_message"
            xsi:type="string">Magento\Indexer\Model\Message
            \Invalid</item>
    </argument>
</arguments>
</type>

//vendor/magento/module-tax/etc/adminhtml/di.xml
<type name="Magento\Framework\Notification\MessageList">
    <arguments>
        <argument name="messages" xsi:type="array">
            <item name="tax" xsi:type="string">Magento
                \Tax\Model\System\Message\Notifications</item>
        </argument>
    </arguments>
</type>
```

What this means is that the `Magento\Indexer\Model\Message\Invalid` and `Magento\Tax\Model\System\Message\Notifications` string items are being added to the `messages` argument and are being made available within the `MessageList` constructor.

In the preceding DI example, we only had the `$messages` parameter defined as one argument of the `array` type, and the rest were its array items.

Let's take a look at a DI example for another type definition. This time, it is the one found under the `vendor/magento/module-backend/etc/di.xml` file and which is defined as follows:

```
<type name="Magento\Backend\Model\Url">
    <arguments>
        <argument name="scopeResolver" xsi:type="object">
          Magento\Backend\Model\Url\ScopeResolver</argument>
        <argument name="authSession" xsi:type="object">
          Magento\Backend\Model\Auth\Session\Proxy</argument>
        <argument name="formKey" xsi:type="object">
          Magento\Framework\Data\Form\FormKey\Proxy</argument>
        <argument name="scopeType" xsi:type="const">
          Magento\Store\Model\ScopeInterface::SCOPE_STORE
          </argument>
        <argument name="backendHelper" xsi:type="object">
          Magento\Backend\Helper\Data\Proxy</argument>
    </arguments>
</type>
```

Here, you will see a type with several different arguments passed to the constructor of the `Magento\Backend\Model\Url` class. If you now take a look at the constructor of the `Url` class, you will see that it is defined in the following way:

```
public function __construct(
    \Magento\Framework\App\Route\ConfigInterface $routeConfig,
    \Magento\Framework\App\RequestInterface $request,
    \Magento\Framework\Url\SecurityInfoInterface $urlSecurityInfo,
    \Magento\Framework\Url\ScopeResolverInterface $scopeResolver,
    \Magento\Framework\Session\Generic $session,
    \Magento\Framework\Session\SidResolverInterface $sidResolver,
    \Magento\Framework\Url\RouteParamsResolverFactory
        $routeParamsResolverFactory,
    \Magento\Framework\Url\QueryParamsResolverInterface
        $queryParamsResolver,
    \Magento\Framework\App\Config\ScopeConfigInterface
        $scopeConfig,
    $scopeType,
    \Magento\Backend\Helper\Data $backendHelper,
    \Magento\Backend\Model\Menu\Config $menuConfig,
    \Magento\Framework\App\CacheInterface $cache,
    \Magento\Backend\Model\Auth\Session $authSession,
    \Magento\Framework\Encryption\EncryptorInterface $encryptor,
    \Magento\Store\Model\StoreFactory $storeFactory,
    \Magento\Framework\Data\Form\FormKey $formKey,
    array $data = []
) {
    //Method body here...
}
```

The `__construct` method here clearly has more parameters than what's defined in the `di.xml` file. What this means is that the type argument entries in `di.xml` do not necessarily cover all the class `__construct` parameters. The arguments that are defined in `di.xml` simply impose the types of individual parameters defined in the PHP class itself. This works as long as the `di.xml` parameters are of the same type or descendants of the same type.

Ideally, we would not pass the class type but interface into the PHP constructor and then set the type in `di.xml`. This is where the `type`, `preference`, and `virtualType` play a major role in `di.xml`. We have seen the role of `type`. Now, let's go ahead and see what `preference` does.

Configuring class preferences

A great number of Magento's core classes pass interfaces around constructors. The benefit of this is that the object manager, with the help of di.xml, can decide which class to actually instantiate for a given interface.

Let's imagine the `Foggyline\Di\Console\Command\DiTestCommand` class with a constructor, as follows:

```
public function __construct(
    \Foggyline\Di\Model\TestInterface $myArg1,
    $myArg2,
    $name = null
)
{
    //Method body here...
}
```

Note how `$myArg1` is type hinted as the `\Foggyline\Di\Model\TestInterface` interface. The object manager knows that it needs to look into the entire di.xml for possible `preference` definitions.

We can define `preference` within the module's di.xml file, as follows:

```
<preference
        for="Foggyline\Di\Model\TestInterface"
        type="Foggyline\Di\Model\Cart"/>
```

Here, we are basically saying that when someone asks for an instance of `Foggyline\Di\Model\TestInterface`, give it an instance of the `Foggyline\Di\Model\Cart` object. For this to work, the `Cart` class has to implement `TestInterface` itself. Once the preference definition is in place, `$myArg1` shown in the preceding example becomes an object of the `Cart` class.

Additionally, the `preference` element is not reserved only to point out the preferred classes for some interfaces. We can use it to set the preferred class for some other class.

Now, let's have a look at the `Foggyline\Di\Console\Command\DiTestCommand` class with a constructor:

```
public function __construct(
    \Foggyline\Di\Model\User $myArg1,
    $myArg2,
    $name = null
)
{
    //Method body here...
}
```

Note how $myArg1 is now type hinted as the `\Foggyline\Di\Model\User` class. Like in the previous example, the object manager will look into `di.xml` for possible `preference` definitions.

Let's define the `preference` element within the module's `di.xml` file, as follows:

```
<preference
    for="\Foggyline\Di\Model\User"
    type="Foggyline\Di\Model\Cart"/>
```

What this `preference` definition is saying is that whenever an instance of the `User` class is requested, pass an instance of the `Cart` object. This will work only if the `Cart` class extends from `User`. This is a convenient way of rewriting a class, where the class is being passed directly into another class constructor in place of the interface.

Since the class `__construct` parameters can be type hinted as either classes or interfaces and further manipulated via the `di.xml` preference definition, a question rises as to what is better. Is it better to use interfaces or specific classes? While the answer might not be fully clear, it is always preferable to use interfaces to specify the dependencies we are injecting into the system.

Using virtual types

Along with `type` and `preference`, there is another powerful feature of `di.xml` that we can use. The `virtualType` element enables us to define virtual types. Creating a virtual type is like creating a subclass of an existing class except for the fact that it's done in `di.xml` and not in code.

Virtual types are a way of injecting dependencies into some of the existing classes without affecting other classes. To explain this via a practical example, let's take a look at the following virtual type defined in the `app/etc/di.xml` file:

```
<virtualType name="Magento\Framework\Message\Session\Storage"
  type="Magento\Framework\Session\Storage">
    <arguments>
        <argument name="namespace" xsi:type="string">
          message</argument>
    </arguments>
</virtualType>
<type name="Magento\Framework\Message\Session">
    <arguments>
        <argument name="storage" xsi:type="object">
          Magento\Framework\Message\Session\Storage</argument>
    </arguments>
</type>
```

The `virtualType` definition in the preceding example is `Magento\Framework\Message\Session\Storage`, which extends from `Magento\Framework\Session\Storage` and overwrites the `namespace` parameter to the `message` string value. In `virtualType`, the `name` attribute defines the globally unique name of the virtual type, while the `type` attribute matches the real PHP class that the virtual type is based on.

Now, if you look at the `type` definition, you will see that its `storage` argument is set to the object of `Magento\Framework\Message\Session\Storage`. The `Session\Storage` file is actually a virtual type. This allows `Message\Session` to be customized without affecting other classes that also declare a dependency on `Session\Storage`.

Virtual types allow us to effectively change the behavior of a dependency when it is used in a specific class.

Summary

In this chapter, we had a look at the object manager and dependency injection, which are the foundations of Magento object management. We learned the meaning of the `type` and `preference` elements of dependency injection and how to use them to manipulate class construct parameters. Though there is much more to be said about dependency injection in Magento, the presented information should suffice and help us with other aspects of Magento.

In the next chapter, we will extend our journey into `di.xml` via the concept of plugins.

6
Plugins

In this chapter, we will take a look at a feature of Magento called **plugins**. Before we start with plugins, we first need to understand the term interception because the two terms are used somewhat interchangeably when dealing with Magento.

Interception is a software design pattern that is used when we want to insert code dynamically without necessarily changing the original class behavior. This works by dynamically inserting code between the calling code and the target object.

The interception pattern in Magento is implemented via plugins. They provide the before, after, and around listeners, which help us extend the observed method behavior.

In this chapter, we will cover the following topics:

- Creating a plugin
- Using the `before` listener
- Using the `after` listener
- Using the `around` listener
- The plugin sort order

Before we start creating a plugin, it is worth noting their limitations. Plugins cannot be created for just any class or method, as they do not work for the following:

- Final classes
- Final methods
- The classes that are created without a dependency injection

Let's go ahead and create a plugin using a simple module called `Foggyline_Plugged`.

Creating a plugin

Start by creating the app/code/Foggyline/Plugged/registration.php file with partial content, as follows:

```
\Magento\Framework\Component\ComponentRegistrar::register(
    \Magento\Framework\Component\ComponentRegistrar::MODULE,
    'Foggyline_Plugged',
    __DIR__
);
```

Then, create the app/code/Foggyline/Plugged/etc/module.xml file with partial content, as follows:

```
<config xmlns:xsi="http://www.w3.org/2001/XMLSchema-instance"
  xsi:noNamespaceSchemaLocation="urn:magento:framework:Module/
  etc/module.xsd">
    <module name="Foggyline_Plugged" setup_version="1.0.0">
        <sequence>
            <module name="Magento_Catalog"/>
        </sequence>
    </module>
</config>
```

The preceding file is simply a new module declaration with the dependency set against the Magento_Catalog module, as we will be observing its class. We will not go into the details of module declaration right now, as that will be covered later in the following chapters.

Now, create the app/code/Foggyline/Plugged/etc/di.xml file with partial content, as follows:

```
<config xmlns:xsi="http://www.w3.org/2001/XMLSchema-instance"
  xsi:noNamespaceSchemaLocation="urn:magento:framework:
  ObjectManager/etc/config.xsd">
    <type name="Magento\Catalog\Block\Product\AbstractProduct">
        <plugin name="foggyPlugin1"
          type="Foggyline\Plugged\Block\Catalog\Product\
          AbstractProductPlugin1"
          disabled="false" sortOrder="100"/>
        <plugin name="foggyPlugin2"
          type="Foggyline\Plugged\Block\Catalog\Product\
          AbstractProductPlugin2"
          disabled="false" sortOrder="200"/>
```

```
            <plugin name="foggyPlugin3"
              type="Foggyline\Plugged\Block\Catalog\Product\
              AbstractProductPlugin3"
              disabled="false" sortOrder="300"/>
        </type>
    </config>
```

Plugins are defined within the module `di.xml` file. To define a plugin, by using the `type` element and its `name` attribute, we first map the class that we want to observe. In this case, we are observing the `Magento\Catalog\Block\Product\AbstractProduct` class. Note that even though the file and class name imply an abstract type of class, the `AbstractProduct` class is not abstract.

In the `type` element, we then define one or more plugins using the `plugin` element.

The `plugin` element has the following four attributes assigned to it:

- `name`: Using this attribute, you can provide a unique and recognizable name value that is specific to the plugin

- `sortOrder`: This attribute determines the order of execution when multiple plugins are observing the same method

- `disabled`: The default value of this attribute is set to `false`, but if it is set to `true`, it will disable the plugin

- `type`: This attribute points to the class that we will be using to implement the `before`, `after`, or `around` listener

After doing this, create the `app/code/Foggyline/Plugged/Block/Catalog/Product/AbstractProductPlugin1.php` file with partial content, as follows:

```php
namespace Foggyline\Plugged\Block\Catalog\Product;

class AbstractProductPlugin1
{
    public function beforeGetAddToCartUrl(
        $subject,
        $product, $additional = []
    )
    {
        var_dump('Plugin1 - beforeGetAddToCartUrl');
    }

    public function afterGetAddToCartUrl($subject)
    {
```

```
        var_dump('Plugin1 - afterGetAddToCartUrl');
    }

    public function aroundGetAddToCartUrl(
        $subject,
        \Closure $proceed,
        $product,
        $additional = []
    )
    {
        var_dump('Plugin1 - aroundGetAddToCartUrl');
        return $proceed($product, $additional);
    }
}
```

As per the type definition in the di.xml file, the plugin observes the Magento\
Catalog\Block\Product\AbstractProduct class, and this class has a method
called getAddToCartUrl, which is defined as follows:

```
public function getAddToCartUrl($product, $additional = [])
{
    //method body here...
}
```

The AbstractProductPlugin1 class does not have to be extended from another class
for the plugin to work. We define the before, after and around listeners for the
getAddToCartUrl method by using the naming convention, as follows:

```
<before> + <getAddToCartUrl> => beforeGetAddToCartUrl
<after> + <getAddToCartUrl> => afterGetAddToCartUrl
<around> + <getAddToCartUrl> => aroundGetAddToCartUrl
```

We will go into the details of each listener later. Right now we need to
finish the module by creating the AbstractProductPlugin2.php and
AbstractProductPlugin3.php files as a copy of AbstractProductPlugin1.php
and along with that, simply changing all the number values within their code from 1
to 2 or 3.

It's a good practice to organize the listeners into folders matching the structure of
the observed class location. For example, if a module is called Foggyline_Plugged
and we are observing the method in the Magento\Catalog\Block\Product\
AbstractProduct class, we should consider putting the plugin class into the
Foggyline/Plugged/Block/Catalog/Product/AbstractProductPlugin.php file.
This is a not a requirement. Rather, it is a nice convention for other developers to
easily manage the code.

Once the module is in place, we need to execute the following commands on the console:

```
php bin/magento module:enable Foggyline_Plugged
php bin/magento setup:upgrade
```

This will make the module visible to Magento.

If we now open the storefront in a browser for a category page, we will see the results of all the var_dump function calls.

Let's go ahead and take a look at each and every listener method in detail.

Using the before listener

The before listeners are used when we want to change the arguments of an original method or add some behavior before an original method is called.

Looking back at the beforeGetAddToCartUrl listener method definition, you will see that it has three properties assigned in sequence—$subject, $product, and $additional.

With the before method listener, the first property is always the $subject property, which contains the instance of the object type being observed. Properties following the $subject property match the properties of the observed getAddToCartUrl method in a sequential order.

This simple rule used for transformation is as follows:

```
getAddToCartUrl($product, $additional = [])
beforeGetAddToCartUrl($subject, $product, $additional = [])
```

The before listener methods do not need to have a return value.

If we run get_class($subject) in the beforeGetAddToCartUrl listener method that we previously saw, we will have the following result:

```
\Magento\Catalog\Block\Product\ListProduct\Interceptor
    extends \Magento\Catalog\Block\Product\ListProduct
        extends \Magento\Catalog\Block\Product\AbstractProduct
```

What this shows is that even though we are observing the AbstractProduct class, the $subject property is not directly of that type. Rather, it is of the ListProduct\Interceptor type. This is something that you should keep in mind during development.

Using the after listener

The `after` listeners are used when we want to change the values returned by an original method or add some behavior after an original method is called.

Looking back at the `afterGetAddToCartUrl` listener method definition, you will see that it has only one `$subject` property assigned.

With the `after` method listener, the first and only property is always the `$subject` property, which contains the instance of the object type being observed and not the return value of the observed method.

This simple rule used for transformation is as follows:

```
getAddToCartUrl($product, $additional = [])
afterGetAddToCartUrl($subject)
```

The `after` listener methods do not need to have a return value.

Like the `before` interceptor method, the `$subject` property in this case is not directly of the `AbstractProduct` type. Rather, it is of the parent `ListProduct\Interceptor` type.

Using the around listener

The `around` listeners are used when we want to change both the arguments and the returned values of an original method or add some behavior before and after an original method is called.

Looking back at the `aroundGetAddToCartUrl` listener method definition, you will see that it has four properties assigned in sequence—`$subject`, `$proceed`, `$product`, and `$additional`.

With the `after` method listener, the first property is always the `$subject` property, which contains the instance of the object type being observed and not the return value of the observed method. The second property is always the `$proceed` property of `\Closure`. The properties following the `$subject` and `$proceed` match the properties of the observed `getAddToCartUrl` method in the sequential order too.

This simple rule used for transformation is as follows:

```
getAddToCartUrl($product, $additional = [])
aroundGetAddToCartUrl(
    $subject,
    \Closure $proceed,
    $product,
    $additional = []
)
```

The `around` listener methods must have a return value. The return value is formed in such way that the parameters following the `$closure` parameter in the `around` listener method definition are passed to the `$closure` function call in a sequential order, as follows:

```
return $proceed($product, $additional);
//or
$result = $proceed($product, $additional);
return $result;
```

The plugin sort order

Looking back, when we defined a plugin in the `di.xml` file, one of the attributes that we set for every plugin definition was `sortOrder`. It was set to `100`, `200` to `300` for `foggyPlugin1`, `foggyPlugin2` and `foggyPlugin3` respectively.

The flow of the code execution for the preceding plugins is as follows:

- `Plugin1 - beforeGetAddToCartUrl`
- `Plugin1 - aroundGetAddToCartUrl`
- `Plugin2 - beforeGetAddToCartUrl`
- `Plugin2 - aroundGetAddToCartUrl`
- `Plugin3 - beforeGetAddToCartUrl`
- `Plugin3 - aroundGetAddToCartUrl`
- `Plugin3 - afterGetAddToCartUrl`
- `Plugin2 - afterGetAddToCartUrl`
- `Plugin1 - afterGetAddToCartUrl`

In other words, if multiple plugins are listening to the same method, the following execution order is used:

- The `before` plugin functions with the lowest `sortOrder` value
- The `around` plugin functions with the lowest `sortOrder` value
- The `before` plugin functions following the `sortOrder` value from the lowest to the highest
- The `around` plugin functions following the `sortOrder` value from the lowest to the highest
- The `after` plugin functions with the highest `sortOrder` value
- The `after` plugin functions following the `sortOrder` value from the highest to the lowest

Special care needs to be taken when it comes to the `around` listener, as it is the only listener that needs to return a value. If we omit the return value, we risk breaking the execution flow in such a way that the other around plugins for the same method won't be executed.

Summary

In this chapter, we had a look at a powerful feature of Magento called plugins. We created a small module with three plugins; each plugin had a different sort order. This enabled us to trace the execution flow of multiple plugins that observe the same method. We explored in detail the `before`, `after`, and `around` listener methods, while having a strong emphasis on the parameter order. The finalized module used in this chapter can be found at `https://github.com/ajzele/B05032-Foggyline_ Plugged`.

In the next chapter, we are going to dive deep into backend development.

7
Backend Development

Backend development is a term that is most commonly used to describe work closely related to the server side. This usually implies the actual server, application code, and the database. For example, if we open a storefront of a web shop, add a few products to the cart, and then check out, the application will store the information provided. This information is managed on a server with a server-side language, such as PHP, and then saved in a database. In *Chapter 4, Models and Collections*, we took a look at the backbone of backend development. In this chapter, we will explore other backend-related aspects.

We will use the `Foggyline_Office` module that was defined in one of the previous chapters as we go through the following topics:

- Cron jobs
- Notification messages
- Sessions and cookies
- Logging
- The profiler
- Events and observers
- Caches
- Widgets
- Custom variables
- i18n (internationalization)
- Indexers

These individual isolated units of functionality are mostly used in everyday backend-related development.

Cron jobs

Speaking of `cron` jobs, it is worth noting one important thing. A `Magento cron` job is not the same as an operating system `cron` job. An operating system `cron` is driven by a `crontab` (short for `cron` table) file. The `crontab` file, is a configuration file that specifies shell commands that need to be run periodically on a given schedule.

A `Magento cron` job is driven by a periodic execution of PHP code that handles entries in the `cron_schedule` table. The `cron_schedule` table is where `Magento` `cron` jobs are queued once they are picked up from the individual `crontab.xml` file.

The `Magento cron` jobs cannot be executed without the operating system `cron` job being set to execute the `php bin/magento cron:run` command. Ideally, an operating system `cron` job should be set to trigger `Magento`'s `cron:run` every minute. `Magento` will then internally execute its `cron` jobs according to the way an individual `cron` job is defined in the `crontab.xml` file.

To define a new `cron` job in `Magento cron`, we first need to define a `crontab.xml` file in the module. Let's create a `app/code/Foggyline/Office/etc/crontab.xml` file with the following content:

```xml
<?xml version="1.0"?>
<config xmlns:xsi="http://www.w3.org/2001/XMLSchema-instance"
  xsi:noNamespaceSchemaLocation=
  "urn:magento:module:Magento_Cron:etc/crontab.xsd">
    <group id="default">
        <job name="foggyline_office_logHello" instance=
          "Foggyline\Office\Model\Cron" method="logHello">
            <schedule>*/2 * * * *</schedule>
        </job>
    </group>
</config>
```

Note that the XSD schema location points to `crontab.xsd` from within the `Magento_Cron` module.

The `id` attribute of a `group` element is set to the `default` value. In its modules, `Magento` defines two different groups, namely default and index. We used the `default` value, as this is the one that gets executed when the standard `php bin/magento cron:run` command is triggered on the console.

Within the `group` element, we have individual jobs defined under the `job` element. The `job` element requires us to specify the `name`, `instance`, and `method` attributes. The `name` attribute has to be unique within the `group` element. The value of the `instance` and `method` attributes should point to the class that will be instantiated and the method within the class that needs to be executed.

The `schedule` element nested within the `cron` job specifies the desired time of job execution. It uses the same time expression as that of the entries in an operating system `crontab` file. The specific example that we will look at defines an expression (`*/2 * * * *`) that is executed every two minutes.

Once we have defined the `crontab.xml` file, we need to define the `Foggyline\Office\Model\Cron` class file, as follows:

```
namespace Foggyline\Office\Model;

class Cron
{
    protected $logger;

    public function __construct(
        \Psr\Log\LoggerInterface $logger
    )
    {
        $this->logger = $logger;
    }

    public function logHello()
    {
        $this->logger->info('Hello from Cron job!');
        return $this;
    }
}
```

The preceding code simply defines a `logHello` method used by the `cron` job. In the `logHello` method, we used the `logger` method that was instantiated via the constructor. The `logger` method will make a log entry in the `var/log/system.log` file once it is executed.

Once the command is executed, you will see the `Ran` jobs by schedule message in the console. Additionally, the `cron_schedule` table should get filled with all the `Magento cron` jobs that were defined.

At this point, we should trigger the `php bin/magento cron:run` command in the console.

The `cron_schedule` table contains the following columns:

- `schedule_id`: The auto-increment `primary` field.
- `job_code`: The value of the job `name` attribute, as defined in `crontab.xml` file, which equals to `foggyline_office_logHello` table in our example.
- `status`: Defaults to the pending value for the newly created entries in the table and allows for a `pending`, `running`, `success`, `missed` or `error` value. Its value changes as the `cron` job traverses through its life cycle.
- `messages`: Stores the possible exception error message if the exception has occurred during a job's execution.
- `created_at`: The `timestamp` value that denotes when a job was created.
- `scheduled_at`: The `timestamp` value that denotes when a job was scheduled for execution.
- `executed_at`: The `timestamp` value that denotes when a job's execution started.
- `finished_at`: The `timestamp` value that denotes when a job has finished executing.

Unless we have already set the operating system `cron` to trigger the `php bin/magento cron:run` command, we need to trigger it on our own a few times every two minutes in order to actually execute the job. The first time a command is run, if the job does not exist in the `cron_schedule` table, `Magento` will merely queue it, but it won't execute it. The subsequent `cron` runs will execute the command. Once we are sure that the `cron` job entry in the `cron_schedule` table has the `finished_at` column value filled, we will see an entry that looks like `[2015-11-21 09:42:18] main.INFO: Hello from Cron job! [] []` in the `var/log/system.log` file.

> While developing and testing `cron` jobs in `Magento`, we might need to truncate the `cron_schedule` table, delete `Magento`'s `var/cache` value, and execute the `php bin/magento cron:run` command repetitively until we get it tested and working.

Notification messages

`Magento` implements the notification message mechanism via the `Messages` module. The `Messages` module conforms to `\Magento\Framework\Message\ManagerInterface`. Though the interface itself does not impose any session relation, an implementation adds interface-defined types of messages to a session and allows access to those messages later. In the `app/etc/di.xml` file, there is a preference defined for `\Magento\Framework\Message\ManagerInterface` towards the `Magento\Framework\Message\Manager` class.

`Message\ManagerInterface` specifies four types of messages, namely `error`, `warning`, `notice`, and `success`. The types of messages are followed by several key methods in the `Message\Manager` class, such as `addSuccess`, `addNotice`, `addWarning`, `addError`, and `addException`. The `addException` method is basically a wrapper for `addError` that accepts an `exception` object as a parameter.

Let's try to run the following code in the `execute` method of `app/code/Foggyline/Office/Controller/Test/Crud.php`:

```
$resultPage = $this->resultPageFactory->create();
$this->messageManager->addSuccess('Success-1');
$this->messageManager->addSuccess('Success-2');
$this->messageManager->addNotice('Notice-1');
$this->messageManager->addNotice('Notice-2');
$this->messageManager->addWarning('Warning-1');
$this->messageManager->addWarning('Warning-2');
$this->messageManager->addError('Error-1');
$this->messageManager->addError('Error-2');
return $resultPage;
```

Once this code executed, the result, as shown in the following screenshot, will appear on the page in the browser:

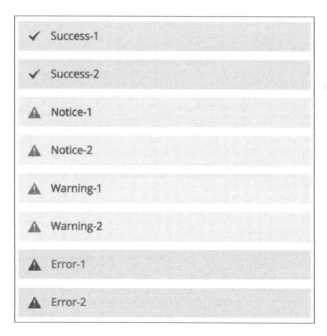

Notification messages appear both in the frontend and admin area.

The frontend layout `vendor/magento/module-theme/view/frontend/layout/default.xml` file defines it as follows:

```xml
<page layout="3columns"
  xmlns:xsi="http://www.w3.org/2001/XMLSchema-instance"
  xsi:noNamespaceSchemaLocation=
  "../../../../../../../lib/internal/Magento/Framework
  /View/Layout/etc/page_configuration.xsd">
    <update handle="default_head_blocks"/>
    <body>
        <!-- ... -->
        <referenceContainer name="columns.top">
            <container name="page.messages" htmlTag="div"
              htmlClass="page messages">
                <block class="Magento\Framework\View\Element
                  \Messages" name="messages" as="messages"
                  template="Magento_Theme::messages.phtml"/>
            </container>
        </referenceContainer>
        <!-- ... -->
    </body>
</page>
```

The `template` file that renders the messages is `view/frontend/templates/messages.phtml` in the `Magento_Theme` module. By looking at the `Magento\Framework\View\Element\Messages` class, you will see that the `_toHtml` method branches into `if-else` statements, depending on whether template is set or not. In case the template is not set, `_toHtml` internally calls the `_renderMessagesByType` method, which renders messages in the HTML format that are grouped by type.

The `view/adminhtml/layout/default.xml` admin layout file in the `Magento_AdminNotification` module defines it as follows:

```xml
<page xmlns:xsi="http://www.w3.org/2001/XMLSchema-instance"
  xsi:noNamespaceSchemaLocation="urn:magento:
  framework:View/Layout/etc/page_configuration.xsd">
    <body>
        <referenceContainer name="notifications">
            <block class="Magento\AdminNotification\Block
              \System\Messages" name="system_messages"
              as="system_messages" before="-" template=
              "Magento_AdminNotification::system/messages.phtml"/>
        </referenceContainer>
    </body>
</page>
```

The `template` file that renders the messages is `view/adminhtml/templates/system/messages.phtml` in the `Magento_AdminNotification` module. When you look at the `Magento\AdminNotification\Block\System\Messages` class, you will see that its `_toHtml` is calling the `_toHtml` parent method, where the parent belongs to the `\Magento\Framework\View\Element\Template` class. This means that the output is relying on the `view/adminhtml/templates/system/messages.phtml` file in the `Magento_AdminNotification` module.

Session and cookies

Sessions in `Magento` conform to `Magento\Framework\Session\SessionManagerInterface`. In the `app/etc/di.xml` file, there is a definition preference for the `SessionManagerInterface` class which points to the `Magento\Framework\Session\Generic` class type. The `Session\Generic` class is just an empty class that extends the `Magento\Framework\Session\SessionManager` class, which in turn implements the `SessionManagerInterface` class.

There is one important object that gets instantiated in the `SessionManager` instance that conforms to `\Magento\Framework\Session\Config\ConfigInterface`. On looking at `app/etc/di.xml` file, we can see a preference for `ConfigInterface` pointing to a `Magento\Framework\Session\Config` class type.

> To fully understand the session behavior in `Magento`, we should study the inner workings of both the `SessionManager` and `Session\Config` classes.

`Magento` uses cookies to keep track of a session. These cookies have a default lifetime of 3,600 seconds. When a session is established, a cookie with the name of `PHPSESSID` is created in the browser. The value of the cookie equals the session name. By default, sessions are stored in files in the `var/session` directory of `Magento`'s root installation.

If you have a look at these session files, you will see that session information is being stored in serialized strings that are divided into groupings such as _ session_validator_data, _session_hosts, default, customer_website_1, and checkout, as shown in the following screenshot:

```
_session_validator_data
    |a:4:{s:11:"remote_addr";s:9:"127.0.0.1";s:8:
_session_hosts
    |a:1:{s:12:"magento2.loc";b:1;}
default
    |a:3:{s:9:"_form_key";s:16:"u3sNaa26Ii21nveV"
customer_website_1
    |a:0:{}
checkout
    |a:0:{}
```

This is not the finite list of grouping. Modules that implement their own session handling bits can add their own groups.

We can store and retrieve information in a session by simply using expressions like the following ones:

```
$this->sessionManager->setFoggylineOfficeVar1('Office1');
$this->sessionManager->getFoggylineOfficeVar1();
```

The preceding expressions will create and get an entry from the session under the default group.

We can get the entire content of the default session group simply by using the $this->sessionManager->getData() expression, which will return an array of data that is similar to the following one:

```
array(3) {
  ["_form_key"] => string(16) "u3sNaa26Ii21nveV"
  ["visitor_data"] => array(14) {
    ["last_visit_at"] => string(19) "2015-08-19 07:40:03"
    ["session_id"] => string(26) "8p82je0dkqq1o00lanlr6bj6m2"
    ["visitor_id"] => string(2) "35"
    ["server_addr"] => int(2130706433)
    ["remote_addr"] => int(2130706433)
    ["http_secure"] => bool(false)
    ["http_host"] => string(12) "magento2.loc"
    ["http_user_agent"] => string(121) "Mozilla/5.0 …"
    ["http_accept_language"] => string(41) "en-US,en;"
    ["http_accept_charset"] => string(0) ""
```

```
    ["request_uri"] => string(38)
      "/index.php/foggyline_office/test/crud/"
    ["http_referer"] => string(0) ""
    ["first_visit_at"] => string(19) "2015-08-19 07:40:03"
    ["is_new_visitor"] => bool(false)
  }
  ["foggyline_office_var_1"] => string(7) "Office1"
}
```

As you can see, the `foggyline_office_var_1` value is right there among other session values.

There are several useful methods of `ConfigInterface` that we can use to fetch session configuration information; a few of these methods are as follows:

- `getCookieSecure`

- `getCookieDomain`

- `getCookieHttpOnly`

- `getCookieLifetime`

- `getName`

- `getSavePath`

- `getUseCookies`

- `getOptions`

Here's a result example of the `getOptions` method call on the `Session\Config` instance:

```
array(9) {
  ["session.save_handler"] => string(5) "files"
  ["session.save_path"] => string(39)
    "/Users/branko/www/magento2/var/session/"
  ["session.cookie_lifetime"] => int(3600)
  ["session.cookie_path"] => string(1) "/"
  ["session.cookie_domain"] => string(12) "magento2.loc"
  ["session.cookie_httponly"] => bool(true)
  ["session.cookie_secure"] => string(0) ""
  ["session.name"] => string(9) "PHPSESSID"
  ["session.use_cookies"] => bool(true)
}
```

Cookies often go hand in hand with sessions. Besides being used to link to a certain session, cookies are often used to store some information on the client side, thus tracking or identifying the return users and customers.

Besides the pure PHP approach with the `setcookie` function, we can manage cookies in `Magento` through an instance of `Magento\Framework\Stdlib\CookieManagerInterface`. When you look at `app/etc/di.xml` file, you will see that the preference for `CookieManagerInterface` points to a class of the `Magento\Framework\Stdlib\Cookie\PhpCookieManager` type.

The following restrictions are worth noting when it comes to `Magento` cookies:

- We can set maximum of 50 cookies in the system. Otherwise, `Magento` will throw an `Unable to send the cookie. Maximum number of cookies would be exceeded` exception.

- We can store a cookie with a maximum size of 4096 bytes. Otherwise, `Magento` will throw an `Unable to send the cookie. Size of \'%name\' is %size bytes` exception.

By imposing these restrictions, `Magento` ensures that we are compatible with most browsers.

The `CookieManagerInterface` class, among other things, specifies the `setSensitiveCookie` method requirement. This method sets a value in a private cookie with the given `$name` `$value` pairing. Sensitive cookies have **HttpOnly** set to true and thus cannot be accessed by JavaScript.

As we will soon demonstrate in the following examples, to set a public or private cookie, we can help ourselves by using instances of the following:

- `\Magento\Framework\Stdlib\Cookie\CookieMetadataFactory`

- `\Magento\Framework\Stdlib\CookieManagerInterface`

- `\Magento\Framework\Session\Config\ConfigInterface`

We can set public cookies in the following way:

```
$cookieValue = 'Just some value';
$cookieMetadata = $this->cookieMetadataFactory
    ->createPublicCookieMetadata()
    ->setDuration(3600)
    ->setPath($this->sessionConfig->getCookiePath())
    ->setDomain($this->sessionConfig->getCookieDomain())
    ->setSecure($this->sessionConfig->getCookieSecure())
    ->setHttpOnly($this->sessionConfig->getCookieHttpOnly());

$this->cookieManager
  ->setPublicCookie('cookie_name_1', $cookieValue,
    $cookieMetadata);
```

The preceding code will result in a cookie, as shown in the following screenshot:

We can set private cookies in the following way:

```
$cookieValue = 'Just some value';

$cookieMetadata = $this->cookieMetadataFactory
    ->createSensitiveCookieMetadata()
    ->setPath($this->sessionConfig->getCookiePath())
    ->setDomain($this->sessionConfig->getCookieDomain());

$this->cookieManager
  ->setSensitiveCookie('cookie_name_2', $cookieValue,
    $cookieMetadata);
```

The preceding code will result in a cookie, as shown in the following screenshot:

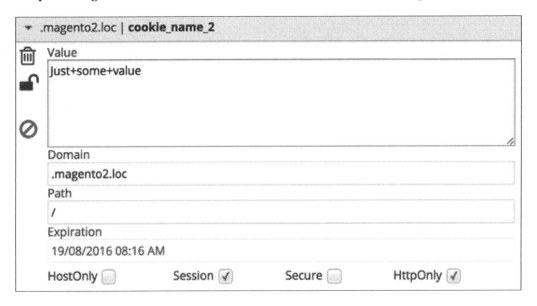

Interestingly, both the public and private cookies in the preceding example show that **HttpOnly** is checked off because by default, a Magento admin has **Stores | Settings | Configuration | General | Web | Default Cookie Settings | Use HTTP Only** set to **Yes**. Since we are using the setHttpOnly method in the public cookie example, we simply picked up the config value via $this->sessionConfig-> getCookieHttpOnly() and passed it on. If we comment out that line, we will see that the public cookie does not really set **HttpOnly** by default.

Logging

Magento supports the messages logging mechanism via its \Psr\Log\ LoggerInterface class. The LoggerInterface class has a preference defined within app/etc/di.xml file for the Magento\Framework\Logger\Monolog class type. The actual crux of implementation is actually in the Monolog parent class named Monolog\Logger, which comes from the Monolog vendor.

The LoggerInterface class uses the following eight methods to write logs to the eight RFC 5424 levels:

- debug
- info
- notice

- warning

- error

- critical

- alert

- emergency

To use a logger, we need to pass the `LoggerInterface` class to a constructor of a class from within we want to use it and then simply make one of the following method calls:

```
$this->logger->log(\Monolog\Logger::DEBUG, 'debug msg');
$this->logger->log(\Monolog\Logger::INFO, 'info msg');
$this->logger->log(\Monolog\Logger::NOTICE, 'notice msg');
$this->logger->log(\Monolog\Logger::WARNING, 'warning msg');
$this->logger->log(\Monolog\Logger::ERROR, 'error msg');
$this->logger->log(\Monolog\Logger::CRITICAL, 'critical msg');
$this->logger->log(\Monolog\Logger::ALERT, 'alert msg');
$this->logger->log(\Monolog\Logger::EMERGENCY, 'emergency msg');
```

Alternatively, the preferred shorter version through individual log level type methods is as follows:

```
$this->logger->debug('debug msg');
$this->logger->info('info msg');
$this->logger->notice('notice msg');
$this->logger->warning('warning msg');
$this->logger->error('error msg');
$this->logger->critical('critical msg');
$this->logger->alert('alert msg');
$this->logger->emergency('emergency msg');
```

Both approaches result in the same two log files being created in `Magento`, which are as follows:

- `var/log/debug.log`

- `var/log/system.log`

The `debug.log` file contains only the debug level type of the log, while the rest are saved under `system.log`.

Entries within these logs will then look like this:

```
[2015-11-21 09:42:18] main.DEBUG: debug msg {"is_exception":false}
  []
[2015-11-21 09:42:18] main.INFO: info msg [] []
[2015-11-21 09:42:18] main.NOTICE: notice msg [] []
[2015-11-21 09:42:18] main.WARNING: warning msg [] []
[2015-11-21 09:42:18] main.ERROR: error msg [] []
[2015-11-21 09:42:18] main.CRITICAL: critical msg [] []
[2015-11-21 09:42:18] main.ALERT: alert msg [] []
[2015-11-21 09:42:18] main.EMERGENCY: emergency msg [] []
```

Each of these `logger` methods can accept an entire array of arbitrary data called context, as follows:

```
$this->logger->info('User logged in.', ['user'=>'Branko',
  'age'=>32]);
```

The preceding expression will produce the following entry in `system.log`:

```
[2015-11-21 09:42:18] main.INFO: User logged in.
  {"user":"Branko","age":32} []
```

 We can manually delete any of the `.log` files from the `var/log` directory, and `Magento` will automatically create it again when needed.

`Magento` also has another logging mechanism in place, where it logs the following actions in the `log_*` tables in a database:

- `log_customer`
- `log_quote`
- `log_summary`
- `log_summary_type`
- `log_url`
- `log_url_info`
- `log_visitorz`
- `log_visitor_info`
- `log_visitor_online`

It is worth noting that this database logging is not related in any way to `Psr` logger that was described previously. While `Psr` logger serves developers within the code to group and log certain messages according to the `Psr` standard, the database logging logs the live data that is a result of `user/customer` interaction in the browser.

By default, `Magento` keeps database logs for around 180 days. This is a configurable option that can be controlled in the `Magento` admin area under the **Stores | Settings | Configuration | Advanced | System | Log Cleaning** tab with other log related options, as shown in the following screenshot:

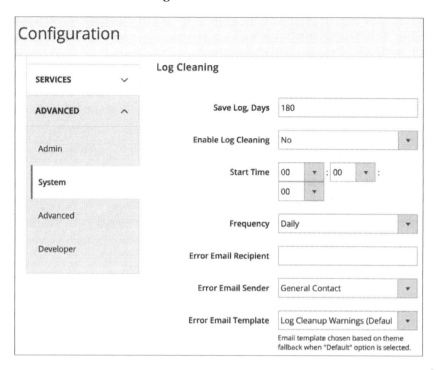

Configuration options that are shown in the preceding screenshot only bare meaning operating system `cron` is triggering `Magento cron`.

 We can execute two commands on terminal: `php bin/magento log:status` to get the current state information about log tables and `php bin/magento log:clean` to force the clearing of tables.

The profiler

`Magento` has an in-built profiler that can be used to identify performance problems on the server side. In a nutshell, the profiler can tell us the execution time of certain chunks of code. There is nothing that great with its behavior. We can only get the execution time of code blocks or individual expressions that have been wrapped by the profiler's start and stop methods. On its own, `Magento` calls for the profiler extensively across its code. However, we can't see it in effect as the profiler output is disabled by default.

`Magento` supports three profiler outputs, namely `html`, `csvfile`, and `firebug`.

To enable the profiler, we can edit `.htaccess` and add one of the following expressions:

- `SetEnv MAGE_PROFILER "html"`
- `SetEnv MAGE_PROFILER "csvfile"`
- `SetEnv MAGE_PROFILER "firebug"`

The HTML type of profiler will show its output into the footer area of a page that we open in the browser, as shown in the following screenshot:

Timer Id	Time	Avg	Cnt	Emalloc	RealMem
cache_frontend_create	0.046384	0.023192	2	1,479,184	1,572,864
cache_load	0.014226	0.004742	3	454,796	524,288
magento	0.168286	0.168286	1	4,086,732	3,670,016
· cache_load	0.013186	0.001884	7	430,260	524,288
· store.resolve	0.080572	0.080572	1	2,132,144	2,097,152
· · EVENT:model_load_before	0.002523	0.002523	1	133,904	0
· · · cache_load	0.001933	0.000967	2	40,436	0

The `csv` file type of profiler will output into `var/log/profiler.csv`, as shown in the following screenshot:

```
cache_frontend_create,0.056534,0.028267,2,"1,479,196","1,572,864"
cache_load,0.008312,0.002771,3,"454,796","524,288"
magento,0.152288,0.152288,1,"4,086,812","3,670,016"
magento->cache_load,0.010538,0.001505,7,"430,256","786,432"
magento->store.resolve,0.075128,0.075128,1,"2,132,084","1,835,008"
magento->store.resolve->EVENT:model_load_before,0.002179,0.002179,1,"133,912","262,144"
magento->store.resolve->EVENT:model_load_before->cache_load,0.001416,0.000708,2,"40,436",0
```

The firebug type of profiler will output into `var/log/profiler.csv`, as shown in the following screenshot:

The profiler outputs the following pieces of information:

- `Time` profiler shows the time spent from `Profiler::start` to `Profiler::stop`.

- `Avg` profiler shows the average time spent from `Profiler::start` to `Profiler::stop` for cases where `Cnt` is greater than one.

- `Cnt` profiler shows the integer value of how many times we have started the profiler with the same timer name. For example, if we have called `\Magento\Framework\Profiler::start('foggyline:office');` twice somewhere in the code, then `Cnt` will show the value of 2.

- `Emalloc` profiler stands for the amount of memory allocated to PHP. It is a mix of the core PHP `memory_get_usage` function without the true parameter passed to it and the timer values.

- `RealMem` profiler also stands for the amount of memory allocated to PHP whose final value is also obtained via the `memory_get_usage` function minus the timer values, but this time with the true parameter passed to it.

We can easily add our own `Profiler::start` calls anywhere in the code. Every `Profiler::start` should be followed by some code expressions and then finalized with a `Profiler::stop` call, as follows:

```
\Magento\Framework\Profiler::start('foggyline:office');
sleep(2); /* code block or single expression here */
\Magento\Framework\Profiler::stop('foggyline:office');
```

Depending on where we call the profiler in the code, the resulting output should be similar to the one shown in the following screenshot:

. . CONTROLLER_ACTION:foggyline_office_test_crud	2.077258	2.077258	1	239,732	262,144
. . . action_body	2.077231	2.077231	1	238,752	262,144
. . . . foggyline:office	2.000966	2.000966	1	1,308	0
. . . . postdispatch	0.052955	0.052955	1	55,952	0

Events and observers

`Magento` implements the observer pattern through `\Magento\Framework\Event\ManagerInterface`. In `app/etc/di.xml`, there is a preference for `ManagerInterface` that points to the `Magento\Framework\Event\Manager\Proxy` class type. The `Proxy` class further extends the `\Magento\Framework\Event\Manager` class that implements the actual event dispatch method.

Events are dispatched by calling a dispatch method on the instance of the `Event\Manager` class and passing the name and some data, which is optional, to it. Here's an example of a `Magento` core event:

```
$this->eventManager->dispatch(
    'customer_customer_authenticated',
    ['model' => $this->getFullCustomerObject($customer),
        'password' => $password]
);
```

The `$this->eventManager` is an instance of the previously mentioned `Event\`
`Manager` class. In this case, the event name equals to `customer_customer_`
`authenticated`, while the data passed to the event is the array with two elements.
The preceding event is fired when the authenticate method is called on `\Magento\`
`Customer\Model\AccountManagement`, that is, when a customer logs in.

Dispatching an event only makes sense if we expect someone to observe it and
execute their code when the event is dispatched. Depending on the area from
which we want to observe events, we can define observers in one of the
following XML files:

- `app/code/{vendorName}/{moduleName}/etc/events.xml`

- `app/code/{vendorName}/{moduleName}/etc/frontend/events.xml`

- `app/code/{vendorName}/{moduleName}/etc/adminhtml/events.xml`

Let's define an observer that will log an e-mail address of an authenticated user
into a `var/log/system.log` file. We can use the `Foggyline_Office` module and
add some code to it. As we are interested in the storefront, it makes sense to put the
observer in the `etc/frontend/events.xml` module.

Let's define the `app/code/Foggyline/Office/etc/frontend/events.xml` file with
content, as follows:

```
<config xmlns:xsi="http://www.w3.org/2001/XMLSchema-instance"
  xsi:noNamespaceSchemaLocation="urn:magento:framework:
  Event/etc/events.xsd">
    <event name="customer_customer_authenticated">
        <observer name="foggyline_office_customer_authenticated"
            instance="Foggyline\Office\Observer\LogCustomerEmail" />
    </event>
</config>
```

Here, we are specifying a `foggyline_office_customer_authenticated`
observer for the `customer_customer_authenticated` event. The observer is
defined in the `LogCustomerEmail` class that is placed in the `Observer` module
directory. The `Observer` class has to implement the `Magento\Framework\Event\`
`ObserverInterface` class. The `Observer` interface defines a single execute method.
The execute method hosts the observer code and is executed when the `customer_`
`customer_authenticated` event is dispatched.

Let's go ahead and define the `Foggyline\Office\Observer\LogCustomerEmail` class in the `app/code/Foggyline/Office/Observer/LogCustomerEmail.php` file, as follows:

```php
namespace Foggyline\Office\Observer;

use Magento\Framework\Event\ObserverInterface;

class LogCustomerEmail implements ObserverInterface
{
    protected $logger;

    public function __construct(
        \Psr\Log\LoggerInterface $logger
    )
    {
        $this->logger = $logger;
    }

    /**
     * @param \Magento\Framework\Event\Observer $observer
     * @return self
     */
    public function execute(\Magento\Framework\Event\Observer
      $observer)
    {
        //$password = $observer->getEvent()->getPassword();
        $customer = $observer->getEvent()->getModel();
        $this->logger->info('Foggyline\Office: ' . $customer->
          getEmail());
        return $this;
    }
}
```

The `execute` method takes a single parameter called `$observer` of the `\Magento\Framework\Event\Observer` type. The event that we are observing is passing two pieces of data within the array, namely the `model` and `password`. We can access this by using the `$observer->getEvent()->get{arrayKeyName}` expression. The `$customer` object is an instance of the `Magento\Customer\Model\Data\CustomerSecure` class, which contains properties such as `email`, `firstname`, `lastname`, and so on. Thus, we can extract the e-mail address from it and pass it to logger's `info` method.

Now that we know how to observe existing events, let's see how we can dispatch our own events. We can dispatch events from almost anywhere in the code, with or without data, as shown in the following example:

```
$this->eventManager->dispatch('foggyline_office_foo');
// or
$this->eventManager->dispatch(
    'foggyline_office_bar',
    ['var1'=>'val1', 'var2'=>'val2']
);
```

It is worth noting that there are two types of events; we can group them in the following way according to the way their name is assigned:

- **Static**: `$this->eventManager->dispatch('event_name', ...)`
- **Dynamic**: `$this->eventManager->dispatch({expression}.'_event_name', ...)`

The static events have a fixed string for a name, while the dynamic ones have a name that is determined during the runtime. Here's a nice example of the core Magento functionality from the `afterLoad` method that is defined under `lib/internal/Magento/Framework/Data/AbstractSearchResult.php`, which showcases how to use both types of events:

```
protected function afterLoad()
{
    $this->eventManager->dispatch
      ('abstract_search_result_load_after', ['collection' =>
      $this]);
    if ($this->eventPrefix && $this->eventObject) {
        $this->eventManager->dispatch($this->eventPrefix .
        '_load_after', [$this->eventObject => $this]);
    }
}
```

We can see a *static* event (`abstract_search_result_load_after`) and a dynamic event (`$this->eventPrefix . '_load_after'`). The `$this->eventPrefix` is an expression that gets evaluated during the runtime. We should be careful when using dynamic events as they are triggered under multiple situations. Some interesting dynamic events are the one defined on classes like the following ones:

- `Magento\Framework\Model\AbstractModel`
    - `$this->_eventPrefix . '_load_before'`
    - `$this->_eventPrefix . '_load_after'`
    - `$this->_eventPrefix . '_save_commit_after'`

- ◦ `$this->_eventPrefix . '_save_before'`
- ◦ `$this->_eventPrefix . '_save_after'`
- ◦ `$this->_eventPrefix . '_delete_before'`
- ◦ `$this->_eventPrefix . '_delete_after'`
- ◦ `$this->_eventPrefix . '_delete_commit_after'`
- ◦ `$this->_eventPrefix . '_clear'`

- • `\Magento\Framework\Model\ResourceModel\Db\Collection\AbstractCollection`
  - ◦ `$this->_eventPrefix . '_load_before'`
  - ◦ `$this->_eventPrefix . '_load_after'`

- • `\Magento\Framework\App\Action\Action`
  - ◦ `'controller_action_predispatch_' . $request->getRouteName()`
  - ◦ `'controller_action_predispatch_' . $request->getFullActionName()`
  - ◦ `'controller_action_postdispatch_' . $request->getFullActionName()`
  - ◦ `'controller_action_postdispatch_' . $request->getRouteName()`

- • `Magento\Framework\View\Result\Layout`
- • `'layout_render_before_' . $this->request-> getFullActionName()`

These events are fired on the `model`, `collection`, `controller`, and `layout` classes, which are probably among the most used backend elements that often require observing and interacting. Even though we can say that the full event name is known during the runtime along with the dynamic event, this can be assumed even before the runtime.

For example, assuming that we want to observe `'controller_action_predispatch_' . $request->getFullActionName()` for the `Foggyline_Office` module's `Crud` controller action, the actual full event name will be `'controller_action_predispatch_foggyline_office_test_crud'`, given that `$request->getFullActionName()` will resolve to `foggyline_office_test_crud` during the runtime.

Cache(s)

`Magento` has eleven out-of-the-box cache types, according to the following list. These are used across many levels within the system:

- **Configuration**: Various XML configurations that were collected across modules and merged
- **Layouts**: Layout building instructions
- **Blocks HTML output**: Page blocks HTML
- **Collections data**: Collection data files
- **Reflection data**: API interfaces reflection data
- **Database DDL operations**: Results of DDL queries, such as describing tables or indexes
- **EAV types and attributes**: Entity types declaration cache
- **Page cache**: Full page caching
- **Translations**: Translation files
- **Integrations configuration**: Integration configuration file
- **Integrations API configuration**: Integrations API configuration file
- **Web services configuration**: REST and SOAP configurations, generated WSDL file

There is also **Additional Cache Management** that manages the cache for the following files:

- Previously generated product image files
- Themes JavaScript and CSS files combined to one file
- Preprocessed view files and static files

Each of these caches can be cleared separately.

We can easily define our own cache type. We can do so by first creating an `app/code/Foggyline/Office/etc/cache.xml` file with content, as follows:

```
<config xmlns:xsi="http://www.w3.org/2001/XMLSchema-instance"
  xsi:noNamespaceSchemaLocation="urn:magento:framework:Cache/etc/
  cache.xsd">
    <type name="foggyline_office"
        instance="Foggyline\Office\Model\Cache">
      <label>Foggyline Office Example</label>
      <description>Example cache from Foggyline Office
        module.</description>
    </type>
</config>
```

When defining a new cache type, we need to specify its name and instance attributes. The name attribute of the type element should be set to foggyline_ office and should be unique across Magento. This value should match the TYPE_ IDENTIFIER constant value on the Foggyline\Office\Model\Cache class, which will be created soon. The instance attribute holds the class name that we will use for caching.

Then, we will define the Foggyline\Office\Model\Cache class in the app/code/ Foggyline/Office/Model/Cache.php file with the following content:

```
namespace Foggyline\Office\Model;

class Cache extends \Magento\Framework\Cache\Frontend\Decorator\
TagScope
{
    const TYPE_IDENTIFIER = 'foggyline_office';

    const CACHE_TAG = 'OFFICE';

    public function __construct(
        \Magento\Framework\App\Cache\Type\FrontendPool
          $cacheFrontendPool
    )
    {
        parent::__construct(
            $cacheFrontendPool->get(self::TYPE_IDENTIFIER),
              self::CACHE_TAG
        );
    }
}
```

The Cache class extends from TagScope and specifies its own values for TYPE_ IDENTIFIER and CACHE_TAG, passing them along to the parent constructor in the __construct method. With these two files (cache.xml and Cache), we have basically defined a new cache type.

Once we have specified the cache.xml file and the referenced cache class, we should be able to see our cache type in the Magento admin under the **System | Tools | Cache Management** menu, as shown in the following screenshot:

Cache Management			Flush Cache Storage	**Flush Magento Cache**
☐	Database DDL operations	Results of DDL queries, such as describing tables or indexes.	DB_DDL	DISABLED
☐	EAV types and attributes	Entity types declaration cache.	EAV	DISABLED
☐	Foggyline Office Example	Example cache from Foggyline Office module.	OFFICE	DISABLED

On its own, simply defining a new cache does not mean that it will get filled and used by `Magento`.

If you would like to use the cache anywhere within your code, you can do so by first passing the instance of the cache class to the constructor, as follows:

```
protected $cache;

public function __construct(
    \Foggyline\Office\Model\Cache $cache
)
{
    $this->cache = $cache;
}
```

Then, you can execute a chunk of code, as follows:

```
$cacheId = 'some-specific-id';
$objInfo = null;
$_objInfo = $this->cache->load($cacheId);

if ($_objInfo) {
    $objInfo = unserialize($_objInfo);
} else {
    $objInfo = [
        'var1'=> 'val1',
        'var2' => 'val2',
        'var3' => 'val3'
    ];
    $this->cache->save(serialize($objInfo), $cacheId);
}
```

The preceding code shows how we first try to load the value from the existing cache entry, and if there is none, we save it. If the cache type is set to `disabled` under the **Cache Management** menu, then the preceding code will never save and pull the data from the cache, as it is not in effect.

If you take a look at the `var/cache` folder of `Magento` at this point, you will see something similar to what's shown in the following screenshot:

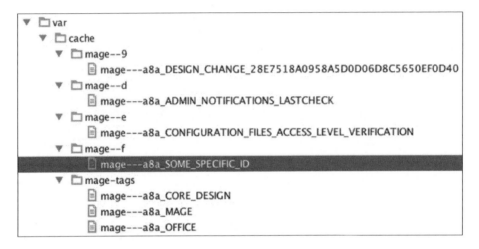

`Magento` created two cache entries for us, namely `var/cache/mage-tags/mage---a8a_OFFICE` and `var/cache/mage--f/mage---a8a_SOME_SPECIFIC_ID`. The `mage---a8a_OFFICE` file has only a single line of entry in this specific case, and the entry is the `a8a_SOME_SPECIFIC_ID` string, which obviously points to the other file. The `mage---a8a_SOME_SPECIFIC_ID` file contains the actual serialized `$objInfo` array.

The `a8a_` prefix and other prefixes in the `cache` file names are not really relevant to us; this is something that `Magento` adds on its own. What is relevant to us is the passing of proper individual cache tags to the chunks or variables that we want to cache, like in the preceding example, and the `TYPE_IDENTIFIER` and `CACHE_TAG` tags that we set for the `Cache` class.

Widgets

`Magento` provides support for widgets. Though the word "widget" might imply frontend development skills and activities, we will look at them as a part of the backend development flow because creating useful and robust widgets requires a significant amount of backend knowledge.

`Magento` provides several out-of-the-box widgets; some of them are as follows:

- CMS page link
- CMS static block
- Catalog category link
- Catalog new products list
- Catalog product link
- Catalog products list
- Orders and returns
- Recently compared products
- Recently viewed products

To create a fully custom widget, we start by defining `app/code/Foggyline/Office/etc/widget.xml` with content, as follows:

```xml
<widgets xmlns:xsi="http://www.w3.org/2001/XMLSchema-instance"
    xsi:noNamespaceSchemaLocation="urn:magento:module:
    Magento_Widget:etc/widget.xsd">
    <widget id="foggyline_office"
        class="Foggyline\Office\Block\Widget\Example"
            placeholder_image="Magento_Cms::images/
                widget_block.png">
        <label translate="true">Foggyline Office</label>
        <description translate="true">Example Widget</description>
        <parameters>
            <parameter name="var1" xsi:type="select"
              visible="true" source_model="Magento\Config\Model
              \Config\Source\Yesno">
                <label translate="true">Yes/No var1</label>
            </parameter>
            <parameter name="var2" xsi:type="text" required="true"
              visible="true">
                <label translate="true">Number var2</label>
                <depends>
                    <parameter name="var1" value="1"/>
                </depends>
                <value>5</value>
            </parameter>
        </parameters>
    </widget>
</widgets>
```

The `id` widget has been set to `foggyline_office`, while the class powering widget has been set to `Foggyline\Office\Block\Widget\Example`. the `widget` class is basically a `block` class that extends from `\Magento\Framework\View\Element\AbstractBlock` and implements `\Magento\Widget\Block\BlockInterface`. The `label` and `description` element set values appear under the `Magento` admin when we select the widget for use.

The parameters of a widget are its configurable options that translate into HTML form elements, depending on the `type` and `source_model` options that we have selected. In the following example, we will demonstrate the usage of the `select` and `text` elements to retrieve input from a user, as shown in the following screenshot:

Let's proceed by creating the actual `Widget\Example` class in the `app/code/Foggyline/Office/Block/Widget/Example.php` file with content, as follows:

```php
namespace Foggyline\Office\Block\Widget;

class Example extends \Magento\Framework\View\Element\Text
    implements \Magento\Widget\Block\BlockInterface
{
    protected function _beforeToHtml()
    {
        $this->setText(sprintf(
            'example widget: var1=%s, var2=%s',
            $this->getData('var1'),
            $this->getData('var2')
        ));
```

```
        return parent::_beforeToHtml();
    }
}
```

What is happening here is that we are using `Element\Text` as a block type and not `Element\Template` because we want to simplify the example, as `Element\Template` will require the `phtml` template to be defined as well. By using `Element\Text`, we can simply define `_beforeToHtml` and call the `setText` method to set the text string of the block's output. We will build the output string by picking up the `var1` and `var2` variables, which were passed as parameters to the block.

Now, if we open the `Magento` admin area, go to **Content | Elements | Pages**, and select **Home Page** to edit, we should be able to click on the **Insert Frontend App** button and add our widget to the page. Alternatively, if we are not editing the page content in the `WYSIWYG` mode, we can also add the widget manually to the page by using the following expression:

```
{{widget type="Foggyline\\Office\\Block\\Widget\\Example" var1="1"
    var2="5"}}
```

Finally, we should see the example widget: `var1=1`, `var2=5` string in the browser while visiting the home page of the storefront.

We can use frontend apps to create highly configurable and embeddable widgets that users can easily assign to a CMS page or block.

Custom variables

Variables are a handy little feature of a core `Magento_Variable` module. `Magento` allows you to create custom variables and then use them in e-mail templates, the `WYSIWYG` editor, or even code expressions.

The following steps outline how we can create a new variable manually:

1. In the `Magento` admin area, navigate to **System | Other Settings | Custom Variables**.
2. Click on the **Add New Variable** button.
3. While keeping in mind the **Store View** switcher, fill in the required **Variable Code** and **Variable Name** options, and preferably one of the optional options, either **Variable HTML Value** or **Variable Plain Value**.
4. Click on the **Save** button.

Now that we have created the custom variable, we can use it in an e-mail template or the WYSIWYG editor by calling it using the following expression:

```
{{customVar code=foggyline_hello}}
```

The preceding expression will call for the value of the custom variable with code foggyline_hello.

Variables can be used within various code expressions, though it is not recommended to rely on the existence of an individual variable, as an admin user can delete it at any point. The following example demonstrates how we can use an existing variable in the code:

```
$storeId =0;

$variable = $this->_variableFactory->create()->setStoreId(
    $storeId
)->loadByCode(
    'foggyline_hello'
);

$value = $variable->getValue(
    \Magento\Variable\Model\Variable::TYPE_HTML
);
```

The $this->_variableFactory is an instance of \Magento\Variable\Model\ VariableFactory.

If used in the right way, variables can be useful. Storing information such as phone numbers or specialized labels that are used in CMS pages, blogs, and e-mail templates is a nice example of using custom variables.

i18n

i18n is the abbreviation for **internationalization**. Magento adds i18n support out of the box, thus adapting to various languages and regions without application changes. Within app/functions.php, there is a __() translation function, which is defined as follows:

```
function __()
{
    $argc = func_get_args();

    $text = array_shift($argc);
    if (!empty($argc) && is_array($argc[0])) {
```

```
        $argc = $argc[0];
    }

    return new \Magento\Framework\Phrase($text, $argc);
}
```

This `translation` function accepts a variable number of arguments and passes them to a constructor of the `\Magento\Framework\Phrase` class and returns its instance. The `Phrase` class has the `__toString` method, which then returns the translated string.

Here are a few examples of how we can use the `__()` function:

- `__('Translate me')`

- `__('Var1 %1, Var2 %2, Var %3', time(), date('Y'), 32)`

- `__('Copyright %1 <a href="%2">Magento</a>', date('Y'), 'http://magento.com')`

Strings passed through the `translation` function are expected to be found under the local CSV files, such as `app/code/{vendorName}/{moduleName}/i18n/{localeCode}.csv`. Let's imagine for a moment that we have two different store views defined in the `Magento` admin area under **Stores** | **Settings** | **All Stores**. One store has **Store** | **Settings** | **Configuration** | **General** | **Locale Options** | **Locale** set to **English (United Kingdom)** and the other one to **German (Germany)**. The local code for **English (United Kingdom)** is `en_GB`, and for **German (Germany)**, it is `de_DE`.

For the `de_DE` locale, we will add translation entries in the `app/code/Foggyline/Office/i18n/de_DE.csv` file, as follows:

```
"Translate me","de_DE Translate me"
"Var1 %1, Var2 %2, Var %3","de_DE Var1 %1, Var2 %2, Var %3"
"Copyright %1 <a href=""%2"">Magento</a>","de_DE Copyright %1 <a
  href=""%2"">Magento</a>"
```

For the `en_GB` locale, we will add translation entries in the `app/code/Foggyline/Office/i18n/en_GB.csv` file, as follows:

```
"Translate me","en_GB Translate me"
"Var1 %1, Var2 %2, Var %3", "en_GB Var1 %1, Var2 %2, Var %3"
"Copyright %1 <a href=""%2"">Magento</a>","en_GB Copyright %1 <a
href=""%2"">Magento</a>"
```

Looking at the two CSV files, a pattern emerges. We can see that the CSV files function in the following way:

- Individual translation strings are provided according to every line of CSV
- Each line further comprises two individual strings that are separated by a comma
- Both individual strings are surrounded by quotes
- If a string contains quotes, it is escaped by a double quote so that it does not break translation
- The %1, %2, %3...%n pattern is used to mark variable placeholders that we provided during application runtime through the code

Magento supports several commands related to its bin/magento console tool:

i18n

```
i18n:collect-phrases    Discovers phrases in the codebase
i18n:pack               Saves language package
i18n:uninstall          Uninstalls language packages
```

If we execute a console command as follows, Magento will recursively look for translatable expressions within PHP, PHTML, or XML files that have phrases to translate:

```
php bin/magento i18n:collect-phrases -o
"/Users/branko/www/magento2/app/code/Foggyline/Office/i18n/en_GB.csv"
/Users/branko/www/magento2/app/code/Foggyline/Office
```

The output of the preceding command will basically overwrite the app/code/ Foggyline/Office/i18n/en_GB.csv file, which has all the Foggyline/Office module translatable phrases. This is a nice way of aggregating all the translatable phrases into appropriate locale files, such as en_GB.csv in this case.

The translation CSV files can also be placed under the individual theme. For example, let's imagine a situation where we add content to app/design/frontend/ Magento/blank/i18n/en_GB.csv, as follows:

```
"Translate me","Theme_en_GB Translate me"
"Var1 %1, Var2 %2, Var %3", "Theme_en_GB Var1 %1, Var2 %2, Var %3"
"Copyright %1 <a href=""%2"">Magento</a>","Theme_en_GB Copyright
%1 <a href=""%2"">Magento</a>"
```

Now, a `Translate me` string output of the storefront for the `en_GB` locale would resolve to `Theme_en_GB Translate me` and not to the `en_GB Translate me` string.

> Theme CSV translations take higher precedence than module CSV translations, thus enabling developers to override individual module translations.

Along with CSV translation files, `Magento` also supports a feature called **inline translation**. We can activate the inline translation in the `Magento` admin area by navigating to **Store | Settings | Configuration | Advanced | Developer | Translate Inline**. This feature can be turned on separately for admin and storefront, as shown in the following screenshot:

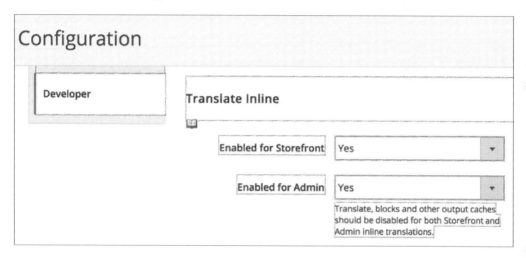

As shown in the preceding screenshot, when a feature is activated, red dotted borders appear around the HTML elements. Hovering over an individual element shows a little book icon near the individual element at the bottom left corner. Clicking on the book icon opens a popup, as shown in the following screenshot:

Translate

Shown:	Theme_en_GB Translate me
Translated:	Theme_en_GB Translate me
Original:	Translate me
Location:	Text
Scope:	theme2
Store View Specific:	☐
Custom:	Theme_en_GB Translate

Please refresh the page to see your changes after submitting this form.

SUBMIT   CLOSE

It is important to note that these red dotted borders and the book icon will only appear for strings that we passed through the __() translate function.

Here, we can see various pieces of information about the string, such as the Shown, Translated, and Original string. There is also an input field called Custom, where we can add a new translation. Inline translation strings are stored in the translation table in the database.

 Inline translation takes higher precedence than theme CSV translation files.

Indexer(s)

Indexing is the process of transforming data by reducing it to flattened data with less database tables. This process is run for products, categories, and so on in order to improve the performance of a web store. Since data constantly changes, this is not a one-time process. Rather, it is a periodic one. The `Magento_Indexer` module is a base of the `Magento` Indexing functionality.

The `Magento` console tool supports the following indexer commands.

```
indexer
    indexer:info          Shows allowed Indexers
    indexer:reindex       Reindexes Data
    indexer:set-mode      Sets index mode type
    indexer:show-mode     Shows Index Mode
    indexer:status        Shows status of Indexer
```

On running `php bin/magento indexer:info`, you will get a list of all the Magento indexers; the default ones are as follows:

```
catalog_category_product      Category Products
catalog_product_category      Product Categories
catalog_product_price         Product Price
catalog_product_attribute     Product EAV
foggyline_office_employee     Employee Flat Data
cataloginventory_stock        Stock
catalogrule_rule              Catalog Rule Product
catalogrule_product           Catalog Product Rule
catalogsearch_fulltext        Catalog Search
```

You will see all the indexers listed in the Magento admin in the **System | Tools | Index Management** menu.

From within the admin area, we can only change the indexer mode. There are two modes of indexers:

- **Update on Save**: Index tables are updated right after the dictionary data is changed

- **Update by Schedule**: Index tables are updated by `cron` jobs according to the configured schedule

Since indexers cannot be run manually from admin, we have to rely either on their manual execution or the `cron` execution.

Manual execution is done via the following console command:

```
php bin/magento indexer:reindex
```

The preceding command will run all the indexers at once. We can fine-tune it further to execute individual indexes by running a console command that is similar to the following line of code:

```
php bin/magento indexer:reindex catalogsearch_fulltext
```

Cron-executed indexers are defined via the `Magento_Indexer` module, as follows:

- `indexer_reindex_all_invalid`: This will execute every minute of every hour every day. It runs the `reindexAllInvalid` method on an instance of the `Magento\Indexer\Model\Processor` class.

- `indexer_update_all_views`: This will execute every minute of every hour every day. It runs the `updateMview` method on an instance of the `Magento\Indexer\Model\Processor` class.

- `indexer_clean_all_changelogs`: This will execute the 0th minute of every hour every day. It runs the `clearChangelog` method on an instance of the `Magento\Indexer\Model\Processor` class.

These `cron` jobs use an operating system `cron` job setup in such a way that the `Magento` `cron` job is triggered every minute.

The following three statuses is what an indexer can have:

- `valid`: The data is synchronized and no re-indexing is required
- `invalid`: The original data was changed and the index should be updated
- `working`: The index process is running

While we won't go into the details of actually creating a custom indexer within this chapter, it is worth noting that `Magento` defines its indexers in the `vendor/magento/module-*/etc/indexer.xml` file. This might come in handy for cases where we want a deeper understanding of the inner workings of an individual indexer. For example, the `catalog_product_flat` indexer is implemented via the `Magento\Catalog\Model\Indexer\Product\Flat` class, as defined within the `vendor/magento/module-catalog/etc/indexer.xml` file. By studying the `Flat` class implementation in depth, you can learn how data is taken from EAV tables and flattened into a simplified structure.

Summary

In this chapter, we covered some of the most relevant aspects of Magento, which was beyond models and classes, regarding backend development. We had a look at `crontab.xml`, which helps us schedule `jobs` (commands) so that they can be run periodically. Then, we tackled notification messages, which enable us to push styled messages to users via a browser. The *Session and cookies* section gave us an understanding of how `Magento` tracks user information from a browser to a session. Logging and profiling showed us a simple yet effective mechanism to keep track of performance and possible issues across code. The *Events and observers* section introduced us to a powerful pattern that `Magento` implements across the code, where we can trigger custom code execution when a certain event is fired. The section on caching guided us through the available cache types, and we studied how to create and use our own cache type. Through the section on frontend apps (widgets), we learned how to create our own miniature apps that can be called into CMS pages and blocks. Custom variables gave us an insight into a simple yet interesting feature, where we can define a variable via the admin interface and then use it within CMS page, block, or e-mail template. The section on i18n showed us how to use the Magento translation feature to translate any string on three different levels, namely the module CSV file, the theme CSV file, and inline translation. Finally, we had a look at indexers and their mode and status; we learned how to control their execution.

The next chapter will tackle frontend development. We will learn how create our own theme and use blocks and layouts to affect the output.

8
Frontend Development

Frontend development is a term most commonly tied to producing HTML, CSS, and JavaScript for a website or web application. Interchangeably, it addresses accessibility, usability, and performance toward reaching a satisfying user experience. Various levels of customization we want to apply to our web store require different development skill levels. We can make relatively simple changes to our store using just CSS. These would be the changes where we accept the structure of the store and focus only on visuals like changing colors and images. This might be a good starting point for less experienced developers and those new to the Magento platform. A more involved approach would be to make changes to the output generated by Magento modules. This usually means tiny bits of PHP knowledge, mostly *copy-paste-modify* of existing code fragments. A skill level above this one would imply knowledge of making structural changes to our store. This usually means mastering Magento's moderately sophisticated layout engine, where we make changes through XML definitions. The final and highest skill level for Magento frontend development implies the modification of existing or new custom functionality development.

Throughout this chapter, we will take a deep dive through the following sections:

- Rendering flow
- View elements
- Block architecture and life cycle
- Templates
- XML layouts
- Themes
- JavaScript
- CSS

Rendering flow

The Magento application entry point is its `index.php` file. All of the HTTP requests go through it.

Let's analyze the (trimmed) version of the `index.php` file as follows:

```
//PART-1-1
require __DIR__ . '/app/bootstrap.php';

//PART-1-2
$bootstrap = \Magento\Framework\App\Bootstrap::create(BP,
    $_SERVER);

//PART-1-3
$app = $bootstrap->
    createApplication('Magento\Framework\App\Http');

//PART-1-4
$bootstrap->run($app);
```

`PART-1-1` of the preceding code simply includes `/app/bootstrap.php` into the code. What happens inside the bootstrap is the inclusion of `app/autoload.php` and `app/functions.php`. The functions file contains a single `__()` function, used for translation purposes, returning an instance of the `\Magento\Framework\Phrase` object. Without going into the details of the auto-load file, it is suffice to say it handles the auto-loading of all our class files across Magento.

`PART-1-2` is simply a static create method call to obtain the instance of the `\Magento\Framework\App\Bootstrap` object, storing it into the `$bootstrap` variable.

`PART-1-3` is calling the `createApplication` method on the `$bootstrap` object. What is happening within `createApplication` is nothing more than using object manager to create and return the object instance of the class we are passing to it. Since we are passing the `\Magento\Framework\App\Http` class name to the `createApplication` method, our `$app` variable becomes the instance of that class. What this means, effectively, is that our web store app is an instance of `Magento\Framework\App\Http`.

`PART-1-4` is calling the run method on the `$bootstrap` object, passing it the instance of the `Magento\Framework\App\Http` class. Although it looks like a simple line of code, this is where things get complicated, as we will soon see.

Let's analyze the (trimmed) version of the `\Magento\Framework\App\Bootstrap ->` run method as follows:

```
public function run(\Magento\Framework\AppInterface $application)
{
    //PART-2-1
    $this->initErrorHandler();
    $this->initObjectManager();
    $this->assertMaintenance();
    $this->assertInstalled();

    //PART-2-2
    $response = $application->launch();

    //PART-2-3
    $response->sendResponse();
}
```

In the preceding code, PART-2-1 handles the sort of housekeeping bits. It initializes the custom error handler, initializes the object manager, checks if our application is in maintenance mode, and checks that it is installed.

PART-2-2 looks like a simple line of code. Here, we are calling the `launch` method on `$application`, which is the `Magento\Framework\App\Http` instance. Without going into the inner workings of the `launch` method for the moment, let's just say it returns the instance of the `Magento\Framework\App\Response\Http\Interceptor` class defined under `var/generation/Magento/Framework/App/Response/Http/Interceptor.php`. Note that this is an automatically generated wrapper class, extending the `\Magento\Framework\App\Response\Http` class. Effectively, ignoring `Interceptor`, we can say that `$response` is an instance the `\Magento\Framework\App\Response\Http` class.

Finally, PART-2-3 calls the `sendResponse` method on `$response`. Though `$response` is an instance of the `\Magento\Framework\App\Response\Http` class, the actual `sendResponse` method is found further down the parent tree on the `\Magento\Framework\HTTP\PhpEnvironment\Response` class. The `sendResponse` method calls another parent class method called `send`. The `send` method can be found under the `Zend\Http\PhpEnvironment\Response` class. It triggers the `sendHeaders` and `sendContent` methods. This is where the actual output gets sent to the browser, as the `sendHeaders` method is using PHP's `header` function and `echo` construct to push the output.

To reiterate on the preceding, the flow of execution as we understand it comes down to the following:

- `index.php`
- `\Magento\Framework\App\Bootstrap -> run`
- `\Magento\Framework\App\Http -> launch`
- `\Magento\Framework\App\Response\Http -> sendResponse`

Though we have just made it to the end of the bootstrap's `run` method, it would be unfair to say we covered the rendering flow, as we barely touched it.

We need to take a step back and take a detailed look at PART-2-2, the inner workings of the `launch` method. Let's take a look at the (trimmed) version of the `\Magento\Framework\App\Http -> launch` method as follows:

```
public function launch()
{
    //PART-3-1
    $frontController = $this->_objectManager->get
        ('Magento\Framework\App\FrontControllerInterface');

    //PART-3-2
    $result = $frontController->dispatch($this->_request);

    if ($result instanceof \Magento\Framework\Controller
      \ResultInterface) {
        //PART-3-3
        $result->renderResult($this->_response);
    } elseif ($result instanceof \Magento\Framework\App
      \Response\HttpInterface) {
        $this->_response = $result;
    } else {
        throw new \InvalidArgumentException('Invalid return
            type');
    }

    //PART-3-4
    return $this->_response;
}
```

PART-3-1 creates the instance of the object whose class conforms to \Magento\ Framework\App\FrontControllerInterface. If we look under app/etc/di.xml, we can see there is a preference for FrontControllerInterface in favor of the \ Magento\Framework\App\FrontController class. However, if we were to debug the code and check for the actual instance class, it would show Magento\Framework\ App\FrontController\Interceptor. This is Magento adding an interceptor wrapper that then extends \Magento\Framework\App\FrontController, which we expected from the di.xml preference entry.

Now that we know the real class behind the $frontController instance, we know where to look for the dispatch method. The dispatch method is another important step in understanding the rendering flow process. We will look into its inner workings in a bit more detail later on. For now, let's focus back on the $result variable of PART-3-2. If we were to debug the variable, the direct class behind it would show as Magento\Framework\View\Result\Page\Interceptor, defined under the dynamically created var/generation/Magento/Framework/View/ Result/Page/Interceptor.php file. Interceptor is the wrapper for the \Magento\ Framework\View\Result\Page class. Thus, it is safe to say that our $result variable is an instance of the Page class.

The Page class extends \Magento\Framework\View\Result\Layout, which further extends \Magento\Framework\Controller\AbstractResult and implements \ Magento\Framework\Controller\ResultInterface. Quite a chain we have here, but it is important to understand it.

Notice PART-3-3. Since our $result is an instance of \Magento\Framework\ Controller\ResultInterface, we fall into the first if condition that calls the renderResult method. The renderResult method itself is declared within the \ Magento\Framework\View\Result\Layout class. Without going into the details of renderResult, suffice to say that it adds HTTP headers, and content to the $this->_ response object passed to it. That same response object is what the launch method returns, as we described before in PART-2-2.

Though PART-3-3 does not depict any return value, the expression $result->renderResult($this->_response) does not do any output on its own. It modifies $this->_response that we finally return from the launch method as shown in PART-3-4.

To reiterate on the preceding, the flow of execution as we understand it comes down to the following:

- index.php
- \Magento\Framework\App\Bootstrap -> run
- \Magento\Framework\App\Http -> launch

- `\Magento\Framework\App\FrontController -> dispatch`

- `\Magento\Framework\View\Result\Page -> renderResult`

- `\Magento\Framework\App\Response\Http -> sendResponse`

As we mentioned while explaining PART-3-2, the `dispatch` method is another important step in the rendering flow process. Let's take a look at the (trimmed) version of the `\Magento\Framework\App\FrontController -> dispatch` method as follows:

```
public function dispatch(\Magento\Framework\App\RequestInterface
    $request)
{
    //PART-4-1
    while (!$request->isDispatched() && $routingCycleCounter++ <
        100) {
        //PART-4-2
        foreach ($this->_routerList as $router) {
            try {
                //PART-4-3
                $actionInstance = $router->match($request);
                if ($actionInstance) {
                    $request->setDispatched(true);
                    //PART-4-4
                    $result = $actionInstance->dispatch($request);
                    break;
                }
            } catch (\Magento\Framework\Exception
                \NotFoundException $e) {}
        }
    }
    //PART-4-4
    return $result;
}
```

PART-4-1 and PART-4-2 in the preceding code shows (almost) the entire `dispatch` method body contained within a loop. The loop does 100 iterations, further looping through all available router types, thus giving each router 100 times to find a route `match`.

The router list loop includes routers of the following class types:

- `Magento\Framework\App\Router\Base`

- `Magento\UrlRewrite\Controller\Router`

- `Magento\Cms\Controller\Router`

- `Magento\Framework\App\Router\DefaultRouter`

All of the listed routers implement \Magento\Framework\App\RouterInterface, making them all have the implementation of the match method.

A module can further define new routers if they choose so. As an example, imagine if we are developing a Blog module. We would want our module catching all requests on a URL that starts with a /blog/ part. This can be done by specifying the custom router, which would then show up on the preceding list.

PART-4-3 shows the $actionInstance variable storing the result of the router match method call. As per RouterInterface requirements, the match method is required to return an instance whose class implements \Magento\Framework\App\ActionInterface. Let's imagine we are now hitting the URL /foggyline_office/test/crud/ from the module we wrote in *Chapter 4, Models and Collections.* In this case, our $router class would be \Magento\Framework\App\Router\Base and our $actionInstance would be of the class \Foggyline\Office\Controller\Test\Crud\Interceptor. Magento automatically adds Interceptor, through the dynamically generated var/generation/Foggyline/Office/Controller/Test/Crud/Interceptor.php file. This Interceptor class further extends our module \Foggyline\Office\Controller\Test\Crud class file. The Crud class extends \Foggyline\Office\Controller\Test, which further extends \Magento\Framework\App\Action\Action, which implements \Magento\Framework\App\ActionInterface. After a lengthy parent-child tree, we finally got to ActionInterface, which is what our match method is required to return.

PART-4-4 shows the dispatch method being called on $actionInstance. This method is implemented within \Magento\Framework\App\Action\Action, and is expected to return an object that implements \Magento\Framework\App\ResponseInterface. Internal to dispatch, the execute method is called, thus running the code within our Crud controller action execute method.

Assuming our Crud controller action execute method does not return nothing, the $result object becomes an instance of Magento\Framework\App\Response\Http\Interceptor, which is wrapped around \Magento\Framework\App\Response\Http.

Let's imagine our Crud class has been defined as follows:

```
/**
 * @var \Magento\Framework\View\Result\PageFactory
 */
protected $resultPageFactory;

public function __construct(
    \Magento\Framework\App\Action\Context $context,
```

```
        \Magento\Framework\View\Result\PageFactory $resultPageFactory
    )
    {
        $this->resultPageFactory = $resultPageFactory;
        return parent::__construct($context);
    }

    public function execute()
    {
        $resultPage = $this->resultPageFactory->create();
        //...
        return $resultPage;
    }
```

Debugging the $result variable now shows it's an instance of \Magento\
Framework\View\Result\Page\Interceptor. This Interceptor gets dynamically
generated by Magento under var/generation/Magento/Framework/View/Result/
Page/Interceptor.php and is merely a wrapper for \Magento\Framework\
View\Result\Page. This Page class further extends the \Magento\Framework\
View\Result\Layout class, and implements \Magento\Framework\App\
ResponseInterface.

Finally, PART-4-4 shows the $result object of type \Magento\Framework\View\
Result\Page being returned from the FrontController dispatch method.

To reiterate on the preceding, the flow of execution as we understand it comes down
to the following:

- index.php
- \Magento\Framework\App\Bootstrap -> run
- \Magento\Framework\App\Http -> launch
- \Magento\Framework\App\FrontController -> dispatch
- \Magento\Framework\App\Router\Base -> match
- \Magento\Framework\App\Action\Action -> dispatch
- \Magento\Framework\View\Result\Page -> renderResult
- \Magento\Framework\App\Response\Http -> sendResponse

In a nutshell, what we as frontend developers should know is that returning the
Page type object from our controller action will automatically call the renderResult
method on that object. Page and Layout is where all the theme translations, layout,
and template loading are triggering.

View elements

Magento's primary view elements are its UI Components, containers, and blocks. The following is a brief overview of each of them.

Ui components

Under the `vendor/magento/framework/View/Element/` folder, we can find `UiComponentInterface` and `UiComponentFactory`. The full set of `Ui` components is located under the `vendor/magento/framework/View/Element/` directory. Magento implements `UiComponent` through a separate module called `Magento_Ui`. Thus, the components themselves are located under the `vendor/magento/module-ui/Component/` directory.

Components implement `UiComponentInterface`, which is defined under the `vendor/magento/framework/View/Element/UiComponentInterface.php` file as follows:

```
namespace Magento\Framework\View\Element;

use Magento\Framework\View\Element\UiComponent\ContextInterface;

interface UiComponentInterface extends BlockInterface
{
    public function getName();
    public function getComponentName();
    public function getConfiguration();
    public function render();
    public function addComponent($name, UiComponentInterface
        $component);
    public function getComponent($name);
    public function getChildComponents();
    public function getTemplate();
    public function getContext();
    public function renderChildComponent($name);
    public function setData($key, $value = null);
    public function getData($key = '', $index = null);
    public function prepare();
    public function prepareDataSource(array & $dataSource);
    public function getDataSourceData();
}
```

Notice how `BlockInterface` extends `BlockInterface`, whereas `BlockInterface` defines only one method requirement as follows:

```
namespace Magento\Framework\View\Element;

interface BlockInterface
{
    public function toHtml();
}
```

Since `Block` is an element of the interface, `UiComponent` can be looked at as an advanced block. Let's take a quick look at the `_renderUiComponent` method of the `\Magento\Framework\View\Layout` class, (partially) defined as follows:

```
protected function _renderUiComponent($name)
{
    $uiComponent = $this->getUiComponent($name);
    return $uiComponent ? $uiComponent->toHtml() : '';
}
```

This shows that `UiComponent` is rendered in the same way as block, by calling the `toHtml` method on the component. The `vendor/magento/module-ui/view/base/ui_component/etc/definition.xml` file contains an extensive list of several `UiComponents` as follows:

- `dataSource`: `Magento\Ui\Component\DataSource`
- `listing`: `Magento\Ui\Component\Listing`
- `paging`: `Magento\Ui\Component\Paging`
- `filters`: `Magento\Ui\Component\Filters`
- `container`: `Magento\Ui\Component\Container`
- `form`: `Magento\Ui\Component\Form`
- `price`: `Magento\Ui\Component\Form\Element\DataType\Price`
- `image`: `Magento\Ui\Component\Form\Element\DataType\Media`
- `nav`: `Magento\Ui\Component\Layout\Tabs\Nav`

... and many more

These components are mostly used to construct a listing and filters in the admin area. If we do a string search for `uiComponent` across the entire Magento, we would mostly find entries like the one in `vendor/magento/module-cms/view/adminhtml/layout/cms_block_index.xml` with content as follows:

```
<page xmlns:xsi="http://www.w3.org/2001/XMLSchema-instance"
   xsi:noNamespaceSchemaLocation="urn:magento:framework:View/Layout
   /etc/page_configuration.xsd">
      <body>
          <referenceContainer name="content">
              <uiComponent name="cms_block_listing"/>
          </referenceContainer>
      </body>
</page>
```

The value `cms_block_listing` of `uiComponent`'s `name` attribute refers to the name of the `vendor/magento/module-cms /view/adminhtml/ui_component/cms_block_listing.xml` file. Within the `cms_block_listing.xml` file, we have a listing component defined across more than a few hundreds lines of XML. Listing component then `dataSource`, `container`, `bookmark`, `filterSearch`, `filters`, and so on. We will not go into the details of these declarations, as our focus here is on more general frontend bits.

Containers

Containers have no block classes related to them. Container renders all of its children automatically. They allow the configuration of some attributes. Simply attach any element to a container and it will render it automatically. With a container, we can define wrapping tags, CSS classes, and more.

We cannot create instances of containers because they are an abstract concept, whereas we can create instances of blocks.

Containers are rendered via the `_renderContainer` method of the `Magento\Framework\View\Layout` class, defined as follows:

```
protected function _renderContainer($name)
{
    $html = '';
    $children = $this->getChildNames($name);
    foreach ($children as $child) {
        $html .= $this->renderElement($child);
    }
```

```
if ($html == '' || !$this->structure->getAttribute($name,
    Element::CONTAINER_OPT_HTML_TAG)) {
        return $html;
}


$htmlId = $this->structure->getAttribute($name,
    Element::CONTAINER_OPT_HTML_ID);
if ($htmlId) {
        $htmlId = ' id="' . $htmlId . '"';
}


$htmlClass = $this->structure->getAttribute($name,
    Element::CONTAINER_OPT_HTML_CLASS);
if ($htmlClass) {
        $htmlClass = ' class="' . $htmlClass . '"';
}


$htmlTag = $this->structure->getAttribute($name,
    Element::CONTAINER_OPT_HTML_TAG);

$html = sprintf('<%1$s%2$s%3$s>%4$s</%1$s>', $htmlTag,
    $htmlId, $htmlClass, $html);


return $html;
    }
}
```

Containers support the following extra attributes: htmlTag, htmlClass, htmlId, and label. To make a little demonstration of a container in action, let us make sure we have a module from *Chapter 4, Models and Collections* in place, and then create the view/frontend/layout/foggyline_office_test_crud.xml file within the module root folder app/code/Foggyline/Office/ with content as follows:

```
<page xmlns:xsi="http://www.w3.org/2001/XMLSchema-instance"
  layout="1column"
        xsi:noNamespaceSchemaLocation="urn:magento:framework:View
            /Layout/etc/page_configuration.xsd">
    <head>
        <title>Office CRUD #layout</title>
    </head>
    <body>
        <container name="foobar" htmlTag="div" htmlClass="foo-
            bar">
            <block class="Magento\Framework\View\Element\Text"
                name="foo">
                <action method="setText">
```

```
                    <argument name="text" xsi:type="string">
                        <![CDATA[<p>The Foo</p>]]></argument>
                </action>
            </block>
            <block class="Magento\Framework\View\Element\Text"
                name="bar">
                <action method="setText">
                    <argument name="text" xsi:type="string">
                        <![CDATA[<p>The Bar</p>]]></argument>
                </action>
            </block>
        </container>
    </body>
</page>
```

The preceding XML defines a single container named `foobar`, and within the container there are two block elements named `foo` and `bar`. It should kick in when we open `http://{our-shop-url}/index.php/foggyline_office/test/crud/` in the browser.

Notice how the container itself is not nested within any other element, rather directly into the body. We could have easily nested into some other container as shown:

```
<body>
    <referenceContainer name="content">
        <container name="foobar" htmlTag="div" htmlClass="foo-
            bar">
```

Either way, we should see the strings **The Foo** and **The Bar** shown in the browser, with a full-page layout loaded, as shown in the following screenshot:

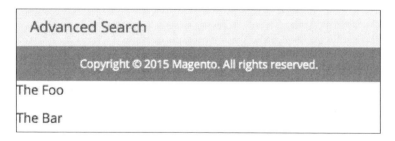

Blocks

Although containers determine the layout of the page, they do not contain actual content directly. Pieces that contain the content and are nested within containers are called **blocks**. Each block can contain any number of child content blocks or child containers. Thus, mostly every web page in Magento is formed as a mix of blocks and containers. Layout defines a sequence of blocks on the page, not their location. The look and feel of the blocks is determined by CSS and how the page is rendered. When we speak of blocks, we almost always implicitly refer to templates as well. Templates are the thing that actually draw elements within a page; blocks are the thing that contain the data. In other words, templates are PHTML or HTML files pulling data through variables or methods sent on a linked PHP block class.

Magento defines the `Magento\Framework\View\Result\Page` type under `app/etc/di.xml` as follows:

```
<type name="Magento\Framework\View\Result\Page">
    <arguments>
        <argument name="layoutReaderPool"
          xsi:type="object">pageConfigRenderPool</argument>
        <argument name="generatorPool"
          xsi:type="object">pageLayoutGeneratorPool</argument>
        <argument name="template"
          xsi:type="string">Magento_Theme::root.phtml</argument>
    </arguments>
</type>
```

Notice the template argument is set to `Magento_Theme::root.phtml`. When `Page` gets initialized, it picks up the `vendor/magento/module-theme/view/base/templates/root.phtml` file. `root.phtml` is defined as follows:

```
<!doctype html>
<html <?php echo $htmlAttributes ?>>
    <head <?php echo $headAttributes ?>>
        <?php echo $requireJs ?>
        <?php echo $headContent ?>
        <?php echo $headAdditional ?>
    </head>
    <body data-container="body" data-mage-init='{"loaderAjax": {},
      "loader": { "icon": "<?php echo $loaderIcon; ?>"}}' <?php
      echo $bodyAttributes ?>>
        <?php echo $layoutContent ?>
    </body>
</html>
```

Variables within `root.phtml` are assigned during the `Magento\Framework\View\Result\Page` render method call as (partially) as shown:

```
protected function render(ResponseInterface $response)
{
    $this->pageConfig->publicBuild();
    if ($this->getPageLayout()) {
        $config = $this->getConfig();
        $this->addDefaultBodyClasses();
        $addBlock = $this->getLayout()->getBlock
            ('head.additional');
        $requireJs = $this->getLayout()->getBlock('require.js');
        $this->assign([
            'requireJs' => $requireJs ? $requireJs->toHtml() :
                null,
            'headContent' => $this->pageConfigRenderer->
                renderHeadContent(),
            'headAdditional' => $addBlock ? $addBlock->toHtml() :
                null,
            'htmlAttributes' => $this->pageConfigRenderer->
                renderElementAttributes($config::ELEMENT_TYPE_HTML),
            'headAttributes' => $this->pageConfigRenderer->
                renderElementAttributes($config::ELEMENT_TYPE_HEAD),
            'bodyAttributes' => $this->pageConfigRenderer->
                renderElementAttributes($config::ELEMENT_TYPE_BODY),
            'loaderIcon' => $this->getViewFileUrl('images/loader-
                2.gif'),
        ]);

        $output = $this->getLayout()->getOutput();
        $this->assign('layoutContent', $output);
        $output = $this->renderPage();
        $this->translateInline->processResponseBody($output);
        $response->appendBody($output);
    } else {
        parent::render($response);
    }
    return $this;
}
```

The expression `$this->assign` is what assigns variables like `layoutContent` to the `root.phtml` template. `layoutContent` is generated based on base layouts, together with all layout updates for the current page.

Whereas base layouts include the following XMLs within `vendor/magento/module-theme/view/`:

- `base/page_layout/empty.xml`
- `frontend/page_layout/1column.xml`
- `frontend/page_layout/2columns-left.xml`
- `frontend/page_layout/2columns-right.xml`
- `frontend/page_layout/3columns.xml`

The expression `$this->getLayout()->getOutput()` is what gets all blocks marked for output. It basically finds elements in a layout, renders them, and returns the string with its output. Along the way, the event `core_layout_render_element` gets fired, giving us one possible way of affecting the output result. At this point, most of the elements on the page are rendered. This is important because blocks play a big role here. The rendering system will take `empty.xml` into account, as it too consists of a list of containers, and every container has some blocks attached to it by other layout updates.

> In a nutshell, each container has blocks assigned to it. Each block usually (but not always) renders a template. The template itself may or may not call other blocks, and so on. Blocks are rendered when they are called from the template.

Block architecture and life cycle

Blocks are another one of the primary view elements in Magento. At the root of the parent tree structure, blocks extend from the `Magento\Framework\View\Element\AbstractBlock` class and implement `Magento\Framework\View\Element\BlockInterface`.

`BlockInterface` sets only one requirement, the implementation of the `toHtml` method. This method should return blocks HTML output.

Looking inside `AbstractBlock`, we can see it has a number of methods declared. Among the most important ones are the following methods:

- `_prepareLayout`: Prepares a global layout. We can redefine this method in child classes for changing the layout.
- `addChild`: Creates a new block, sets it as a child of the current block, and returns the newly created block.

- `_toHtml`: Returns an empty string. We need to override this method in descendants to produce HTML.

- `_beforeToHtml`: Returns `$this`. Executes before rendering HTML, but after trying to load a cache.

- `_afterToHtml`: Processing block HTML after rendering. Returns a HTML string.

- `toHtml`: Produces and returns a block's HTML output. This method should not be overridden. We can override the `_toHtml` method in descendants if needed.

The `AbstractBlock` execution flow can be described as follows:

- `_prepareLayout`
- `toHtml`
- `_beforeToHtml`
- `_toHtml`
- `_afterToHtml`

It starts with `_prepareLayout` and flows through a set of methods until it reaches `_afterToHtml`. This is, in essence, what we need to know about block execution flow.

The most important block types are:

- `Magento\Framework\View\Element\Text`
- `Magento\Framework\View\Element\Text\ListText`
- `Magento\Framework\View\Element\Messages`
- `Magento\Framework\View\Element\Template`

All of these blocks are basically an implementation of an abstract block. Since the `_toHtml` method in `AbstractBlock` returns only an empty string, all of these descendants are implementing their own version of the `_toHtml` method.

To demonstrate the usage of these blocks, we can use our previously created `app/code/Foggyline/Office/view/frontend/layout/foggyline_office_test_crud.xml` file.

The `Text` block has a `setText` method we can use to set its content. The way we instantiate the `Text` block and set its text value through the layout file is shown as follows:

```
<block class="Magento\Framework\View\Element\Text"
  name="example_1">
    <action method="setText">
        <argument name="text"
          xsi:type="string"><![CDATA[<p>Text_1</p>]]></argument>
    </action>
</block>
```

The `ListText` block extends from `Text`. However, it does not really support the use of `setText` to set its content. This is obvious just by looking at its code, where the `$this->setText('')` expression is immediately called within its `_toHtml` method implementation. Instead, what happens is that the `_toHtml` method loops through any child blocks it might have and calls the layout's `renderElement` method on it. Basically, we might compare the `ListText` block to `container`, as it has nearly the same purpose. However, unlike container, block is a class so we can manipulate it from PHP. The following is an example of using `ListText`, containing a few child `Text` blocks:

```
<block class="Magento\Framework\View\Element\Text\ListText"
  name="example_2">
    <block class="Magento\Framework\View\Element\Text"
      name="example_2a">
        <action method="setText">
            <argument name="text" xsi:type="string">
              <![CDATA[<p>Text_2A</p>]]></argument>
        </action>
    </block>
    <block class="Magento\Framework\View\Element\Text"
      name="example_2b">
        <action method="setText">
            <argument name="text" xsi:type="string">
              <![CDATA[<p>Text_2B</p>]]></argument>
        </action>
    </block>
</block>
```

The `Messages` block supports four methods that we can use to add content to output: `addSuccess`, `addNotice`, `addWarning`, and `addError`. The following is an example instantiating the `Messages` block through the layout update file:

```
<block class="Magento\Framework\View\Element\Messages"
  name="example_3">
    <action method="addSuccess">
        <argument name="text" xsi:type="string">
          <![CDATA[<p>Text_3A: Success</p>]]></argument>
    </action>
    <action method="addNotice">
        <argument name="text" xsi:type="string">
          <![CDATA[<p>Text_3B: Notice</p>]]></argument>
    </action>
    <action method="addWarning">
        <argument name="text" xsi:type="string">
          <![CDATA[<p>Text_3C: Warning</p>]]></argument>
    </action>
    <action method="addError">
        <argument name="text" xsi:type="string">
          <![CDATA[<p>Text_3D: Error</p>]]></argument>
    </action>
</block>
```

The preceding example should be taken with caution, since calling these setter methods in layout is not the proper way to do it. The default `Magento_Theme` module already defines the `Messages` block that uses `vendor/magento/module-theme/view/frontend/templates/messages.phtml` for message rendering. Thus, for most of the part there is no need to define our own messages block.

Finally, let's look at the example of the `Template` block as follows:

```
<block class="Magento\Framework\View\Element\Template"
    name="example_4" template="Foggyline_Office::office
      /no4/template.phtml"/>
```

The preceding XML will instantiate the `Template` type of block and render the content of the `view/frontend/templates/office/no4/template.phtml` file within the `app/code/Foggyline/Office/` directory.

On the PHP level, instantiating a new block can be accomplished using the layout object, or directly through the object manager. The layout approach is the preferred way. With regard to the previous examples in XML, let's see their alternatives in PHP (assuming `$resultPage` is an instance of `\Magento\Framework\View\Result\PageFactory`).

The following is an example of instantiating the `Text` type of block and adding it as a child of the content container:

```
$block = $resultPage->getLayout()->createBlock(
    'Magento\Framework\View\Element\Text',
    'example_1'
)->setText(
    '<p>Text_1</p>'
);

$resultPage->getLayout()->setChild(
    'content',
    $block->getNameInLayout(),
    'example_1_alias'
);
```

The `ListText` version is done in PHP as follows:

```
$blockLT = $resultPage->getLayout()->createBlock(
    'Magento\Framework\View\Element\Text\ListText',
    'example_2'
);

$resultPage->getLayout()->setChild(
    'content',
    $blockLT->getNameInLayout(),
    'example_2_alias'
);

$block2A = $resultPage->getLayout()->createBlock(
    'Magento\Framework\View\Element\Text',
    'example_2a'
)->setText(
    '<p>Text_2A</p>'
);

$resultPage->getLayout()->setChild(
    'example_2',
    $block2A->getNameInLayout(),
    'example_2a_alias'
);

$block2B = $resultPage->getLayout()->createBlock(
    'Magento\Framework\View\Element\Text',
    'example_2b'
```

```
)->setText(
    '<p>Text_2B</p>'
);

$resultPage->getLayout()->setChild(
    'example_2',
    $block2B->getNameInLayout(),
    'example_2b_alias'
);
```

Notice how we first made an instance of the `ListText` block and assigned it as a child of an element named content. Then we created two individual `Text` blocks and assigned them as a child of an element named example_2, which is our `ListText`.

Next, let's define the `Messages` block as follows:

```
$messagesBlock = $resultPage->getLayout()->createBlock(
    'Magento\Framework\View\Element\Messages',
    'example_3'
);

$messagesBlock->addSuccess('Text_3A: Success');
$messagesBlock->addNotice('Text_3B: Notice');
$messagesBlock->addWarning('Text_3C: Warning');
$messagesBlock->addError('Text_3D: Error');

$resultPage->getLayout()->setChild(
    'content',
    $messagesBlock->getNameInLayout(),
    'example_3_alias'
);
```

Finally, let's look at the `Template` block type, which we initiate as follows:

```
$templateBlock = $resultPage->getLayout()->createBlock(
    'Magento\Framework\View\Element\Template',
    'example_3'
)->setTemplate(
    'Foggyline_Office::office/no4/template.phtml'
);

$resultPage->getLayout()->setChild(
    'content',
    $templateBlock->getNameInLayout(),
    'example_4_alias'
);
```

Whenever possible, we should set our blocks using XML layouts.

Now that we know how to utilize the most common types of Magento blocks, let's see how we can create our own block type.

Defining our own `block` class is as simple as creating a custom class file that extends `Template`. This `block` class should be placed under our module `Block` directory. Using our `Foggyline_Office` module, let's create a file, `Block/Hello.php`, with content as follows:

```
namespace Foggyline\Office\Block;

class Hello extends \Magento\Framework\View\Element\Template
{
    public function helloPublic()
    {
        return 'Hello #1';
    }

    protected function helloProtected()
    {
        return 'Hello #2';
    }

    private function helloPrivate()
    {
        return 'Hello #3';
    }
}
```

The preceding code simply creates a new custom block class. We can then call this `block` class through our layout file as follows:

```
<block class="Foggyline\Office\Block\Hello"
    name="office.hello" template="office/hello.phtml"/>
```

Finally, within our module `app/code/Foggyline/Office/` directory, we create a template file, `view/frontend/templates/office/hello.phtml`, with content as follows:

```
<?php /* @var $block Foggyline\Office\Block\Hello */ ?>
<h1>Hello</h1>
<p><?php echo $block->helloPublic() ?></p>
<p><?php //echo $block->helloProtected() ?></p>
<p><?php //echo $block->helloPrivate() ?></p>
```

To further understand what is happening here within the template file, let's take a deeper look at templates themselves.

Templates

Templates are snippets of HTML mixed with PHP. The PHP part includes elements such as variables, expressions, and `class` method calls. Magento uses the PHTML file extension for template files. Templates are located under an individual module's `view/{_area_}/templates/` directory.

In our previous example, we referred to our module template file with an expression like `Foggyline_Office::office/hello.phtml`. Since templates can belong to different modules, we should prepend the template with the module name as a best practice. This will help us locate template files and avoid file conflicts.

A simple naming formula goes like this: we type the name of the module, double single colon, and then the name. Thus making a template path like `office/hello.phtml` equaling to `Foggyline_Office::office/hello.phtml`.

Within the PHTML template file we often have various PHP expressions like `$block->helloPublic()`. Notice the block class `Foggyline\Office\Block\Hello` in the preceding XML. An instance of this block class becomes available to us in `hello.phtml` through the `$block` variable. Thus, an expression like `$block->helloPublic()` is effectively calling the `helloPublic` method from an instance of the `Hello` class. The `Hello` class is not one of the Magento core classes, but it does extend `\Magento\Framework\View\Element\Template`.

Our `hello.phtml` template also has two more expressions: `$block->helloProtected()` and `$block->helloPrivate()`. However, these are not executed as template files can only see public methods from their `$block` instances.

The `$this` variable is also available within the PHTML template as an instance of the `Magento\Framework\View\TemplateEngine\Php` class.

In the preceding template code example, we could have easily replaced `$block->helloPublic()` with the `$this->helloPublic()` expression. The reason why this would work lies in the template engine `Php` class, (partially) defined as follows:

```php
public function __call($method, $args)
{
    return call_user_func_array([$this->_currentBlock, $method],
        $args);
}

public function __isset($name)
{
```

```
        return isset($this->_currentBlock->{$name});
    }

    public function __get($name)
    {
        return $this->_currentBlock->{$name};
    }
```

Given that templates are included in the context of the engine rather than in the context of the block, `__call` redirects methods calls to the current block. Similarly, `__isset` redirects `isset` calls to the current block and `__get` allows read access to properties of the current block.

Though we can use both `$block` and `$this` for the same purpose within the template file, we should really opt for using `$block`.

Another important aspect of templates is their fallback mechanism. Fallback is the process of defining a full template path given only its relative path. For example, `office/hello.phtml` falls back to the `app/code/Foggyline/Office/view/frontend/templates/office/hello.phtml` file.

Path resolution starts from the `_toHtml` method defined on the `Magento\Framework\View\Element\Template` class. The `_toHtml` method then calls `getTemplateFile` within the same class, which in turn calls `getTemplateFileName` on `resolver`, which is an instance of `\Magento\Framework\View\Element\Template\File\Resolver`. Looking further, resolver's `getTemplateFileName` further calls `getTemplateFileName` on `_viewFileSystem`, which is an instance of `\Magento\Framework\View\FileSystem`. The method `getFile` is further called on an instance of `\Magento\Framework\View\Design\FileResolution\Fallback\TemplateFile`. `getFile` further triggers the resolve method on the `Magento\Framework\View\Design\FileResolution\Fallback\Resolver\Simple` instance, which further calls the `getRule` method on the `Magento\Framework\View\Design\Fallback\RulePool` instance. The `RulePoll` class is the final class in the chain here. `getRule` finally calls the `createTemplateFileRule` method, which creates the rule that detects where the file is located.

While running the `getRule` method, Magento checks against the following types of fallback rules:

- `file`
- `locale`
- `template`
- `static`
- `email`

It is worth spending some time to study the inner workings of the `RulePool` class, as it showcases detailed fallbacks for the listed rules.

Layouts

Up to this point, we briefly touched on layout XMLs. Layout XML is a tool to build the pages of the Magento application in a modular and flexible manner. It enables us to describe the page layout and content placement. Looking at XML root nodes, we differentiate two types of layouts:

- `layout`: XML wrapped in `<layout>`
- `page`: XML wrapped in `<page>`

`Page` layouts represent a full page in HTML, whereas `layout` layouts represent a part of a page. The `layout` type is a subset of the `page` layout type. Both types of layout XML files are validated by the XSD schema found under the `vendor/magento/framework/View/Layout/etc/` directory:

- `layout` – `layout_generic.xsd`
- `page` – `page_configuration.xsd`

Based on the application components that provide `<layout>` and `<page>` elements , we can further section them as base and theme layouts.

The base layouts are provided by the modules, usually at the following locations:

- `<module_dir>/view/frontend/layout`: page configuration and generic layout files
- `<module_dir>/view/frontend/page_layout`: page layout files

The theme layouts are provided by the themes, usually at the following locations:

- `<theme_dir>/<Namespace>_<Module>/layout`: page configuration and generic layout files
- `<theme_dir>/<Namespace>_<Module>/page_layout`: page layout files

Magento will load and merge all module and theme XML files on the appropriate page. Once files are merged and XML instructions are processed, the result is rendered and sent to the browser for display. Having two different layout XML files, where both reference the same block, means that the second one with the same name in the sequence will replace the first one.

When the XML files are loaded, Magento applies an inheritance theme at the same time. We can apply a theme and it will look for the parent until a theme without a parent is reached.

In addition to the merging of files from each module, layout files from within module directories can also be extended or overridden by themes. Overriding layout XML is not a good practice, but it might be necessary sometimes.

To *override* the base layout files provided by the module within the `<module_dir>/view/frontend/layout/`directory.

We need to create an XML file with the same name in the `app/design/frontend/<vendor>/<theme>/<Namespace_Module>/layout/override/base/`**directory**.

To *override* the theme layout files provided by the parent theme within the `<parent_theme_dir>/<Namespace>_<Module>/layout/`**directory**.

We need to create an XML file with the same name in the `app/design/frontend/<vendor>/<theme >/<Namespace_Module>/layout/override/theme/<Parent_Vendor>/<parent_theme>/`**directory**.

Layouts can be both overridden and extended.

The recommended way to customize layout is to extend it through a custom theme. We can do so by simply adding a custom XML layout file with the same name in the `app/design/frontend/{vendorName}/{theme}/{vendorName}_{moduleName}/layout/` directory.

Layouts, as we saw in previous examples, support a large number of directives: page page, head, block, and so on. The practical use of these directives and how they mix together is a challenge on its own. Giving full details on each and every directive is beyond the scope of this book. However, what we can do is to show how to figure out the use of an individual directive, which we might need at a given time. For that purpose, it is highly recommended to use an IDE environment like **NetBeans PHP** or **PhpStorm** that provide autocomplete on XMLs that include XSD.

The following is an example of defining an external schema to PhpStorm, where we are simply saying that the `urn:magento:framework:View/Layout/etc/page_configuration.xsd` alias belongs to the `vendor/magento/framework/View/Layout/etc/page_configuration.xsd` file:

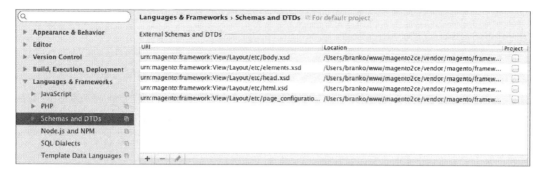

This way, PhpStorm will know how to provide autocomplete while we type around XML files.

As an example, let's take a look at how we could use the css directive to add an external CSS file to our page. With an IDE that supports autocomplete as soon as we type the css directive within the page | head element, autocomplete might throw out something like the following:

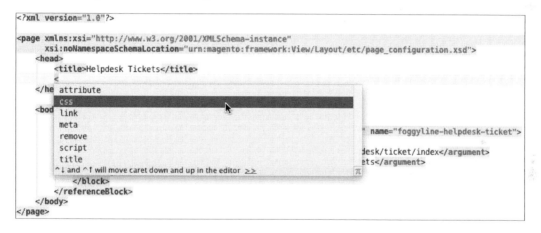

A list of available attributes is shown, such as src, sizes, ie_condtion, src_type, and so on. IDEs like PhpStorm will allow us to right-click an element or its attribute and *go to the definition*. Looking into the definition for the src attribute gets us into the vendor/magento/framework/View/Layout/etc/head.xsd file that defines the css element as follows:

```
<xs:complexType name="linkType">
    <xs:attribute name="src" type="xs:string" use="required"/>
    <xs:attribute name="defer" type="xs:string"/>
    <xs:attribute name="ie_condition" type="xs:string"/>
    <xs:attribute name="charset" type="xs:string"/>
```

```
          <xs:attribute name="hreflang" type="xs:string"/>
          <xs:attribute name="media" type="xs:string"/>
          <xs:attribute name="rel" type="xs:string"/>
          <xs:attribute name="rev" type="xs:string"/>
          <xs:attribute name="sizes" type="xs:string"/>
          <xs:attribute name="target" type="xs:string"/>
          <xs:attribute name="type" type="xs:string"/>
          <xs:attribute name="src_type" type="xs:string"/>
      </xs:complexType>
```

All of these are attributes we can set on the `css` element, and as such get their
autocomplete as shown:

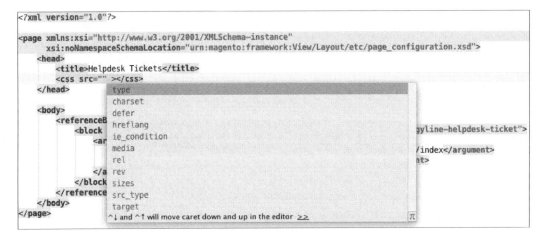

Although it is not required to use a robust IDE with Magento, it certainly helps to
have one that understands XML and XSD files to the level of providing autocomplete
and validation.

Themes

By default, Magento comes with two themes, named `Blank` and `Luma`. If we log in to
the Magento admin area, we can see a list of available themes under the **Content |
Design | Themes** menu, as shown in the following screenshot:

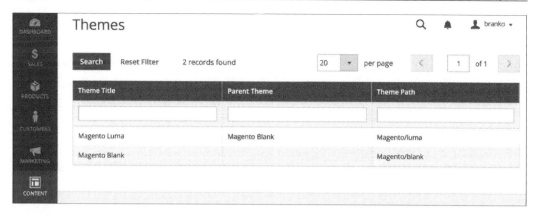

Magento themes support a parent-child relationship, something we noted previously, that is visible on the preceding image within the **Parent Theme** column.

Creating a new theme

The following steps outline the process of creating our own theme:

1. Under {Magento root directory}/app/design/frontend, create a new directory bearing our vendor name, Foggyline.

2. Within the vendor directory, create a new directory bearing the theme name, jupiter.

3. Within the jupiter directory, create the registration.php file with content as follows:

```php
<?php
\Magento\Framework\Component\ComponentRegistrar::register(
    \Magento\Framework\Component\ComponentRegistrar::THEME,
    'frontend/Foggyline/jupiter',
    __DIR__
);
```

4. Copy vendor/magento/theme-frontend-blank/theme.xml into our theme, app/design/frontend/Foggyline/jupiter/theme.xml, changing the content as follows:

```xml
<theme xmlns:xsi="http://www.w3.org/2001/XMLSchema-
    instance" xsi:noNamespaceSchemaLocation="urn:magento:
    framework:Config/etc/theme.xsd">
    <title>Foggyline Jupiter</title>
    <parent>Magento/blank</parent>
    <media>
```

```
        <preview_image>media/preview.jpg</preview_image>
    </media>
</theme>
```

5. Create the `app/design/frontend/Foggyline/jupiter/media/preview.jpg` image file to serve as the theme preview image (the one used in the admin area).

6. Optionally, create separate directories for static files such as styles, fonts, JavaScript, and images. These are stored within the `web` subdirectory of our theme `app/design/frontend/Foggyline/jupiter/` folder like follows:

   ○ `web/css/`

   ○ `web/css/source/`

   ○ `web/css/source/components/`

   ○ `web/images/`

   ○ `web/js/`

   Within the theme `web` directory, we store general theme static files. If our theme contains module-specific static files, these are stored under the corresponding `vendor` module subdirectories, like `app/design/frontend/Foggyline/jupiter/{vendorName_moduleName}/web/`.

7. Optionally, we can create the theme `logo.svg` image under our theme `web/images/` folder.

Once we are done with the preceding steps, looking back into the admin area under the **Content | Design | Themes** menu, we should now see our theme listed as shown in the following screenshot:

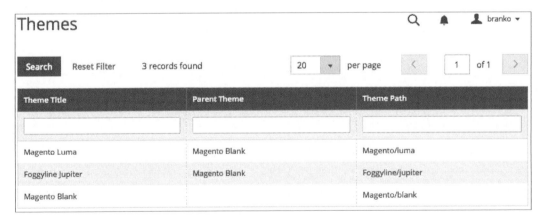

Whereas clicking on the row in the table next to our theme name would open a screen like the following:

Notice how the previous two screens do not show any options to apply the theme. They are only listing out available themes and some basic information next to each theme. Our custom theme shows an interesting relationship, where a parent and a child theme can belong to different vendors.

Applying the theme requires the following extra steps:

1. Make sure our theme appears in the theme list, under the **Content | Design | Themes** menu.
2. Go to **Stores | Settings | Configuration | General | Design**.

3. In the **Store View** drop-down field, we select the store view where we want to apply the theme, as shown in the upper-left corner of the following image:

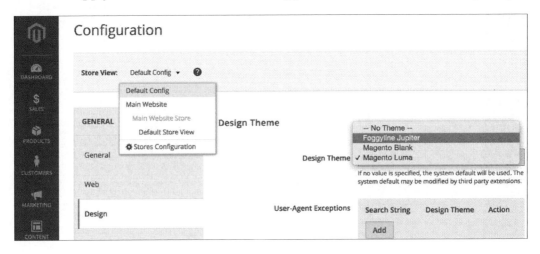

4. On the **Design Theme** tab, we select our newly created theme in the **Design Theme** drop-down, as shown on the right-hand side of the preceding image. Click **Save Config**.

5. Under **System | Tools | Cache Management**, select and refresh the invalid cache types and click on the **Flush Catalog Images Cache, Flush JavaScript/ CSS Cache**, and **Flush Static Files Cache** buttons.

6. Finally, to see our changes applied, reload the storefront pages in the browser.

There is a lot more to be said about themes that can fit in a book of its own. However, we will move on to the other important bits.

JavaScript

Magento makes use of quite a large number of JavaScript libraries, such as:

- Knockout: `http://knockoutjs.com`
- Ext JS: `https://www.sencha.com/products/extjs/`
- jQuery: `https://jquery.com/`
- jQuery UI: `https://jqueryui.com/`
- modernizr: `http://www.modernizr.com/`
- Prototype: `http://www.prototypejs.org/`
- RequireJS: `http://requirejs.org/`

- script.aculo.us: `http://script.aculo.us/`
- moment.js: `http://momentjs.com/`
- Underscore.js: `http://underscorejs.org/`
- gruntjs: `http://gruntjs.com/`
- AngularJS: `https://angularjs.org/`
- jasmine: `http://jasmine.github.io/`

… and a few others

Though a frontend developer is not required to know the ins and outs of every library, it is recommended to at least have a basic insight into most of them.

It is worth running `find {MAGENTO-DIR}/ -name \*.js > js-list.txt` on the console to get a full list of each and every JavaScript file in Magento. Spending a few minutes glossing over the list might serve as a nice future memo when working with JavaScript bits in Magento.

The RequireJS and jQuery libraries are probably the *most interesting* ones, as they often step into the spotlight during frontend development. RequireJS plays a big role in Magento, as it loads other JavaScript files. Using a modular script loader like RequireJS improves the speed of code. Speed improvement comes from removing JavaScript from the header and asynchronously or lazy loading JavaScript resources in the background.

JavaScript resources can be specified as follows:

- Library level for all libraries in the Magento code base (`lib/web`).
- Module level for all libraries in a module (`app/code/{vendorName}/{moduleName}/view/{area}/web`).
- Theme for all libraries in a theme (`app/design/{area}/{vendorName}/{theme}/{vendorName}_{moduleName}/web`).
- All libraries in a theme (`app/design/{area}/{vendorName}/{theme}/web`). Though possible, it is not recommended using this level to specify JavaScript resources.

It is recommended to specify JavaScript resources in the templates rather than in the layout updates. This way, we ensure processing of the resources through RequireJS.

To work with the RequireJS library, specify the mapping of JavaScript resources; that is, assign the aliases to resources. Use `requires-config.js` to create the mapping.

To make our configurations more precise and specific for different modules/themes, we can identify mapping in the `requires-config.js` file at several levels depending on our needs. Configurations are collected and executed in the following order:

- Library configurations
- Configurations at the module level
- Configurations at the theme module level for the ancestor themes
- Configurations at the theme module level for a current theme
- Configurations at the theme level for the ancestor themes
- Configurations at the theme level for the current theme

When we speak of JavaScript in Magento, we can hear various terms like component and widget. We can easily divide those terms by describing the type of JavaScript in Magento as per the following list:

- **JavaScript component (JS component)**: This can be any single JavaScript file decorated as an **AMD** (short for **Asynchronous Module Definition**) module
- **Ui component**: A JavaScript component located in the `Magento_Ui` module
- **jQuery UI widget**: A JavaScript component/widget provided by the jQuery UI library used in Magento
- **jQuery widget**: A custom widget created using jQuery UI Widget Factory and decorated as an AMD module

There are two ways we can initialize a JavaScript component in template files:

- Using the `data-mage-init` attribute
- Using the `<script>` tag

The `data-mage-init` attribute is parsed on a DOM ready event. Since it is initialized on a certain element, the script is called only for that particular element, and is not automatically initialized for other elements of the same type on the page. An example of `data-mage-init` usage would be something like the following:

```
<div data-mage-init='{ "<componentName>": {...} }'></div>
```

The `<script>` tag initialization is done without relation to any specific element, or in relation to a specific element but no direct access to the element. The script tag has to have an attribute, `type="text/x-magento-init"`. An example of `<script>` tag initialization would be something like the following:

```
<script type="text/x-magento-init">
    // specific element but no direct access to the element
    "<element_selector>": {
        "<jsComponent1>": ...,
        "<jsComponent2>": ...
    },
    // without relation to any specific element
    "*": {
        "<jsComponent3>": ...
    }
</script>
```

Depending on the situation and desired level of expressiveness, we can either opt for usage of `data-mage-init` or attribute or `<script>` tag.

Creating a custom JS component

Let's go through a practical example of creating a JS component within our `Foggyline_Office` module in a form of the jQuery widget as follows:

First, we add our entry to `app/code/Foggyline/Office/view/frontend/requirejs-config.js`, as shown:

```
var config = {
    map: {
        '*': {
            foggylineHello:
                'Foggyline_Office/js/foggyline-hello'
        }
    }
};
```

Then we add the actual JavaScript `app/code/Foggyline/Office/view/frontend/web/js/foggyline-hello.js` with content as follows:

```
define([
    "jquery",
    "jquery/ui"
], function($){
    "use strict";
```

```
$.widget('mage.foggylineHello', {
    options: {
    },
    _create: function () {
        alert(this.options);
        //my code here
    }
});

return $.mage.foggylineHello;
});
```

Finally, we call our JavaScript component within some PHTML template, let's say `app/code/Foggyline/Office/view/frontend/templates/office/hello.phtml`, as show:

```
<div data-mage-init='{"foggylineHello":{"myVar1": "myValue1",
"myVar2": "myValue2"}}'>Foggyline</div>
```

Once we refresh the frontend, we should see the result of `alert(this.options)` in the browser showing `myVar1` and `myVar2`.

The `data-mage-init` part basically triggers as soon as the page loads. It is not triggered via some click or similar event on top of the `div` element; it is triggered on page load.

If we don't see the desired result in the browser, we might need to fully clear the cache in the admin area.

CSS

Magento uses a PHP port of the official LESS processor to parse the `.less` files into `.css` files. LESS is a CSS preprocessor that extends the CSS language by adding various features to it, like variables, mixins, and functions. All of this makes CSS more maintainable, extendable, and easier to theme. Frontend developers are thus expected to write LESS files that Magento then converts to appropriate CSS variants.

> It is worth running `find {MAGENTO-DIR}/ -name \*.less > less-list.txt` on the console to get a full list of each and every LESS file in Magento. Spending a few minutes glossing over the list might serve as a nice future memo when working with style sheet bits in Magento.

We can customize the storefront look and feel through one of the following approaches:

- Override the default LESS files – only if our theme inherits from the default or any other theme, in which case we can override the actual LESS files
- Create our own LESS files using the built-in LESS preprocessor
- Create our own CSS files, optionally having compiled them using a third-party CSS preprocessor

Within the individual frontend theme directory, we can find style sheets at the following locations:

- {vendorName}_{moduleName}/web/css/source/
- {vendorName}_{moduleName}/web/css/source/module/
- web/css/
- web/css/source/

CSS files can be included in a page through templates and layout files. A recommended way is to include them through layout files. If we want our style sheets to be available through all pages on the frontend, we can add using the default_head_blocks.xml file. If we look at the blank theme, it uses vendor/magento/theme-frontend-blank/Magento_Theme/layout/default_head_blocks.xml defined as follows:

```
<page xmlns:xsi="http://www.w3.org/2001/XMLSchema-instance"
   xsi:noNamespaceSchemaLocation="urn:magento:framework:View/Layout
   /etc/page_configuration.xsd">
    <head>
        <css src="css/styles-m.css"/>
        <css src="css/styles-l.css" media="screen and (min-width:
           768px)"/>
        <css src="css/print.css" media="print"/>
    </head>
</page>
```

All it takes is for us to copy this file in the same location under our custom theme; assuming it's the jupiter theme from the preceding examples, that would be app/design/frontend/Foggyline/jupiter/Magento_Theme/layout/default_head_blocks.xml. Then we simply modify the file to include our CSS.

When run, Magento will try to find the included CSS files. If a CSS file is not found, it then searches for the same filenames with a .less extension. This is part of the built-in preprocessing mechanism.

Summary

In this chapter, we started off by looking into the three aspects of the rendering flow process: the view, result object, and pages. Then we took a detailed look at three primary view elements: `ui-components`, `containers`, and `blocks`. We further studied blocks in depth, looking into their architecture and life cycle. We moved on to templates, looking into their locations, rendering, and fallback. Then came XML layouts, as the glue between blocks and templates. All of this gave us a foundation for further looking into theme structure, JavaScript components, and CSS. Along the way, we did a little bit of hands-on with a custom theme and JavaScript components creation. CSS and JavaScript is merely a fragment of what the Magento frontend is all about. Technology-wise, having a solid understanding of XML and even some PHP is more of a requirement than an exception for frontend-related development.

The following chapter will introduce us to Magento's web API where we will learn how to authenticate, make API calls, and even build our own APIs.

9
The Web API

Throughout previous chapters, we learned how to use some of the backend components so that storeowners can manage and manipulate the data such as customers, products, categories, orders, and so on. Sometimes this is not enough, like when we are pulling data in or out from third-party systems. In cases like these, the Magento Web API framework makes it easy to call Magento services through REST or SOAP.

In this chapter, we will cover the following topics:

- User types
- Authentication methods
- REST versus SOAP
- Hands-on with token-based authentication
- Hands-on with OAuth-based authentication
- OAuth-based Web API calls
- Hands-on with session-based authentication
- Creating custom Web APIs
- Search Criteria Interface for list filtering

Before we can start making Web API calls, we must authenticate our identity and have the necessary permissions (authorization) to access the API resource. Authentication allows Magento to identify the caller's user type. Based on the user's (administrator, integration, customer, or guest) access rights, the API calls' resource accessibility is determined.

User types

The list of resources that we can access depends on our user type and is defined within our module `webapi.xml` configuration file.

There are three types of users known to API, listed as follows:

- **Administrator or integration**: Resources for which administrators or integrators are authorized. For example, if administrators are authorized for the `Magento_Cms::page resource,` they can make a POST `/V1/cmsPage` call.
- **Customer**: Resources for which customers are authorized. These are the resources with anonymous or self permission.
- **Guest user**: Resources for which guests are authorized. These are the resources with anonymous permission.

Two files play a crucial role toward defining an API: our module `acl.xml` and `webapi.xml` files.

`acl.xml` is where we define our module **access control list** (**ACL**). It defines an available set of permissions to access the resources. The `acl.xml` files across all Magento modules are consolidated to build an ACL tree that is used to select allowed admin role resources or third-party integration's access (**System | Extensions | Integrations | Add New Integration | Available APIs**).

`webapi.xml` is where we define Web API resources and their permissions. When we create `webapi.xml`, the permissions defined in `acl.xml` are referenced to create access rights for each API resource.

Let's take a look at the following (truncated) `webapi.xml` from the core `Magento_Cms` module:

```
<routes xmlns:xsi="http://www.w3.org/2001/XMLSchema-instance"
  xsi:noNamespaceSchemaLocation=
  "urn:magento:module:Magento_Webapi:etc/webapi.xsd">
    ...
    <route url="/V1/cmsPage" method="POST">
        <service class="Magento\Cms\Api\PageRepositoryInterface"
          method="save" />
        <resources>
            <resource ref="Magento_Cms::page" />
        </resources>
    </route>
    ...
    <route url="/V1/cmsBlock/search" method="GET">
```

```
        <service class="Magento\Cms\Api\BlockRepositoryInterface"
          method="getList" />
        <resources>
            <resource ref="Magento_Cms::block" />
        </resources>
    </route>
    ...
</routes>
```

In the preceding `webapi.xml` file for the CMS page API, only a user with `Magento_Cms::page` authorization can access `POST /V1/cmsPage` or `GET /V1/cmsBlock/search`. We will get back to a more detailed explanation of route later on in our examples; for the moment, our focus is on `resource`. We can assign multiple child `resource` elements under resources. In cases like these, it would be sufficient for a user to have any one of those ACLs assigned to be able to make an API call.

The actual authorization is then granted to either an administrator or integration, defined in the Magento admin, with full group or a specific resource selected in the ACL tree as shown in the following screenshot:

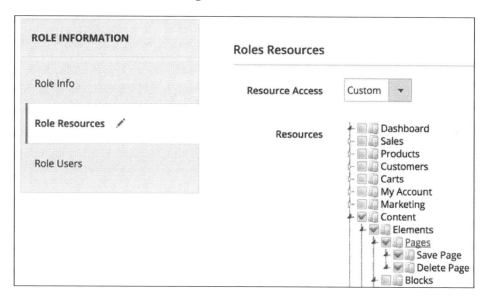

Given that `webapi.xml` and `acl.xml` go hand in hand, let's take a look at the (truncated) `acl.xml` file from the core `Magento_Cms` module:

```
<resources>
    <resource id="Magento_Backend::admin">
        <resource id="Magento_Backend::content">
            <resource id="Magento_Backend::content_elements">
```

```
            <resource id="Magento_Cms::page" ...>
                ...
            </resource>
          </resource>
        </resource>
      </resource>
  </resources>
```

Notice how the position of the Magento_Cms::page resource is nested under Magento_Backend::content_elements, which in turn is nested under Magento_Backend::content, which is further nested under Magento_Backend::admin. This tells Magento where to render the ACL under Magento admin when showing the **Roles Resources** tree as shown in the previous screenshot. This does not mean that the user authorized against the Magento_Cms::page resource won't be able to access the API if all those parent Magento_Backend resources are granted to him as well.

Authorizing against a resource is sort of a flat thing. There is no tree check when authorizing. Thus, each resource is required to have a unique id attribute value on a resource element when defined under acl.xml.

The resources just defined are what we listed before as resources for which administrators or integrators are authorized.

The customer, on the other hand, is assigned a resource named anonymous or self. If we were to do a full <resource ref="anonymous" /> string search across all Magento core modules, several occurrences would show up.

Let's take a look at the (truncated) core module vendor/magento/module-catalog/etc/webapi.xml file:

```
<route url="/V1/products" method="GET">
    <service class=
      "Magento\Catalog\Api\ProductRepositoryInterface"
      method="getList"/>
    <resources>
        <resource ref="anonymous" />
    </resources>
</route>
```

The preceding XML defines an API endpoint path with a value of /V1/products, available via the **HTTP GET** method. It further defines a resource called anonymous, which means either the currently logged-in customer or guest user can call this API endpoint.

anonymous is a special permission that doesn't need to be defined in acl.xml. As such, it will not show up in the permissions tree under Magento admin. This simply means that the current resource in webapi.xml can be accessed without the need for authentication.

Finally, we take a look at the self resource, whose example we can find under the (truncated) vendor/magento/module-customer/etc/webapi.xml file as follows:

```
<route url="/V1/customers/me" method="PUT">
    <service class=
      "Magento\Customer\Api\CustomerRepositoryInterface"
      method="save"/>
    <resources>
        <resource ref="self"/>
    </resources>
    <data>
        <parameter name="customer.id"
          force="true">%customer_id%</parameter>
    </data>
</route>
```

self is a special kind of access that enables a user to access resources they own, assuming we already have an authenticated session with the system. For example, GET /V1/customers/me fetches the logged-in customer's details. This is something that is typically useful for JavaScript-based components/widgets.

Authentication methods

Mobile applications, third-party applications, and JavaScript components/widgets (storefront or admin) are the three main types of clients as seen by Magento. Though a client is basically everything communicating with our APIs, each type of client has a preferred authentication method.

Magento supports three types of authentication methods, listed as follows:

- Token-based authentication
- OAuth-based authentication
- Session-based authentication

Token-based authentication is most suitable for mobile applications, where a token acts like an electronic key providing access to the Web API's. The general concept behind a token-based authentication system is relatively simple. The user provides a username and password during initial authentication in order to obtain a time-limited token from the system. If a token is successfully obtained, all subsequent API calls are then made with that token.

OAuth-based authentication is suitable for third-party applications that integrate with Magento. Once an application is authorized through the **OAuth 1.0a handshake process**, it gains access to Magento Web APIs. There are three key terminologies we must understand here: *user* (resource owner), *client* (consumer), and *server* (service provider). The user or resource owner is the one who is being asked to allow access to its protected resource. Imagine a customer as a user (resource owner) allowing access to its orders to some third-party applications. In such a case, this third-party application would be the client (consumer), whereas Magento and its Web API would be the server (service provider).

Session-based authentication is probably the simplest one to grasp. As a customer, you log in to the Magento storefront with your customer credentials. As an admin, you log in to the Magento admin with your admin credentials. The Magento Web API framework uses your logged-in session information to verify your identity and authorize access to the requested resource.

REST versus SOAP

Magento supports both **SOAP** (short for **Simple Object Access Protocol**) and **REST** (short for **Representational State Transfer**) types of communication with the Web API. Authentication methods themselves are not really bound to any of them. We can use the same authentication method and Web API method calls with both SOAP and REST.

Some of the REST specifics we might outline as follows:

- We run REST Web API calls through cURL commands or a REST client.
- Requests support HTTP verbs: GET, POST, PUT, or DELETE.
- A HTTP header requires an authorization parameter, specifying the authentication token with the **Bearer HTTP authorization scheme**, Authorization: Bearer <TOKEN>. <TOKEN> is the authentication token returned by the Magento token service.
- We can use the HTTP header Accept: application/<FORMAT>, where <FORMAT> is either JSON or XML.

Some of the SOAP specifics we might outline as follows:

- We run SOAP Web API calls through cURL commands or a SOAP client.

- A **Web Service Definition Language (WSDL)** file is generated only for services that we request. There is no one big merged WSDL file for all services.

- The Magento Web API uses WSDL 1.2, compliant with WS-I 2.0 Basic Profile.

- Each Magento service interface that is part of a service contract is represented as a separate service in the WSDL.

- Consuming several services implies specifying them in the WSDL endpoint URL in a comma-separated manner, for example `http://<magento.host>/soap/<optional_store_code>?wsdl&services=<service_name_1>,<service_name_2>`.

- We can get a list of all available services by hitting a URL like `http://<SHOP-URL>/soap/default?wsdl_list` in the browser.

The following REST and SOAP examples will make extensive use of cURL, which is essentially a program that allows you to make HTTP requests from the command line or different language implementations (like PHP). We can further describe cURL as the console browser, or our *view source* tool for the web. Anything we can do with various fancy REST and SOAP libraries, we can do with cURL as well; it is just considered to be a more low-level approach.

Doing SOAP requests with cURL or anything else that does not have WSDL/XML parsing implemented internally is cumbersome. Thus, using PHP SoapClient or something more robust is a must. **SoapClient** is an integrated, actively maintained part of PHP, and is thus generally available.

With negative points being pointed, we will still present all of our API calls with console cURL, PHP cURL, and PHP SoapClient examples. Given that libraries abstract so much functionality, it is absolutely essential that a developer has a solid understanding of cURL, even for making SOAP calls.

Hands-on with token-based authentication

The crux of token-based authentication is as follows:

- Client requests access with a username and password
- Application validates credentials
- Application provides a signed token to the client

The following code example demonstrates the console cURL REST-like request for the customer user:

```
curl -X POST "http://magento2.ce/rest/V1/integration/customer/token"\
    -H "Content-Type:application/json"\
    -d '{"username":"john@change.me", "password":"abc123"}'
```

The following code example demonstrates the PHP cURL REST-like request for the customer user:

```
$data = array('username' => 'john@change.me', 'password' =>
  'abc123');
$data_string = json_encode($data);

$ch = curl_init('http://magento2.ce/rest/V1/integration
  /customer/token');
  curl_setopt($ch, CURLOPT_CUSTOMREQUEST, 'POST');
  curl_setopt($ch, CURLOPT_POSTFIELDS, $data_string);
  curl_setopt($ch, CURLOPT_RETURNTRANSFER, true);
  curl_setopt($ch, CURLOPT_HTTPHEADER, array(
    'Content-Type: application/json',
    'Content-Length: ' . strlen($data_string))
);

$result = curl_exec($ch);
```

The following code example demonstrates the console cURL SOAP-like request for the customer user:

```
curl -X POST -H 'Content-Type: application/soap+xml;
charset=utf-8; action=
  "integrationCustomerTokenServiceV1CreateCustomerAccessToken"'
-d @request.xml http://magento2.ce/index.php/soap/default?services=
  integrationCustomerTokenServiceV1
```

Notice the `-d @request.xml` part. Here, we are saying to the `curl` command to take the content of the `request.xml` file and pass it on as POST body data where the content of the `request.xml` file for the preceding `curl` command is defined as follows:

```
<?xml version="1.0" encoding="UTF-8"?>
<env:Envelope xmlns:env="http://www.w3.org/2003/05/soap-envelope"
  xmlns:ns1="http://magento2.ce/index.php/soap/default?
  services=integrationCustomerTokenServiceV1">
    <env:Body>
```

```
        <ns1:integrationCustomerTokenServiceV1CreateCustomer
          AccessTokenRequest>
            <username>john@change.me</username>
            <password>abc123</password>
        </ns1:integrationCustomerTokenServiceV1CreateCustomer
          AccessTokenRequest>
      </env:Body>
</env:Envelope>
```

The following code example demonstrates the PHP cURL SOAP-like request for the customer user:

```
$data_string = file_get_contents('request.xml');

$ch =
  curl_init('http://magento2.ce/index.php/soap/default?services=
    integrationCustomerTokenServiceV1');
  curl_setopt($ch, CURLOPT_CUSTOMREQUEST, 'POST');
  curl_setopt($ch, CURLOPT_POSTFIELDS, $data_string);
  curl_setopt($ch, CURLOPT_RETURNTRANSFER, true);
  curl_setopt($ch, CURLOPT_HTTPHEADER, array(
    'Content-Type: application/soap+xml; charset=utf-8;
      action="integrationCustomerTokenServiceV1
      CreateCustomerAccessToken"',
    'Content-Length: ' . strlen($data_string))
);

$result = curl_exec($ch);
```

The following code example demonstrates the usage of PHP SoapClient to make a Web API call:

```
$request = new SoapClient(
    'http://magento2.ce/index.php/soap/default?wsdl&services=
      integrationCustomerTokenServiceV1',
    array('soap_version' => SOAP_1_2, 'trace' => 1)
);

$token = $request->integrationCustomerTokenServiceV1Create
  CustomerAccessToken(array('username' => 'john@change.me',
  'password' => 'abc123'));
```

The API call for admin user authentication is nearly identical, and depends on which one of three approaches we take. The difference is merely in using `https://magento2.ce/rest/V1/integration/admin/token` as the endpoint URL in the case of REST, and using `http://magento2.ce/index.php/soap/default?services=integrationCustomerTokenServiceV1`. Additionally, for a SOAP call, we are calling `integrationAdminTokenServiceV1CreateAdminAccessToken` on the `$request` object.

In the case of successful authentication, for both the customer and admin API call, the response would be a random-looking 32-characters-long string that we call token. This token is further saved to the `oauth_token` table in the database, under the token column.

This might be a bit confusing with regard to what the `oauth_token` table has to do with token authentication.

 If we think about it, token-based authentication can be looked at as a simplified version of OAuth, where the user would authenticate using a username and password and then give the obtained time-expiring token to some third-party application to use it.

In the case of failed authentication, the server returns **HTTP 401 Unauthorized**, with a body containing a JSON message:

```
{"message":"Invalid login or password."}
```

Notice how we are able to call the API method, though we are not already authenticated? This means we must be calling an API defined by the anonymous type of resource. A quick look at the API endpoint gives us a hint as to the location of its definition. Looking under the `vendor/magento/module-integration/etc/webapi.xml` file, we can see the following (truncated) XML:

```
<route url="/V1/integration/admin/token" method="POST">
    <service
      class="Magento\Integration\Api\AdminTokenServiceInterface"
      method="createAdminAccessToken"/>
    <resources>
        <resource ref="anonymous"/>
    </resources>
</route>
<route url="/V1/integration/customer/token" method="POST">
    <service
      class="Magento\Integration\Api\
      CustomerTokenServiceInterface"
      method="createCustomerAccessToken"/>
    <resources>
        <resource ref="anonymous"/>
    </resources>
</route>
```

We can clearly see how even token-based authentication itself is defined as API, using the anonymous resource so that everyone can access it. In a nutshell, token-based authentication is a feature of the `Magento\Integration` module.

Now that we have our authentication token, we can start making other API calls. Remember, token simply means we have been authenticated against a given username and password. It does not mean we get full access to all Web API methods. This further depends on whether our customer or user has the proper access role.

Hands-on with OAuth-based authentication

OAuth-based authentication is the most complex, yet most flexible one supported by Magento. Before we get to use it, the merchant must register our external application as integration with the Magento instance. Placing ourselves in the role of merchant, we do so in the Magento admin area under **System | Extensions | Integrations**. Clicking on the **Add New Integration** button opens the screen as shown in the following screenshot:

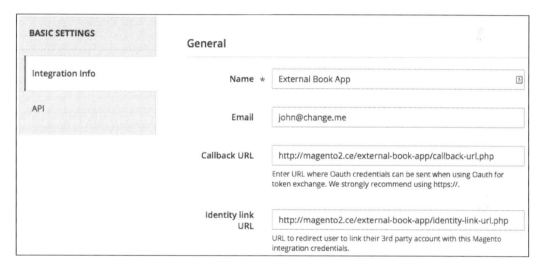

The value `External Book App` is the freely given name of our external application. If we were connecting it with Twitter, we could have easily put its name here. Next to **Name**, we have the **Email, Callback URL**, and **Identity Link URL** fields. The value of e-mail is not really that important. The callback URL and identity link URL define the external application endpoint that receives OAuth credentials. The values of these links point to *external app* that stands as the OAuth client. We will come back to it in a moment.

In the **API** tab under the **Available APIs** pane, we set **Resource Access** to the value of **All** or **Custom**. If set to **Custom**, we can further fine-tune the resources in the **Resources** option we want to allow access to this integration as shown in the following screenshot:

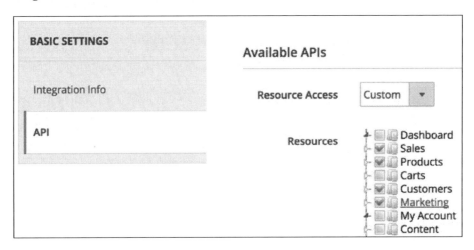

We should always give the minimum required resources to the external application we are using. This way, we minimize possible security risks. The preceding screenshot shows us defining only `Sales`, `Products`, `Customer`, and `Marketing` resources to the integration. This means that the API user would not be able to use content resources, such as save or delete pages.

If we click the **Save** button now, we should be redirected back to the **System | Extensions | Integrations** screen as shown in the following screenshot:

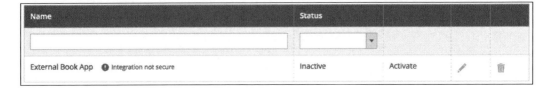

There are three things to focus our attention here. First, we are seeing an **Integration not secure** message. This is because when we defined our callback URL and identity link URL, we used HTTP and not HTTPS protocol. When doing real-world connections, for security reasons, we need to be sure to use HTTPS. Further, we notice how the **Status** column still says **Inactive**.

The **Activate** link, to the right of the **Status** column, is the preceding step before the two-legged OAuth handshake starts. Only an administrator with access to integration listing in the backend can initiate this.

At this point, we need to pull the entire PHP code behind the `External Book App` OAuth client from here, `https://github.com/ajzele/B05032-BookAppOauthClient`, and place it into the root of our Magento installation under the `pub/external-book-app/` folder as shown in the following screenshot:

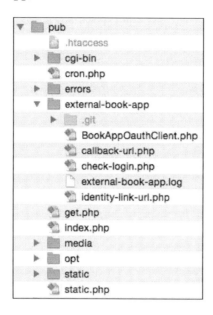

The function of these files is to simulate our own mini-OAuth client. We will not go into much detail about the content of these files, It is more important to look at it as an external OAuth client app. The `callback-url.php` and `identity-link-url.php` files will execute when Magento triggers the callback and identity link URL's as configured under the output image on the previous page.

Once the OAuth client files are in place, we go back to our integrations listing. Here, we click on the **Activate** link. This opens a modal box, asking us to approve access to the API resources as shown in the following screenshot:

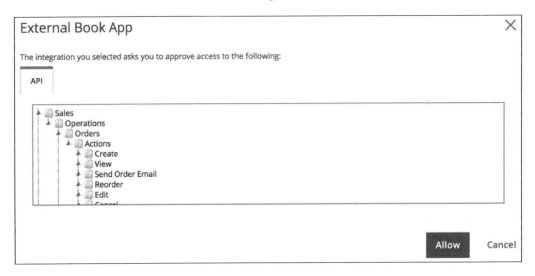

Notice how API resources listed here match those few we set under the **API** tab when creating integration. There are only two actions we can do here really: either click **Cancel** or **Allow** to start the two-legged OAuth handshake. Clicking the **Allow** button does two things in parallel.

First, it instantly posts the credentials to the endpoint (callback URL) specified when creating the External Book App integration. The **HTTP POST** from Magento to the callback URL contains parameters with values similar to the following:

```
Array
(
    [oauth_consumer_key] => cn5anfyvkg7sgm2lrv8cxvq0dxcrj7xm
    [oauth_consumer_secret] => wvmgy0dmlkos2vok04k3h94r40jvi5ye
    [store_base_url] => http://magento2-merchant.loc/index.php/
    [oauth_verifier] => hlnsftola6c7b6wjbtb6wwfx4tow2x6x
)
```

Basically, a HTTP POST request is hitting the callback-url.php file whose content (partial) is as follows:

```
session_id('BookAppOAuth');
session_start();
```

```
$_SESSION['oauth_consumer_key'] = $_POST['oauth_consumer_key'];
$_SESSION['oauth_consumer_secret'] = $_POST['oauth_consumer_secret'];
$_SESSION['store_base_url'] = $_POST['store_base_url'];
$_SESSION['oauth_verifier'] = $_POST['oauth_verifier'];

session_write_close();

header('HTTP/1.0 200 OK');

echo 'Response';
```

We can see that parameters passed by Magento are stored into an external app session named `BookAppOAuth`. Later on, within the `check-login.php` file, these parameters will be used to instantiate the `BookAppOauthClient`, which will further be used to get a request token, which is a pre-authorized token.

Parallel to **Callback URL** HTTP POST, we have a popup window opening as shown in the following screenshot:

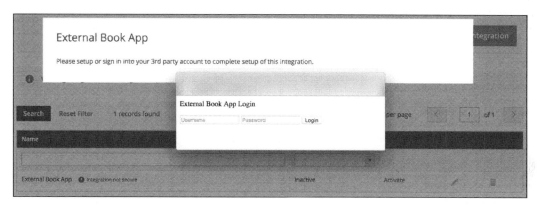

The login form we see in the popup is just some dummy content we placed under the `identity-link-url.php` file. Magento passes two values to this file via HTTP GET. These are `consumer_id` and `success_call_back`. The `consumer_id` value is the ID of our integration we created in the admin area. It is up to the OAuth client app to decide if it wants to do anything with this value or not. The `success_call_back` URL points to our Magento admin `integration/loginSuccessCallback` path. If we take a look at the code of the `identity-link-url.php` file, we can see the form is set to do the POST action on the URL like `check-login.php?consumer_id={$consumerId}&callback_url={$callbackUrl}`.

If we now click the **Login** button, the form will POST data to the `check-login.php` file passing it `consumer_id` and `callback_url` within the URL as GET parameters.

The content of `check-login.php` is defined (partially) as follows:

```php
require '../../vendor/autoload.php';

$consumer = $_REQUEST['consumer_id'];
$callback = $_REQUEST['callback_url'];

session_id('BookAppOAuth');
session_start();

$consumerKey = $_SESSION['oauth_consumer_key'];
$consumerSecret = $_SESSION['oauth_consumer_secret'];
$magentoBaseUrl = rtrim($_SESSION['store_base_url'], '/');
$oauthVerifier = $_SESSION['oauth_verifier'];

define('MAGENTO_BASE_URL', $magentoBaseUrl);

$credentials = new
  \OAuth\Common\Consumer\Credentials($consumerKey,
  $consumerSecret, $magentoBaseUrl);
$oAuthClient = new BookAppOauthClient($credentials);
$requestToken = $oAuthClient->requestRequestToken();

$accessToken = $oAuthClient->requestAccessToken(
    $requestToken->getRequestToken(),
    $oauthVerifier,
    $requestToken->getRequestTokenSecret()
);

header('Location: '. $callback);
```

To keep thing simple, we have no real user login check here. We might have added one above the OAuth-related calls, and then authenticate the user against some username and password before allowing it to use OAuth. However, for simplicity reasons we omitted this part from our sample OAuth client app.

Within the `check-login.php` file, we can see that based on the previously stored session parameters we perform the following:

- Instantiate the `\OAuth\Common\Consumer\Credentials` object passing it the `oauth_consumer_key`, `oauth_consumer_secret`, `store_base_url` stored in the session

- Instantiate the `BookAppOauthClient` object passing its constructor the entire credentials object

- Use the `OauthClient` object to get the request token
- Use the request token to get a long-lived access token

If everything executes successfully, the popup window closes and we get redirected back to the integrations listing. The difference now is that looking at the grid, we have an **Active** status and next to it we have a **Reauthorize** link, as shown in the following screenshot:

What we are really after at this point are **Access Token** and **Access Token Secret**. We can see those if we edit the `External Book App` integration. These values should now be present on the **Integration Details** tab as shown in the following screenshot:

Access Token is the key to all of our further API calls, and with it we successfully finish our authentication bit of OAuth-based authentication.

OAuth-based Web API calls

Once we have obtained OAuth access token, from the preceding steps, we can start making Web API calls to other methods. Even though the Web API coverage is the same for both REST and SOAP, there is a significant difference when making method calls.

For the purpose of giving a more robust example, we will be targeting the customer group save method, (partially) defined in the vendor/magento/module-customer/etc/webapi.xml file as follows:

```
<route url="/V1/customerGroups" method="POST">
    <service class="Magento\Customer\Api\GroupRepositoryInterface"
      method="save"/>
    <resources>
        <resource ref="Magento_Customer::group"/>
    </resources>
</route>
```

To use the access token to make Web API calls, like POST /V1/customerGroups, we need to include these request parameters in the authorization request header in the call:

- oauth_consumer_key, available from the Magento admin area, under the integration edit screen.
- oauth_nonce, random value, uniquely generated by the application for each request.
- oauth_signature_method, name of the signature method used to sign the request. Valid values are: HMAC-SHA1, RSA-SHA1, and PLAINTEXT.
- Even though the Outh protocol supports PLAINTEXT, Magento does not. We will be using HMAC-SHA1.
- oauth_timestamp, integer value, Unix-like timestamp.
- oauth_token, available from the Magento admin area, under the integration edit screen.
- oauth_version, Magento supports Oauth 1.0a, thus we use 1.0.
- oauth_signature, generated signature value, omitted from the signature generation process.

To generate an OAuth 1.0a HMAC-SHA1 signature for a HTTP request takes focused effort, if done manually.

We need to determine the HTTP method and URL of the request, which equals to POST http://magento2-merchant.loc/rest/V1/customerGroups. It is important to use the correct protocol here, so make sure that the https:// or http:// portion of the URL matches the actual request sent to the API.

We then gather all of the parameters included in the request. There are two such locations for these additional parameters: the URL (as part of the query string) and the request body.

In the HTTP request, the parameters are URL encoded, but we need to collect the raw values. In addition to the request parameters, every `oauth_*` parameter needs to be included in the signature, except the `oauth_signature` itself.

The parameters are normalized into a single string as follows:

- Parameters are sorted by name, using lexicographical byte value ordering. If two or more parameters share the same name, they are sorted by their value.

- Parameters are concatenated in their sorted order into a single string. For each parameter, the name is separated from the corresponding value by an = character (ASCII code 61), even if the value is empty. Each name-value pair is separated by an & character (ASCII code 38).

Further, we define the signing key as a value of `{Consumer Key}+{&}+{Access Token Secret}`.

Once we apply the string normalization rules to parameters and determine the signing key, we call `hash_hmac('sha1', $data, {Signing Key}, true)` to get the final `oauth_signature` value.

This should get us the `oauth_signature` as a random 28-characters-long string, similar to this one – `Pi/mGfA0SOlIxO9W30sEch6bjGE=`.

Understanding how to generate the signature string is important, but getting it right every time is tedious and time consuming. We can help ourselves by instantiating the objects of the built-in `\OAuth\Common\Consumer\Credentials` and `\OAuth\OAuth1\Signature\Signature` classes, like (partially) shown as follows:

```
$credentials = new
  \OAuth\Common\Consumer\Credentials($consumerKey,
  $consumerSecret, $magentoBaseUrl);
$signature = new \OAuth\OAuth1\Signature\Signature($credentials);
$signature->setTokenSecret($accessTokenSecret);
$signature->setHashingAlgorithm('HMAC-SHA1');

echo $signature->getSignature($uri, array(
    'oauth_consumer_key' => $consumerKey,
    'oauth_nonce' => 'per-request-unique-token',
    'oauth_signature_method' => 'HMAC-SHA1',
    'oauth_timestamp' => '1437319569',
    'oauth_token' => $accessToken,
    'oauth_version' => '1.0',
), 'POST');
```

Now that we have the `oauth_signature` value, we are ready to do our console `curl` REST example. It comes down to running the following on a console:

```
curl -X POST http://magento2.ce/rest/V1/customerGroups
-H 'Content-Type: application/json'
-H 'Authorization: OAuth
oauth_consumer_key="vw2xi6kaq0o3f7ay60owdpg2f8nt66g6",
oauth_nonce="per-request-token-by-app-1",
oauth_signature_method="HMAC-SHA1",
oauth_timestamp="1437319569",
oauth_token="cney3fmk9p5282bm1khb83q84617dner",
oauth_version="1.0",
oauth_signature="Pi/mGfA0SOlIxO9W30sEch6bjGE="'
-d '{"group": {"code": "The Book Writer", "tax_class_id": "3"}}'
```

Note that the preceding command is merely visually broken into new lines. It should all be single line on a console. Once executed, the API call will create a new customer group called `The Book Writer`. A logical question one might ask looking at the `curl` command is how come we did not normalize the POST data passed as JSON via the `-d` flag switch. This is because parameters in the HTTP POST request body are only taken into consideration for signature generation if content-type is `application/x-www-form-urlencoded`.

The console cURL SOAP requests do not require usage of the OAuth signature. We can execute a SOAP request passing `Authorization: Bearer { Access Token value }` into the request header, like shown in the following example:

```
curl -X POST
http://magento2.ce/index.php/soap/default?services=
customerGroupRepositoryV1 -H 'Content-Type: application/soap+xml;
charset=utf-8; action="customerGroupRepositoryV1Save"' -H
'Authorization: Bearer cney3fmk9p5282bm1khb83q84617dner' -d
@request.xml
```

Where `request.xml` contains content as follows:

```xml
<?xml version="1.0" encoding="UTF-8"?>
<env:Envelope xmlns:env="http://www.w3.org/2003/05/soap-envelope"
  xmlns:ns1="http://magento2.ce/index.php/soap/default?
  services=customerGroupRepositoryV1">
    <env:Body>
        <ns1:customerGroupRepositoryV1SaveRequest>
            <group>
                <code>The Book Writer</code>
                <taxClassId>3</taxClassId>
```

```
            </group>
        </ns1:customerGroupRepositoryV1SaveRequest>
    </env:Body>
</env:Envelope>
```

The following code example demonstrates the PHP cURL SOAP-like request for the customer group `save` method call:

```
$request = new SoapClient(
    'http://magento2.ce/index.php/soap/?wsdl&services=
      customerGroupRepositoryV1',
    array(
        'soap_version' => SOAP_1_2,
        'stream_context' => stream_context_create(array(
            'http' => array(
                'header' => 'Authorization: Bearer
                    cney3fmk9p5282bm1khb83q84617dner')
            )
        )
    )
);

$response = $request->customerGroupRepositoryV1Save(array(
    'group' => array(
        'code' => 'The Book Writer',
        'taxClassId' => 3
    )
));
```

Notice how the method name `customerGroupRepositoryV1Save` actually comprises service name `customerGroupRepositoryV1`, plus the `Save` name of the actual method within the service.

We can get a list of all services defined by opening a URL like `http://magento2.ce/soap/default?wsdl_list` in the browser (depending on our Magento installation).

Hands-on with session-based authentication

Session-based authentication is the third and most simple type of authentication in Magento. We do not have any complexities of token-passing here. As the customer, we log in to the Magento storefront with our customer credentials. As an admin, we log in to the Magento admin with our admin credentials. Magento uses a cookie named PHPSESSID to track the session where our login state is stored. The Web API framework uses our logged-in session information to verify our identity and authorize access to the requested resource.

Customers can access resources that are configured with anonymous or self-permission in the `webapi.xml` configuration file, like GET /rest/V1/customers/me.

If we try to open the http://magento2.ce/rest/V1/customers/me URL while in the browser, but not logged in as the customer, we would get a response as follows:

```
<response>
    <message>Consumer is not authorized to access
      %resources</message>
    <parameters>
        <resources>self</resources>
    </parameters>
</response>
```

If we log in as the customer and then try to open that same URL, we would get a response as follows:

```
<response>
    <id>2</id>
    <group_id>1</group_id>
    <created_at>2015-11-22 14:15:33</created_at>
    <created_in>Default Store View</created_in>
    <email>john@change.me</email>
    <firstname>John</firstname>
    <lastname>Doe</lastname>
    <store_id>1</store_id>
    <website_id>1</website_id>
    <addresses/>
    <disable_auto_group_change>0</disable_auto_group_change>
</response>
```

Admin users can access resources that are assigned to their Magento admin profile.

Creating custom Web APIs

Magento comes with a solid number of API methods that we can call. However, sometimes this is not enough, as our business needs dictate additional logic, and we need to be able to add our own methods to the Web API.

The best part of creating our own API's is that we do not have to be concerned about making them REST or SOAP. Magento abstracts this so that our API methods are automatically available for REST and for SOAP calls.

Adding new API's conceptually evolves around two things: defining business logic through various classes, and exposing it via the `webapi.xml` file. However, as we will soon see, there is a lot of **boilerplate** to it.

Let's create a miniature module called `Foggyline_Slider`, on which we will demonstrate `create (POST)`, `update (PUT)`, `delete (DELETE)`, and `list (GET)` method calls.

Create a module registration file, `app/code/Foggyline/Slider/registration.php`, with content (partial) as follows:

```
\Magento\Framework\Component\ComponentRegistrar::register(
    \Magento\Framework\Component\ComponentRegistrar::MODULE,
    'Foggyline_Slider',
    __DIR__
);
```

Create a module configuration file, `app/code/Foggyline/Slider/etc/module.xml`, with content as follows:

```
<config xmlns:xsi="http://www.w3.org/2001/XMLSchema-instance"
  xsi:noNamespaceSchemaLocation="urn:magento:framework:Module
  /etc/module.xsd">
    <module name="Foggyline_Slider" setup_version="1.0.0"/>
</config>
```

Create an install script where our future models will persist module data. We do so by creating the `app/code/Foggyline/Slider/Setup/InstallSchema.php` file with content (partial) as follows:

```
namespace Foggyline\Slider\Setup;

use Magento\Framework\Setup\InstallSchemaInterface;
use Magento\Framework\Setup\ModuleContextInterface;
use Magento\Framework\Setup\SchemaSetupInterface;

class InstallSchema implements InstallSchemaInterface
{
    public function install(SchemaSetupInterface $setup,
      ModuleContextInterface $context)
    {
        $installer = $setup;
        $installer->startSetup();

        /**
         * Create table 'foggyline_slider_slide'
```

```
        */
        $table = $installer->getConnection()
            ->newTable($installer-
              >getTable('foggyline_slider_slide'))
            ->addColumn(
                'slide_id',
                \Magento\Framework\DB\Ddl\Table::TYPE_INTEGER,
                null,
                ['identity' => true, 'unsigned' => true,
                   'nullable' => false, 'primary' => true],
                'Slide Id'
            )
            ->addColumn(
                'title',
                \Magento\Framework\DB\Ddl\Table::TYPE_TEXT,
                200,
                [],
                'Title'
            )
            ->setComment('Foggyline Slider Slide');
        $installer->getConnection()->createTable($table);
        ...
        $installer->endSetup();


    }
}
```

Now we specify the ACL for our resources. Our resources are going to be CRUD actions we do on our module entities. We will structure our module in a way that slide and image are separate entities, where one slide can have multiple image entities linked to it. Thus, we would like to be able to control access to save and delete actions separately for each entity. We do so by defining the app/code/Foggyline/Slider/etc/acl.xml file as follows:

```
<config xmlns:xsi="http://www.w3.org/2001/XMLSchema-instance"
   xsi:noNamespaceSchemaLocation="urn:magento:framework:Acl/etc/
   acl.xsd">
    <acl>
        <resources>
            <resource id="Magento_Backend::admin">
                <resource id="Magento_Backend::content">
                    <resource id=
                      "Magento_Backend::content_elements">
                        <resource id="Foggyline_Slider::slider"
                           title="Slider" sortOrder="10">
```

```xml
            <resource id="Foggyline_Slider::slide"
                title="Slider Slide" sortOrder="10">
                <resource id=
                    "Foggyline_Slider::slide_save"
                    title="Save Slide"
                    sortOrder="10" />
                <resource id="Foggyline_Slider::
                    slide_delete" title="Delete
                    Slide" sortOrder="20" />
            </resource>
            <resource id="Foggyline_Slider::image"
                title="Slider Image" sortOrder="10">
                <resource id=
                    "Foggyline_Slider::image_save"
                    title="Save Image"
                    sortOrder="10" />
                <resource id=
                    "Foggyline_Slider::image_delete"
                    title="Delete Image"
                    sortOrder="20" />
            </resource>
        </resource>
      </resource>
     </resource>
    </resource>
   </resources>
  </acl>
</config>
```

Now that the ACL has been set, we define our Web API resources within the app/
code/Foggyline/Slider/etc/webapi.xml file (partial) as follows:

```xml
<routes xmlns:xsi="http://www.w3.org/2001/XMLSchema-instance"
  xsi:noNamespaceSchemaLocation=
  "urn:magento:module:Magento_Webapi:etc/webapi.xsd">
    <route url="/V1/foggylineSliderSlide/:slideId" method="GET">
        <service class="Foggyline\Slider\Api\
            SlideRepositoryInterface" method="getById" />
        <resources>
            <resource ref="Foggyline_Slider::slide" />
        </resources>
    </route>
    <route url="/V1/foggylineSliderSlide/search" method="GET">
        <service class="Foggyline\Slider\Api\
            SlideRepositoryInterface" method="getList" />
        <resources>
            <resource ref="anonymous" />
```

```xml
        </resources>
    </route>
    <route url="/V1/foggylineSliderSlide" method="POST">
        <service class="Foggyline\Slider\Api\
          SlideRepositoryInterface" method="save" />
        <resources>
            <resource ref="Foggyline_Slider::slide_save" />
        </resources>
    </route>
    <route url="/V1/foggylineSliderSlide/:id" method="PUT">
        <service class="Foggyline\Slider\Api\
          SlideRepositoryInterface" method="save" />
        <resources>
            <resource ref="Foggyline_Slider::slide_save" />
        </resources>
    </route>
    <route url="/V1/foggylineSliderSlide/:slideId"
      method="DELETE">
        <service class="Foggyline\Slider\Api\
          SlideRepositoryInterface" method="deleteById" />
        <resources>
            <resource ref="Foggyline_Slider::slide_delete" />
        </resources>
    </route>
    <route url="/V1/foggylineSliderImage/:imageId" method="GET">
        <service class="Foggyline\Slider\Api\
          ImageRepositoryInterface" method="getById" />
        <resources>
            <resource ref="Foggyline_Slider::image" />
        </resources>
    </route>
    <route url="/V1/foggylineSliderImage/search" method="GET">
        <service class="Foggyline\Slider\Api\
          ImageRepositoryInterface" method="getList" />
        <resources>
            <resource ref="Foggyline_Slider::image" />
        </resources>
    </route>
    <route url="/V1/foggylineSliderImage" method="POST">
        <service class="Foggyline\Slider\Api\
          ImageRepositoryInterface" method="save" />
        <resources>
            <resource ref="Foggyline_Slider::image_save" />
        </resources>
    </route>
```

```
<route url="/V1/foggylineSliderImage/:id" method="PUT">
    <service class="Foggyline\Slider\Api\
        ImageRepositoryInterface" method="save" />
    <resources>
        <resource ref="Foggyline_Slider::image_save" />
    </resources>
</route>
<route url="/V1/foggylineSliderImage/:imageId"
    method="DELETE">
    <service class="Foggyline\Slider\Api\
        ImageRepositoryInterface" method="deleteById" />
    <resources>
        <resource ref="Foggyline_Slider::image_delete" />
    </resources>
</route>
</routes>
```

Notice how each of those service class attributes point to the interface, not the class. This is the way we should build our exposable services, always having an interface definition behind them. As we will soon see, using di.xml, this does not mean Magento will try to create objects from these interfaces directly.

We now create the app/code/Foggyline/Slider/etc/di.xml file with content (partial) as follows:

```
<config xmlns:xsi="http://www.w3.org/2001/XMLSchema-instance"
    xsi:noNamespaceSchemaLocation=
    "urn:magento:framework:ObjectManager/etc/config.xsd">

    <preference for="Foggyline\Slider\Api\Data\SlideInterface"
        type="Foggyline\Slider\Model\Slide"/>

    <preference for="Foggyline\Slider\Api\
        SlideRepositoryInterface" type=
        "Foggyline\Slider\Model\SlideRepository"/>
    ...
</config>
```

What is happening here is that we are telling Magento something like, "hey, whenever you need to pass around an instance that conforms to the Foggyline\Slider\Api\Data\SlideInterface interface, preferably use the Foggyline\Slider\Model\Slide class for it."

At this point, we still do not have any of those interfaces or model classes actually created. When creating APIs, we should first start by defining interfaces, and then our models should extend from those interfaces.

Interface `Foggyline\Slider\Api\Data\SlideInterface` **is defined within the** `app/code/Foggyline/Slider/Api/Data/SlideInterface.php` **file (partial) as follows:**

```php
namespace Foggyline\Slider\Api\Data;

/**
 * @api
 */
interface SlideInterface
{
    const PROPERTY_ID = 'slide_id';
    const PROPERTY_SLIDE_ID = 'slide_id';
    const PROPERTY_TITLE = 'title';

    /**
     * Get Slide entity 'slide_id' property value
     * @return int|null
     */
    public function getId();

    /**
     * Set Slide entity 'slide_id' property value
     * @param int $id
     * @return $this
     */
    public function setId($id);

    /**
     * Get Slide entity 'slide_id' property value
     * @return int|null
     */
    public function getSlideId();

    /**
     * Set Slide entity 'slide_id' property value
     * @param int $slideId
     * @return $this
     */
    public function setSlideId($slideId);

    /**
     * Get Slide entity 'title' property value
     * @return string|null
     */
```

```php
public function getTitle();

/**
 * Set Slide entity 'title' property value
 * @param string $title
 * @return $this
 */
public function setTitle($title);
}
```

We are going for ultimate simplification here. Our `Slide` entity only really has ID and title values. The `id` and `slide_id` point to the same field in the database and the implementation of their getters and setters should yield the same results.

Although `API/Data/*.php` interfaces become blueprint requirements for our data models, we also have `Api/*RepositoryInterface.php` files. The idea here is to extract create, update, delete, search, and similar data-handling logic away from the data model class into its own class. This way, our model classes become more pure data and business logic classes while the rest of persistence and search-related logic moves into these repository classes.

Our **Slide Repository Interface** is defined within the `app/code/Foggyline/Slider/Api/SlideRepositoryInterface.php` file as follows:

```php
namespace Foggyline\Slider\Api;

/**
 * @api
 */
interface SlideRepositoryInterface
{
    /**
     * Retrieve slide entity.
     * @param int $slideId
     * @return \Foggyline\Slider\Api\Data\SlideInterface
     * @throws \Magento\Framework\Exception\NoSuchEntityException
       If slide with the specified ID does not exist.
     * @throws \Magento\Framework\Exception\LocalizedException
     */
    public function getById($slideId);

    /**
     * Save slide.
     * @param \Foggyline\Slider\Api\Data\SlideInterface $slide
     * @return \Foggyline\Slider\Api\Data\SlideInterface
```

```
 * @throws \Magento\Framework\Exception\LocalizedException
 */
public function save(\Foggyline\Slider\Api\Data\SlideInterface
    $slide);

/**
 * Retrieve slides matching the specified criteria.
 * @param \Magento\Framework\Api\SearchCriteriaInterface
    $searchCriteria
 * @return \Magento\Framework\Api\SearchResultsInterface
 * @throws \Magento\Framework\Exception\LocalizedException
 */
public function
    getList(\Magento\Framework\Api\SearchCriteriaInterface
    $searchCriteria);

/**
 * Delete slide by ID.
 * @param int $slideId
 * @return bool true on success
 * @throws \Magento\Framework\Exception\NoSuchEntityException
 * @throws \Magento\Framework\Exception\LocalizedException
 */
public function deleteById($slideId);
}
```

With interfaces in place, we can move on to model class. In order to persist and fetch data in a database, our Slide entity really needs three files under the Model directory. These are called data *model*, *resource class*, and *collection class*.

The data model class is defined under the app/code/Foggyline/Slider/Model/Slide.php file (partial) as follows:

```
namespace Foggyline\Slider\Model;

class Slide extends \Magento\Framework\Model\AbstractModel
    implements \Foggyline\Slider\Api\Data\SlideInterface
{   /**
 * Initialize Foggyline Slide Model
 *
 * @return void
 */
protected function _construct()
{
```

```php
    /* _init($resourceModel) */
    $this->_init
        ('Foggyline\Slider\Model\ResourceModel\Slide');
}


/**
 * Get Slide entity 'slide_id' property value
 *
 * @api
 * @return int|null
 */
public function getId()
{
    return $this->getData(self::PROPERTY_ID);
}


/**
 * Set Slide entity 'slide_id' property value
 *
 * @api
 * @param int $id
 * @return $this
 */
public function setId($id)
{
    $this->setData(self::PROPERTY_ID, $id);
    return $this;
}


/**
 * Get Slide entity 'slide_id' property value
 *
 * @api
 * @return int|null
 */
public function getSlideId()
{
    return $this->getData(self::PROPERTY_SLIDE_ID);
}


/**
 * Set Slide entity 'slide_id' property value
 *
 * @api
```

```
 * @param int $slideId
 * @return $this
 */
public function setSlideId($slideId)
{
    $this->setData(self::PROPERTY_SLIDE_ID, $slideId);
    return $this;
}


/**
 * Get Slide entity 'title' property value
 *
 * @api
 * @return string|null
 */
public function getTitle()
{
    return $this->getData(self::PROPERTY_TITLE);
}


/**
 * Set Slide entity 'title' property value
 *
 * @api
 * @param string $title
 * @return $this
 */
public function setTitle($title)
{
    $this->setData(self::PROPERTY_TITLE, $title);
}
}
```

Following the model data class is the model resource class, defined in the app/code/ Foggyline/Slider/Model/ResourceModel/Slide.php file (partial) as follows:

```
namespace Foggyline\Slider\Model\ResourceModel;

/**
 * Foggyline Slide resource
 */
class Slide extends
   \Magento\Framework\Model\ResourceModel\Db\AbstractDb
{
    /**
```

```
* Define main table
*
* @return void
*/
protected function _construct()
{
    /* _init($mainTable, $idFieldName) */
    $this->_init('foggyline_slider_slide', 'slide_id');
}
}
```

Finally, the third bit is the model collection class, defined in the app/code/
Foggyline/Slider/Model/ResourceModel/Slide/Collection.php file as follows:

```
namespace Foggyline\Slider\Model\ResourceModel\Slide;

/**
* Foggyline slides collection
*/
class Collection extends
  \Magento\Framework\Model\ResourceModel\Db\Collection\
  AbstractCollection
{
    /**
    * Define resource model and model
    *
    * @return void
    */
    protected function _construct()
    {
        /* _init($model, $resourceModel) */
        $this->_init('Foggyline\Slider\Model\Slide',
            'Foggyline\Slider\Model\ResourceModel\Slide');
    }
}
```

If we were to manually instantiate the model data class now, we would be able to
persist the data in the database. To complete the di.xml requirements, we still lack
one more final ingredient – the Model/SlideRepository class file.

Let us go and create the `app/code/Foggyline/Slider/Model/SlideRepository.php` file with content (partial) as follows:

```php
namespace Foggyline\Slider\Model;

use Magento\Framework\Api\DataObjectHelper;
use Magento\Framework\Api\SearchCriteriaInterface;
use Magento\Framework\Exception\CouldNotDeleteException;
use Magento\Framework\Exception\CouldNotSaveException;
use Magento\Framework\Exception\NoSuchEntityException;
use Magento\Framework\Reflection\DataObjectProcessor;

class SlideRepository implements \Foggyline\Slider\Api\
SlideRepositoryInterface
{
    /**
     * @var \Foggyline\Slider\Model\ResourceModel\Slide
     */
    protected $resource;

    /**
     * @var \Foggyline\Slider\Model\SlideFactory
     */
    protected $slideFactory;

    /**
     * @var \Foggyline\Slider\Model\ResourceModel\Slide\
       CollectionFactory
     */
    protected $slideCollectionFactory;

    /**
     * @var \Magento\Framework\Api\SearchResultsInterface
     */
    protected $searchResultsFactory;

    /**
     * @var \Magento\Framework\Api\DataObjectHelper
     */
    protected $dataObjectHelper;

    /**
     * @var \Magento\Framework\Reflection\DataObjectProcessor
     */
```

```php
    protected $dataObjectProcessor;

    /**
     * @var \Foggyline\Slider\Api\Data\SlideInterfaceFactory
     */
    protected $dataSlideFactory;

    /**
     * @param ResourceModel\Slide $resource
     * @param SlideFactory $slideFactory
     * @param ResourceModel\Slide\CollectionFactory
     *   $slideCollectionFactory
     * @param \Magento\Framework\Api\SearchResultsInterface
     *   $searchResultsFactory
     * @param DataObjectHelper $dataObjectHelper
     * @param DataObjectProcessor $dataObjectProcessor
     * @param \Foggyline\Slider\Api\Data\SlideInterfaceFactory
     *   $dataSlideFactory
     */
    public function __construct(
        \Foggyline\Slider\Model\ResourceModel\Slide $resource,
        \Foggyline\Slider\Model\SlideFactory $slideFactory,
        \Foggyline\Slider\Model\ResourceModel\Slide\
          CollectionFactory $slideCollectionFactory,
        \Magento\Framework\Api\SearchResultsInterface
          $searchResultsFactory,
        \Magento\Framework\Api\DataObjectHelper $dataObjectHelper,
        \Magento\Framework\Reflection\DataObjectProcessor
          $dataObjectProcessor,
        \Foggyline\Slider\Api\Data\SlideInterfaceFactory
          $dataSlideFactory

    )
    {

        $this->resource = $resource;
        $this->slideFactory = $slideFactory;
        $this->slideCollectionFactory = $slideCollectionFactory;
        $this->searchResultsFactory = $searchResultsFactory;
        $this->dataObjectHelper = $dataObjectHelper;
        $this->dataObjectProcessor = $dataObjectProcessor;
        $this->dataSlideFactory = $dataSlideFactory;
    }
    ...
}
```

It might appear that there is a lot going on here, but really we are just passing on some class and interface names to the constructor in order to instantiate the objects we will use across individual service methods defined in the webapi.xml file.

The first service method on our list is getById, defined within SlideRepository. php as follows:

```
/**
 * Retrieve slide entity.
 *
 * @api
 * @param int $slideId
 * @return \Foggyline\Slider\Api\Data\SlideInterface
 * @throws \Magento\Framework\Exception\NoSuchEntityException If
   slide with the specified ID does not exist.
 * @throws \Magento\Framework\Exception\LocalizedException
 */
public function getById($slideId)
{
    $slide = $this->slideFactory->create();
    $this->resource->load($slide, $slideId);
    if (!$slide->getId()) {
        throw new NoSuchEntityException(__('Slide with id %1 does
            not exist.', $slideId));
    }
    return $slide;
}
```

Then we have the save method, defined within SlideRepository.php as follows:

```
/**
 * Save slide.
 *
 * @param \Foggyline\Slider\Api\Data\SlideInterface $slide
 * @return \Foggyline\Slider\Api\Data\SlideInterface
 * @throws \Magento\Framework\Exception\LocalizedException
 */
public function save(\Foggyline\Slider\Api\Data\SlideInterface
  $slide)
{
    try {
        $this->resource->save($slide);
    } catch (\Exception $exception) {
        throw new CouldNotSaveException(__($exception-
            >getMessage()));
    }
    return $slide;
}
```

The save method addresses both POST and PUT requests defined in webapi.xml, thus effectively handling the creation of new slides or an update of existing ones.

Going further, we have the getList method, defined within SlideRepository.php as follows:

```
/**
 * Retrieve slides matching the specified criteria.
 *
 * @param \Magento\Framework\Api\SearchCriteriaInterface
   $searchCriteria
 * @return \Magento\Framework\Api\SearchResultsInterface
 * @throws \Magento\Framework\Exception\LocalizedException
 */
public function
  getList(\Magento\Framework\Api\SearchCriteriaInterface
  $searchCriteria)
{
    $this->searchResultsFactory->setSearchCriteria
      ($searchCriteria);

    $collection = $this->slideCollectionFactory->create();

    foreach ($searchCriteria->getFilterGroups() as $filterGroup) {
        foreach ($filterGroup->getFilters() as $filter) {
            $condition = $filter->getConditionType() ?: 'eq';
            $collection->addFieldToFilter($filter->getField(),
                [$condition => $filter->getValue()]);
        }
    }
    $this->searchResultsFactory->setTotalCount($collection->
      getSize());
    $sortOrders = $searchCriteria->getSortOrders();
    if ($sortOrders) {
        foreach ($sortOrders as $sortOrder) {
            $collection->addOrder(
                $sortOrder->getField(),
                (strtoupper($sortOrder->getDirection()) === 'ASC')
                  ? 'ASC' : 'DESC'
            );
        }
    }
    $collection->setCurPage($searchCriteria->getCurrentPage());
    $collection->setPageSize($searchCriteria->getPageSize());
    $slides = [];
```

```
    /** @var \Foggyline\Slider\Model\Slide $slideModel */
    foreach ($collection as $slideModel) {
        $slideData = $this->dataSlideFactory->create();
        $this->dataObjectHelper->populateWithArray(
            $slideData,
            $slideModel->getData(),
            '\Foggyline\Slider\Api\Data\SlideInterface'
        );
        $slides[] = $this->dataObjectProcessor->
          buildOutputDataArray(
            $slideData,
            '\Foggyline\Slider\Api\Data\SlideInterface'
        );
    }
    $this->searchResultsFactory->setItems($slides);
    return $this->searchResultsFactory;
}
```

Finally, we have the `deleteById` method, defined within `SlideRepository.php` as follows:

```
/**
 * Delete Slide
 *
 * @param \Foggyline\Slider\Api\Data\SlideInterface $slide
 * @return bool
 * @throws CouldNotDeleteException
 */
public function delete(\Foggyline\Slider\Api\Data\SlideInterface
  $slide)
{
    try {
        $this->resource->delete($slide);
    } catch (\Exception $exception) {
        throw new CouldNotDeleteException(__($exception->
          getMessage()));
    }
    return true;
}


/**
 * Delete slide by ID.
 *
 * @param int $slideId
 * @return bool true on success
```

```
 * @throws \Magento\Framework\Exception\NoSuchEntityException
 * @throws \Magento\Framework\Exception\LocalizedException
 */
public function deleteById($slideId)
{
    return $this->delete($this->getById($slideId));
}
```

Keep in mind that we only covered the `Slide` entity in the preceding partial code examples, which is enough to progress further with API call examples.

API call examples

Since all of our defined API's are resource protected, we first need to authenticate as the admin user, assuming the admin user has access to all our custom resources that encompass the ones we defined. For simplicity sake, we will use the token-based authentication method, examples of which are given previously in this chapter. Once authenticated, we should have a 32 random characters long token like `pk8h93nq9cevaw55bohkjbp0o7kpl4d3`, for example.

Once the token key has been obtained, we will test the following API calls using console cURL, PHP cURL, PHP SoapClient, and console SOAP style cURL examples:

- `GET /V1/foggylineSliderSlide/:slideId`, calls the `getById` service method, requires the `Foggyline_Slider::slide` resource

- `GET /V1/foggylineSliderSlide/search`, calls the `getList` service method, requires the `Foggyline_Slider::slide` resource

- `POST /V1/foggylineSliderSlide`, calls the `save` service method, requires the `Foggyline_Slider::slide_save` resource

- `PUT /V1/foggylineSliderSlide/:id`, calls the `save` service method, requires the `Foggyline_Slider::slide_save` resource

- `DELETE /V1/foggylineSliderSlide/:slideId`, calls the `deleteById` service method, requires the `Foggyline_Slider::slide_delete` resource

The getById service method call examples

The console cURL style for executing `GET /V1/foggylineSliderSlide/:slideId` is done as follows:

```
curl -X GET -H 'Content-type: application/json' \
-H 'Authorization: Bearer pk8h93nq9cevaw55bohkjbp0o7kpl4d3' \
http://magento2.ce/rest/V1/foggylineSliderSlide/1
```

The PHP cURL style for executing `GET /V1/foggylineSliderSlide/:slideId` is done as follows:

```
$ch = curl_init('http://magento2.ce/rest/V1/foggylineSliderSlide/1');
curl_setopt($ch, CURLOPT_CUSTOMREQUEST, 'GET');
curl_setopt($ch, CURLOPT_RETURNTRANSFER, true);
curl_setopt($ch, CURLOPT_HTTPHEADER, array(
    'Content-Type: application/json',
    'Authorization: Bearer pk8h93nq9cevaw55bohkjbp0o7kpl4d3'
));

$result = curl_exec($ch);
```

The response for console and PHP cURL style should be a JSON string similar to the following one:

```
{"slide_id":1,"title":"Awesome stuff #1"}
```

The PHP SoapClient style for executing `GET /V1/foggylineSliderSlide/:slideId` is done as follows:

```
$request = new SoapClient(
    'http://magento2.ce/index.php/soap/?
      wsdl&services=foggylineSliderSlideRepositoryV1',
    array(
        'soap_version' => SOAP_1_2,
        'stream_context' => stream_context_create(array(
                'http' => array(
                    'header' => 'Authorization: Bearer
                      pk8h93nq9cevaw55bohkjbp0o7kpl4d3')
            )
        )
    )
);
$response = $request->
  foggylineSliderSlideRepositoryV1GetById(array('slideId'=>1));
```

The response for PHP SoapClient style should be the `stdClass` PHP object as follows:

```
object(stdClass)#2 (1) {
    ["result"]=>
    object(stdClass)#3 (2) {
    ["slideId"]=>
    int(1)
    ["title"]=>
    string(16) "Awesome stuff #1"
    }
}
```

The console SOAP style cURL for executing GET /V1/ foggylineSliderSlide/:slideId is done as follows:

```
curl -X POST \
-H 'Content-Type: application/soap+xml; charset=utf-8;
action="foggylineSliderSlideRepositoryV1GetById"' \
-H 'Authorization: Bearer pk8h93nq9cevaw55bohkjbp0o7kpl4d3' \
-d @request.xml \
http://magento2.ce/index.php/soap/default?services=foggyline
SliderSlideRepositoryV1
```

Where request.xml has content as follows:

```
<?xml version="1.0" encoding="UTF-8"?>
<env:Envelope xmlns:env="http://www.w3.org/2003/05/soap-envelope"
   xmlns:ns1="http://magento2.ce/index.php/soap/default?
   services=foggylineSliderSlideRepositoryV1">
     <env:Body>
         <ns1:foggylineSliderSlideRepositoryV1GetByIdRequest>
             <slideId>1</slideId>
         </ns1:foggylineSliderSlideRepositoryV1GetByIdRequest>
     </env:Body>
</env:Envelope>
```

Notice how we did not really do GET, rather a POST type of request. Also, the URL to which we are pointing our POST is not really the same as with previous requests. This is because Magento SOAP requests are always POST (or PUT) type, as the data is submitted in XML format. XML format in return specifies the service, and the request header action specifies the method to be called on the service.

The response for console SOAP style cURL should be an XML as follows:

```
<?xml version="1.0" encoding="UTF-8"?>
<env:Envelope xmlns:env="http://www.w3.org/2003/05/soap-envelope"
   xmlns:ns1="http://magento2.ce/index.php/soap/default?
   services=foggylineSliderSlideRepositoryV1">
     <env:Body>
         <ns1:foggylineSliderSlideRepositoryV1GetByIdResponse>
             <result>
                 <slideId>1</slideId>
                 <title>Awesome stuff #1</title>
             </result>
         </ns1:foggylineSliderSlideRepositoryV1GetByIdResponse>
     </env:Body>
</env:Envelope>
```

The getList service method call examples

The console cURL style for executing GET /V1/foggylineSliderSlide/search is done as follows:

```
curl -X GET -H 'Content-type: application/json' \

-H 'Authorization: Bearer pk8h93nq9cevaw55bohkjbpOo7kpl4d3' \

"http://magento2.ce/rest/V1/foggylineSliderSlide/search?search_
criteria%5Bfilter_groups%5D%5B0%5D%5Bfilters%5D%5B0%5D%5Bfield%5D=title&
search_criteria%5Bfilter_groups%5D%5B0%5D%5Bfilters%5D%5B0%5D%5Bvalue%5D
=%25some%25&search_criteria%5Bfilter_groups%5D%5B0%5D%5Bfilters%5D%5B0%
5D%5Bcondition_type%5D=like&search_criteria%5Bcurrent_page%5D=1&search_
criteria%5Bpage_size%5D=10&search_criteria%5Bsort_orders%5D%5B0%5D%5Bfiel
d%5D=slide_id&search_criteria%5Bsort_orders%5D%5B0%5D%5Bdirection%5D=ASC"
```

The PHP cURL style for executing GET /V1/foggylineSliderSlide/search is done as follows:

```
$searchCriteriaJSON = '{
    "search_criteria": {
        "filter_groups": [
            {
                "filters": [
                    {
                        "field": "title",
                        "value": "%some%",
                        "condition_type": "like"
                    }
                ]
            }
        ],
        "current_page": 1,
        "page_size": 10,
        "sort_orders": [
            {
                "field": "slide_id",
                "direction": "ASC"
            }
        ]
    }
}';

$searchCriteriaQueryString =
    http_build_query(json_decode($searchCriteriaJSON));
```

```
$ch =
  curl_init('http://magento2.ce/rest/V1/foggylineSliderSlide/
    search?' . $searchCriteriaQueryString);
  curl_setopt($ch, CURLOPT_CUSTOMREQUEST, 'GET');
  curl_setopt($ch, CURLOPT_RETURNTRANSFER, true);
  curl_setopt($ch, CURLOPT_HTTPHEADER, array(
      'Content-Type: application/json',
      'Authorization: Bearer pk8h93nq9cevaw55bohkjbpoo7kpl4d3'
  ));

$result = curl_exec($ch);
```

The response for console and PHP cURL style should be a JSON string similar to the
following one:

```
{"items":[{"slide_id":2,"title":"Just some other
  slider"},{"slide_id":1,"title":"Awesome stuff #1"}],
  "search_criteria":{"filter_groups":[{"filters":
  [{"field":"title","value":"%some%","condition_type":"like"}]}],
  "sort_orders":[{"field":"slide_id","direction":"-
  1"}],"page_size":10,"current_page":1},"total_count":2}
```

The PHP SoapClient style for executing `GET /V1/foggylineSliderSlide/search` is
done as follows:

```
$searchCriteria = [
    'searchCriteria' =>
        [
            'filterGroups' =>
                [
                    [
                        'filters' =>
                            [
                                [
                                    'field' => 'title',
                                    'value' => '%some%',
                                    'condition_type' => 'like',
                                ],
                            ],
                    ],
                ],
            'currentPage' => 1,
            'pageSize' => 10,
            'sort_orders' =>
                [
                    [
```

```
                                     'field' => 'slide_id',
                                     'direction' =>'ASC',
                         ],
                     ],
             ],
    ];

    $request = new SoapClient(
        'http://magento2.ce/index.php/soap/?wsdl&services=
          foggylineSliderSlideRepositoryV1',
        array(
            'soap_version' => SOAP_1_2,
            'trace'=>1,
            'stream_context' => stream_context_create(array(
                    'http' => array(
                        'header' => 'Authorization: Bearer
                          pk8h93nq9cevaw55bohkjbp0o7kpl4d3')
                )
            )
        )
    );

    $response = $request->
        foggylineSliderSlideRepositoryV1GetList($searchCriteria);
```

The response for PHP SoapClient style should be the `stdClass` PHP object
as follows:

```
    object(stdClass)#2 (1) {
      ["result"]=>
      object(stdClass)#3 (3) {
        ["items"]=>
        object(stdClass)#4 (0) {
        }
        ["searchCriteria"]=>
        object(stdClass)#5 (3) {
          ["filterGroups"]=>
          object(stdClass)#6 (1) {
            ["item"]=>
            object(stdClass)#7 (1) {
              ["filters"]=>
              object(stdClass)#8 (1) {
                ["item"]=>
                object(stdClass)#9 (2) {
                  ["field"]=>
```

```
                        string(5) "title"
                        ["value"]=>
                        string(6) "%some%"
                    }
                }
            }
        }
        ["pageSize"]=>
        int(10)
        ["currentPage"]=>
        int(1)
    }
    ["totalCount"]=>
    int(0)
    }
}
```

The console SOAP style cURL for executing GET /V1/foggylineSliderSlide/
search is done as follows:

```
curl -X POST \

-H 'Content-Type: application/soap+xml; charset=utf-8;
action="foggylineSliderSlideRepositoryV1GetList"' \

-H 'Authorization: Bearer pk8h93nq9cevaw55bohkjbp0o7kpl4d3' \

-d @request.xml \

http://magento2.ce/index.php/soap/default?services=foggyline
SliderSlideRepositoryV1
```

Where request.xml has content as follows:

```
<?xml version="1.0" encoding="UTF-8"?>
<env:Envelope xmlns:env="http://www.w3.org/2003/05/soap-envelope"
  xmlns:ns1="http://magento2.ce/index.php/soap/default?
  services=foggylineSliderSlideRepositoryV1">
    <env:Body>
        <ns1:foggylineSliderSlideRepositoryV1GetListRequest>
            <searchCriteria>
                <filterGroups>
                    <item>
                        <filters>
                            <item>
                                <field>title</field>
                                <value>%some%</value>
                            </item>
                        </filters>
```

```
                </item>
            </filterGroups>
            <pageSize>10</pageSize>
            <currentPage>1</currentPage>
        </searchCriteria>
    </ns1:foggylineSliderSlideRepositoryV1GetListRequest>
  </env:Body>
</env:Envelope>
```

Notice we did not really do GET, rather POST. Also, the URL to which we are pointing our POST is not really the same as with previous requests. This is because Magento SOAP requests are always POST type, as the data is submitted in XML format. XML format in return specifies the service, and the request header action specifies the method to be called on the service.

The response for console SOAP style cURL should be an XML as follows:

```
<?xml version="1.0" encoding="UTF-8"?>
<env:Envelope xmlns:env="http://www.w3.org/2003/05/soap-envelope"
  xmlns:ns1="http://magento2.ce/index.php/soap/default?
  services=foggylineSliderSlideRepositoryV1">
    <env:Body>
        <ns1:foggylineSliderSlideRepositoryV1GetListResponse>
            <result>
                <items/>
                <searchCriteria>
                    <filterGroups>
                        <item>
                            <filters>
                                <item>
                                    <field>title</field>
                                    <value>%some%</value>
                                </item>
                            </filters>
                        </item>
                    </filterGroups>
                    <pageSize>10</pageSize>
                    <currentPage>1</currentPage>
                </searchCriteria>
                <totalCount>0</totalCount>
            </result>
        </ns1:foggylineSliderSlideRepositoryV1GetListResponse>
    </env:Body>
</env:Envelope>
```

The save (as new) service method call examples

The console cURL style for executing POST /V1/foggylineSliderSlide is done as follows:

```
curl -X POST -H 'Content-type: application/json' \
-H 'Authorization: Bearer pk8h93nq9cevaw55bohkjbp0o7kpl4d3' \
-d '{"slide": {"title": "API test"}}' \
http://magento2.ce/rest/V1/foggylineSliderSlide/
```

The PHP cURL style for executing POST /V1/foggylineSliderSlide is done as follows:

```
$slide = json_encode(['slide'=>['title'=> 'API test']]);

$ch =
  curl_init('http://magento2.ce/rest/V1/foggylineSliderSlide');
  curl_setopt($ch, CURLOPT_CUSTOMREQUEST, 'POST');
  curl_setopt($ch, CURLOPT_POSTFIELDS, $slide);
  curl_setopt($ch, CURLOPT_RETURNTRANSFER, true);
  curl_setopt($ch, CURLOPT_HTTPHEADER, array(
      'Content-Type: application/json',
      'Content-Length: ' . strlen($slide),
      'Authorization: Bearer pk8h93nq9cevaw55bohkjbp0o7kpl4d3'
  ));

$result = curl_exec($ch);
```

The response for console and PHP cURL style should be a JSON string similar to the following one:

```
{"slide_id":4,"title":"API test"}
```

The PHP SoapClient style for executing POST /V1/foggylineSliderSlide is done as follows:

```
$slide = ['slide'=>['title'=> 'API test']];

$request = new SoapClient(
    'http://magento2.ce/index.php/soap/?wsdl&services-
      foggylineSliderSlideRepositoryV1',
    array(
        'soap_version' => SOAP_1_2,
        'trace'=>1,
        'stream_context' => stream_context_create(array(
                'http' => array(
```

```
                    'header' => 'Authorization: Bearer
                       pk8h93nq9cevaw55bohkjbp0o7kpl4d3')
                )
            )
        )
    );


    $response = $request->
      foggylineSliderSlideRepositoryV1Save($slide);
```

The response for PHP SoapClient style should be the `stdClass` PHP object as follows:

```
object(stdClass)#2 (1) {
  ["result"]=>
  object(stdClass)#3 (2) {
    ["slideId"]=>
    int(6)
    ["title"]=>
    string(8) "API test"
  }
}
```

The console SOAP style cURL for executing POST /V1/foggylineSliderSlide is done as follows:

```
curl -X POST \

-H 'Content-Type: application/soap+xml; charset=utf-8;
action="foggylineSliderSlideRepositoryV1Save"' \

-H 'Authorization: Bearer pk8h93nq9cevaw55bohkjbp0o7kpl4d3' \

-d @request.xml \

http://magento2.ce/index.php/soap/default?services=foggyline
SliderSlideRepositoryV1
```

Where `request.xml` has content as follows:

```
<?xml version="1.0" encoding="UTF-8"?>
<env:Envelope xmlns:env="http://www.w3.org/2003/05/soap-envelope"
  xmlns:ns1="http://magento2.ce/index.php/soap/default?
  services=foggylineSliderSlideRepositoryV1">
    <env:Body>
        <ns1:foggylineSliderSlideRepositoryV1SaveRequest>
            <slide>
                <title>API test</title>
            </slide>
```

```
            </ns1:foggylineSliderSlideRepositoryV1SaveRequest>
        </env:Body>
    </env:Envelope>
```

The response for console SOAP style cURL should be an XML as follows:

```
<?xml version="1.0" encoding="UTF-8"?>
<env:Envelope xmlns:env="http://www.w3.org/2003/05/soap-envelope"
    xmlns:ns1="http://magento2.ce/index.php/soap/default?
    services=foggylineSliderSlideRepositoryV1">
    <env:Body>
        <ns1:foggylineSliderSlideRepositoryV1SaveResponse>
            <result>
                <slideId>8</slideId>
                <title>API test</title>
            </result>
        </ns1:foggylineSliderSlideRepositoryV1SaveResponse>
    </env:Body>
</env:Envelope>
```

The save (as update) service method call examples

The console cURL style for executing PUT /V1/foggylineSliderSlide/:id is done as follows:

```
curl -X PUT -H 'Content-type: application/json' \
-H 'Authorization: Bearer pk8h93nq9cevaw55bohkjbp0o7kpl4d3' \
-d '{"slide": {"slide_id": 2, "title": "API update test"}}' \
http://magento2.ce/rest/V1/foggylineSliderSlide/2
```

The PHP cURL style for executing PUT /V1/foggylineSliderSlide/:id is done as follows:

```
$slideId = 2;
$slide = json_encode(['slide'=>['slide_id'=> $slideId, 'title'=>
    'API update test']]);

$ch =
    curl_init('http://magento2.ce/rest/V1/foggylineSliderSlide/' .
        $slideId);
    curl_setopt($ch, CURLOPT_CUSTOMREQUEST, 'PUT');
    curl_setopt($ch, CURLOPT_POSTFIELDS, $slide);
    curl_setopt($ch, CURLOPT_RETURNTRANSFER, true);
    curl_setopt($ch, CURLOPT_HTTPHEADER, array(
        'Content-Type: application/json',
        'Content-Length: ' . strlen($slide),
```

```
        'Authorization: Bearer pk8h93nq9cevaw55bohkjbp0o7kpl4d3'
    ));

$result = curl_exec($ch);
```

The response for console and PHP cURL style should be a JSON string similar to the following one:

```
{"id":2,"slide_id":2,"title":"API update test"}
```

The PHP SoapClient style for executing `PUT /V1/foggylineSliderSlide/:id` is done as follows:

```
$slideId = 2;
$slide = ['slide'=>['slideId'=> $slideId, 'title'=> 'API update
  test']];

$request = new SoapClient(
    'http://magento2.ce/index.php/soap/?wsdl&services=
      foggylineSliderSlideRepositoryV1',
    array(
        'soap_version' => SOAP_1_2,
        'trace'=>1,
        'stream_context' => stream_context_create(array(
                'http' => array(
                    'header' => 'Authorization: Bearer
                      pk8h93nq9cevaw55bohkjbp0o7kpl4d3')
            )
        )
    )
);

$response = $request->
  foggylineSliderSlideRepositoryV1Save($slide);
```

The response for PHP SoapClient style should be the `stdClass` PHP object as follows:

```
object(stdClass)#2 (1) {
  ["result"]=>
  object(stdClass)#3 (2) {
    ["slideId"]=>
    int(2)
    ["title"]=>
    string(15) "API update test"
  }
}
```

The console SOAP style cURL for executing `PUT /V1/foggylineSliderSlide/:id` is done as follows:

```
curl -X PUT \
-H 'Content-Type: application/soap+xml; charset=utf-8;
action="foggylineSliderSlideRepositoryV1Save"' \
-H 'Authorization: Bearer pk8h93nq9cevaw55bohkjbpOo7kpl4d3' \
-d @request.xml \
http://magento2.ce/index.php/soap/default?services=
foggylineSliderSlideRepositoryV1
```

Where `request.xml` has content as follows:

```
<?xml version="1.0" encoding="UTF-8"?>
<env:Envelope xmlns:env="http://www.w3.org/2003/05/soap-envelope"
  xmlns:ns1="http://magento2.ce/index.php/soap/default?
  services=foggylineSliderSlideRepositoryV1">
    <env:Body>
        <ns1:foggylineSliderSlideRepositoryV1SaveRequest>
            <slide>
                <slideId>2</slideId>
                <title>API update test</title>
            </slide>
        </ns1:foggylineSliderSlideRepositoryV1SaveRequest>
    </env:Body>
</env:Envelope>
```

The response for console SOAP style cURL should be an XML as follows:

```
<?xml version="1.0" encoding="UTF-8"?>
<env:Envelope xmlns:env="http://www.w3.org/2003/05/soap-envelope"
  xmlns:ns1="http://magento2.ce/index.php/soap/default?
  services=foggylineSliderSlideRepositoryV1">
    <env:Body>
        <ns1:foggylineSliderSlideRepositoryV1SaveResponse>
            <result>
                <slideId>2</slideId>
                <title>API update test</title>
            </result>
        </ns1:foggylineSliderSlideRepositoryV1SaveResponse>
    </env:Body>
</env:Envelope>
```

The deleteById service method call examples

The console cURL style for executing DELETE /V1/
foggylineSliderSlide/:slideId is done as follows:

```
curl -X DELETE -H 'Content-type: application/json' \
-H 'Authorization: Bearer pk8h93nq9cevaw55bohkjbp0o7kpl4d3' \
http://magento2.ce/rest/V1/foggylineSliderSlide/3
```

The PHP cURL style for executing DELETE /V1/foggylineSliderSlide/:slideId
is done as follows:

```
$slideId = 4;

$ch =
  curl_init('http://magento2.ce/rest/V1/foggylineSliderSlide/' .
    $slideId);
  curl_setopt($ch, CURLOPT_CUSTOMREQUEST, 'DELETE');
  curl_setopt($ch, CURLOPT_RETURNTRANSFER, true);
  curl_setopt($ch, CURLOPT_HTTPHEADER, array(
      'Content-Type: application/json',
      'Authorization: Bearer pk8h93nq9cevaw55bohkjbp0o7kpl4d3'
  ));


  $result = curl_exec($ch);
```

The response for console and PHP cURL style should be a JSON string similar to the
following one:

```
true
```

The PHP SoapClient style for executing DELETE /V1/
foggylineSliderSlide/:slideId is done as follows:

```
$slideId = 2;

$request = new SoapClient(
    'http://magento2.ce/index.php/soap/?wsdl&services=
      foggylineSliderSlideRepositoryV1',
    array(
        'soap_version' => SOAP_1_2,
        'trace'=>1,
        'stream_context' => stream_context_create(array(
                'http' => array(
                    'header' => 'Authorization: Bearer
                      pk8h93nq9cevaw55bohkjbp0o7kpl4d3')
            )
```

```
        )
      )
);

$response = $request->
  foggylineSliderSlideRepositoryV1DeleteById(array('slideId'=>
  $slideId));
```

The response for PHP SoapClient style should be the `stdClass` PHP object as follows:

```
object(stdClass)#2 (1) {
  ["result"]=>
  bool(true)
}
```

The console SOAP style cURL for executing DELETE /V1/ foggylineSliderSlide/:slideId is done as follows:

```
curl -X POST \

-H 'Content-Type: application/soap+xml; charset=utf-8;
action="foggylineSliderSlideRepositoryV1DeleteById"' \

-H 'Authorization: Bearer pk8h93nq9cevaw55bohkjbp0o7kpl4d3' \

-d @request.xml \

http://magento2.ce/index.php/soap/default?services=
foggylineSliderSlideRepositoryV1
```

Where `request.xml` has content as follows:

```xml
<?xml version="1.0" encoding="UTF-8"?>
<env:Envelope xmlns:env="http://www.w3.org/2003/05/soap-envelope"
  xmlns:ns1="http://magento2.ce/index.php/soap/default?
  services=foggylineSliderSlideRepositoryV1">
    <env:Body>
        <ns1:foggylineSliderSlideRepositoryV1DeleteByIdRequest>
            <slideId>5</slideId>
        </ns1:foggylineSliderSlideRepositoryV1DeleteByIdRequest>
    </env:Body>
</env:Envelope>
```

The response for console SOAP style cURL should be an XML as follows:

```xml
<?xml version="1.0" encoding="UTF-8"?>
<env:Envelope xmlns:env="http://www.w3.org/2003/05/soap-envelope"
  xmlns:ns1="http://magento2.ce/index.php/soap/default?
  services=foggylineSliderSlideRepositoryV1">
    <env:Body>
```

```
            <ns1:foggylineSliderSlideRepositoryV1DeleteByIdResponse>
                <result>true</result>
            </ns1:foggylineSliderSlideRepositoryV1DeleteByIdResponse>
        </env:Body>
    </env:Envelope>
```

The preceding API call examples cover all of our custom-defined APIs for the `Slide` entity.

Looking back at the `$searchCriteria` variable, we used the GET type of HTTP method, passing the entire variable as a query string. If we think about it, we could have specified POST during the Web API resource definition and packed the content of the `$searchCriteria` variable into the request body. Although the GET method approach might look a bit dirtier, imagine if we assigned the anonymous or self role to the resource: we would be able to simply open a lengthy URL in the browser and have the search results. Think of a possible widget use, where a widget would simply do an AJAX request to the URL and fetch the results for guests or the customer.

The full module source code can be found here: `https://github.com/ajzele/B05032-Foggyline_Slider`. Aside from the `Slide` entity, the full module code includes the `Image` entity as well. Since each slide can contain multiple images, we can further test the `Image` API calls analogous to the preceding calls.

Search Criteria Interface for list filtering

Knowing how to do a proper list filtering to fetch the entities that match a certain lookup is essential for the effective use of `getList` services across core Magento and possibly custom-coded API's. An example is fetching the list of customers registered within the last 24 hours for the latest added product.

Let's take a look back at our `app/code/Foggyline/Slider/etc/webapi.xml` file, the bit where we defined the service `method="getList"`. The service class is defined as `Foggyline\Slider\Api\SlideRepositoryInterface`, which is defined as a preference for the `Foggyline\Slider\Model\SlideRepository` class. Finally, within the `SlideRepository` class, we have the actual `getList`. Method `getList` is defined as follows:

```
getList(\Magento\Framework\Api\SearchCriteriaInterface
    $searchCriteria);
```

We can see that the `getList` method takes only one parameter, object instance, that complies with `SearchCriteriaInterface` called `$searchCriteria`.

What this means is we already have the (incomplete) JSON object of the following type to pass to the `getList` method:

```
{
  "search_criteria": {
  }
}
```

In order to further understand the inner workings of `search_criteria`, we need to understand `SearchCriteriaInterface`, which is (partially) defined as follows:

```
interface SearchCriteriaInterface
{
    /* @param \Magento\Framework\Api\Search\FilterGroup[]
      $filterGroups */
    public function setFilterGroups(array $filterGroups = null);

    /* @param \Magento\Framework\Api\SortOrder[] $sortOrders */
    public function setSortOrders(array $sortOrders = null);

    /* @param int $pageSize */
    public function setPageSize($pageSize);

    /* @param int $currentPage */
    public function setCurrentPage($currentPage);
}
```

Every interface getter and setter method expects the values to be found in passed API parameters. What this means is that the `getPageSize()` and `setPageSize()` methods would expect `search_criteria` to have an integer type `page_size` property on it. Similarly, the `getFilterGroups()` and `setFilterGroups()` methods would expect `search_criteria` to have an array of `\Magento\Framework\Api\Search\FilterGroup` passed to it. These insights bring us to an (incomplete) JSON object of the following type to pass to the `getList` method:

```
{
  "search_criteria": {
    "filter_groups": [
    ],
    "current_page": 1,
    "page_size": 10,
    "sort_orders": [
    ]
  }
}
```

Now we have got to the point where we need to determine what goes into `filter_groups` and `sort_orders`, since these are not simple types but compound values.

Looking further into `\Magento\Framework\Api\Search\FilterGroup`, we see the definition of the `getFilters()` and `setFilters()` methods that work with an array of `\Magento\Framework\Api\Filter` objects. What this means is that `filter_groups` has a property filter that is an array of individual filter objects defined as `\Magento\Framework\Api\Filter`. With this in mind, we are now down to the following form of the `search_criteria` JSON object:

```
{
    "search_criteria": {
        "filter_groups": [
            {
                "filters": [
                ]
            }
        ],
        "current_page": 1,
        "page_size": 10,
        "sort_orders": [
        ]
    }
}
```

Looking further into individual `\Magento\Framework\Api\Filter`, through its getters and setters it defines we can conclude properties like `field`, `value`, and `condition_type`. This brings us one step further to finalizing our `search_criteria` JSON object, which is now structured as follows:

```
{
    "search_criteria": {
        "filter_groups": [
            {
                "filters": [
                    {
                        "field": "title",
                        "value": "%some%",
                        "condition_type": "like"
                    }
                ]
            }
        ],
        "current_page": 1,
        "page_size": 10,
```

```
        "sort_orders": [
        ]
    }
  }
}
```

Let us take a look at `sort_orders` as the last outstanding bit. `sort_orders` is of type `\Magento\Framework\Api\SortOrder`, which has getters and setters for the field and direction properties. Knowing this, we are able to fully construct our `search_criteria` JSON object (or array) that we would be passing to the `getList()` service method call, as follows:

```
{
  "search_criteria": {
    "filter_groups": [
      {
        "filters": [
          {
            "field": "title",
            "value": "%some%",
            "condition_type": "like"
          }
        ]
      }
    ],
    "current_page": 1,
    "page_size": 10,
    "sort_orders": [
      {
        "field": "slide_id",
        "direction": -1
      }
    ]
  }
}
```

What happens when we define multiple entries under `filter_groups`, `filters`, or `sort_orders`? The logical expectation would be that these break into AND and OR operators in SQL when they hit the database. Surprisingly, this is not always the case, at least not with our preceding example. Since the actual implementation of the `getList` method is left for us to handle, we can decide how we want to handle the filter groups and filters.

Looking back at our `getList` method, as (partially) shown next, we are not doing anything to imply an OR operator, so everything ends up with an AND condition on the database:

```
foreach ($searchCriteria->getFilterGroups() as $filterGroup) {
    foreach ($filterGroup->getFilters() as $filter) {
        $condition = $filter->getConditionType() ?: 'eq';
        $collection->addFieldToFilter($filter->getField(),
[$condition => $filter->getValue()]);
    }
}
```

The preceding code simply loops through all filter groups, pulling in all filters within the group and calling the same `addFieldToFilter` method for everything. Similar behavior is implemented across core Magento modules. Although the filtering itself follows the `\Magento\Framework\Api\SearchCriteriaInterface` interface, there is no unified Magento-wide approach to force AND and OR operators in filtering.

However, Magento core API's like GET products do implement both AND and OR conditions. In cases like these, filter groups result in OR and filters within the group result in AND conditions.

 Following best practices, we should make sure our modules that implement search criteria do so respecting the `filter_groups/ filters` and OR/AND relationship.

Summary

In this chapter, we covered a lot of ground relating to Magento API's. There is much more left to be said, but the steps outlined here should be enough to get us started even with more advanced API usage. We started the chapter with learning about types of users and the authentication methods supported. Strong emphasis was placed on making several types of API calls, like console cURL, PHP cURL, PHP SoapClient, and console cURL SOAP. This was to encourage developers to understand the inner workings of API calls more deeply than just using high-level libraries.

Throughout the next chapter, we will look into some of the major sections of Magento.

10
The Major Functional Areas

The Magento platform comprises various modules that deliver various bits of functionality. Developers are often more in touch with one group of functionality than others. Examples of some of the most commonly used functionalities include those related to CMS blocks and pages, categories, products, customers, imports, custom product types, custom payment, and shipping modules. This is not to say that other functionalities are less important. In this chapter, we will take a quick look at the functionalities in the Magento admin area, PHP code, and API calls. The chapter is divided into the following sections:

- CMS management
- Catalog management
- Customer management
- Products and customer import
- Custom product types
- Custom offline shipping methods
- Custom offline payment methods

The intention is not to go into the details of each functional area. Rather, the aim is to show the admin interface and the corresponding programmatic and API approach towards basic management.

CMS management

Content is what helps differentiate one store from another. Quality content can boost a store's visibility on search engines, provide informative insight to the customers who buy products, and provide credibility and trust. Magento provides a solid content management system, which can be used to create rich content for a store. We can use it to manage blocks and pages too.

Managing blocks manually

A CMS block is a small modular unit of content that can be positioned almost anywhere on a page. They can even be called into another blocks. Blocks support HTML and JavaScript as its content. Therefore, they are able to display static information such as text, images, and embedded video as well as dynamic information.

Blocks can be created via an admin interface, APIs, or code.

The following steps outline the block creation process from within an admin interface:

1. Log in to the Magento admin area.

2. In the **Content | Elements | Blocks** menu, click on **Add New Block**. This opens a screen that is similar to the one shown in the following screenshot:

3. Fill in some values for the required fields (**Block Title**, **Identifier**, **Store View**, **Status**, and **Content**) and click on the **Save Block** button.

Once the block is saved, you will see the **You saved the block.** success message in the browser. CMS blocks are stored in the `cms_block` and `cms_block_store` tables in a database.

The **Identifier** value is probably the most interesting aspect here. We can use it in a CMS page, another CMS block, or some code to fetch the block that we have just created.

Assuming that we have created a block with the **Identifier** value of `foggyline_hello`, we can call it in the CMS page or another block by using the following expression:

```
{{widget type="Magento\\Cms\\Block\\Widget\\Block"
  template="widget/static_block/default.phtml"
  block_id="foggyline_hello"}}
```

We can also pass the actual integer ID value of a block to the preceding expression, as follows:

```
{{widget type="Magento\\Cms\\Block\\Widget\\Block"
  template="widget/static_block/default.phtml" block_id="2"}}
```

However, this approach requires us to know the actual integer ID of a block.

The preceding expressions show that blocks are included in a page or another block via a widget, which is also known as a frontend app. A widget of the `Magento\Cms\Block\Widget\Block` class type is using the `widget/static_block/default.phtml` template file to render the actual CMS block.

Managing blocks via code

Besides the manual creation of blocks via the admin interface, we can create CMS blocks by using code, as shown in the following code snippet:

```
$model = $this->_objectManager->create('Magento\Cms\Model\Block');
$model->setTitle('Test block');
$model->setIdentifier('test_block');
$model->setContent('Test block!');
$model->setIsActive(true);
$model->save();
```

Here, we used the instance manager to create a new model instance of the `Magento\Cms\Model\Block` class. Then, we set some properties through defined methods and finally called the `save` method.

We can load and update the existing blocks using a code snippet that is similar to the following code:

```
$model = $this->_objectManager->create('Magento\Cms\Model\Block');
//$model->load(3);
$model->load('test_block');
$model->setTitle('Updated Test block');
$model->setStores([0]);
$model->save();
```

The block's `load` method accepts either an integer value of a block ID or a string value of a block identifier.

Finally, we can manage the creation and updating of blocks through the available APIs method. The following code snippet shows how a CMS block is created via a console cURL REST API call:

```
curl -X POST "http://magento2.ce/index.php/rest/V1/cmsBlock" \
    -H "Content-Type:application/json" \
    -H "Authorization: Bearer lcpnsrk4t6al83lymhfs86jabbi9mmt8" \
    -d '{"block": {"identifier": "test_api_block", "title": "Test
    API Block", "content": "API Block Content"}}'
```

The bearer string is just a login token that we obtain by first running the authentication API call, as described in the previous chapter. Once we have the authentication token, we can make a `V1/cmsBlock` POST request, passing a JSON object as data.

Managing blocks via API

We can get the newly created CMS block through an API by executing a snippet of code that looks like this:

```
curl -X GET "http://magento2.ce/index.php/rest/V1/cmsBlock/4" \
    -H "Content-Type:application/json" \
    -H "Authorization: Bearer lcpnsrk4t6al83lymhfs86jabbi9mmt8"
```

We can update the existing CMS block by using an API and executing a snippet of code that is similar to this:

```
curl -X PUT "http://magento2.ce/index.php/rest/V1/cmsBlock/4" \
    -H "Content-Type:application/json" \
    -H "Authorization: Bearer lcpnsrk4t6al83lymhfs86jabbi9mmt8" \
    -d '{"block": {"title": "Updated Test API Block"}}'
```

Here, we used the HTTP PUT method and passed the integer 4 as a part of the V1/ cmsBlock/4 URL. The number 4 represents the ID value of the block in the database.

Managing pages manually

CMS pages are robust content units unlike CMS blocks, which are simply embedded into certain pages. The CMS page can have its own URL. Examples of CMS pages are pages such as **404 Not Found**, **Home page**, **Enable Cookies**, and **Privacy and Cookie Policy**. The idea, when it comes to dealing with CMS pages, is that we can control the content area of a page without affecting site-wide elements such as the header, footer, or sidebars. Magento does not really come with many out-of-the-box CMS pages other than the ones that were listed previously.

Like blocks, pages can also be created via the admin interface, APIs, or code.

The following steps outline the page creation process from within the admin interface:

1. Log in to Magento admin area.

2. In the **Content | Elements | Pages menu**, click on **Add New Page**. This opens a screen that is similar the one shown in the following screenshot:

3. Fill in some values for the required fields (**Page Title, Store View, Status, and Content**) and click on the **Save** Block button.

Once the page is saved, you will see the **You saved this page.** success message in the browser. CMS pages are stored in the `cms_page` and `cms_page_store` tables in the database.

Assuming that we have created a page with **Page Title** value **Info**, we can access this page in a browser via a URL such as `http://magento2.ce/info`. Though we could have to specify the **URL Key** value in the **New Page** edit screen, Magento automatically assigns **URL Key** that matches **Page Title**.

Managing pages via code

Besides the manual creation through the admin interface, we can create CMS pages via code, as shown in the following code snippet:

```
$model = $this->_objectManager->create('Magento\Cms\Model\Page');
$model->setTitle('Test page');
$model->setIdentifier('test-page');
$model->setPageLayout('1column');
$model->setContent('Test page!');
$model->setIsActive(true);
$model->setStores([0]);
$model->save();
```

Here, we used the instance manager to create a new model instance of the `Magento\Cms\Model\Page` class. Then, we set some properties through the defined methods and finally called the `save` method. The **URL Key** that we set through the admin interface is actually an identifier that we set via the `setIdentifier` method call.

Managing pages via API

We can load and update the existing pages by using a code snippet that is similar to the following one:

```
$model = $this->_objectManager->create('Magento\Cms\Model\Page');
//$model->load(6);
$model->load('test-page');
$model->setContent('Updated Test page!');
$model->save();
```

The page model `load` method accepts either an integer ID value of a page identifier (**URL Key**).

Finally, we can manage the creation and updating of pages through the available APIs method. The following code snippet shows how a CMS page is created via a console cURL REST API call:

```
curl -X POST "http://magento2.ce/index.php/rest/V1/cmsPage" \
    -H "Content-Type:application/json" \
    -H "Authorization: Bearer lcpnsrk4t6al83lymhfs86jabbi9mmt8" \
    -d '{"page": {"identifier": "test-api-page", "title": "Test API
    Page", "content": "API Block Content"}}'
```

Once we have the authentication token, we can make a `V1/cmsPage POST` request, passing on the JSON object as data.

We can get the newly created CMS page through an API by executing a snippet of code that is similar to the following one:

```
curl -X GET "http://magento2.ce/index.php/rest/V1/cmsPage/7" \
    -H "Content-Type:application/json" \
    -H "Authorization: Bearer lcpnsrk4t6al83lymhfs86jabbi9mmt8"
```

We can update the existing CMS page through an API by executing a snippet of code that is similar to the following one:

```
curl -X PUT "http://magento2.ce/index.php/rest/V1/cmsPage/7" \
    -H "Content-Type:application/json" \
    -H "Authorization: Bearer lcpnsrk4t6al83lymhfs86jabbi9mmt8" \
    -d '{"page": {"content": "Updated Test API Page",
    "identifier":"updated-page"}}'
```

Here, we used the HTTP PUT method, passing the integer 7 as a part of the `V1/cmsPage/7` URL. The number 7 represents the ID value of the page in the database.

Catalog management

The `Magento_Catalog` module is one of the backbones of the entire Magento platform. It provides robust support for the inventory management of various product types. This module is what manages products, categories and their attributes, the display on the frontend, and many more things.

Managing categories manually

We can access the catalog functionality within the Magento admin area by navigating to **Products** | **Inventory** | **Catalog** or **Products** | **Inventory** | **Category**.

If we start with a blank Magento installation, we will probably start with categories as one of the first entities to be created. We can manually create categories by performing the following steps:

1. Log in to the Magento admin area.

2. Go to the **Products | Inventory | Category** menu. This opens a screen that is similar to the one shown in the following screenshot:

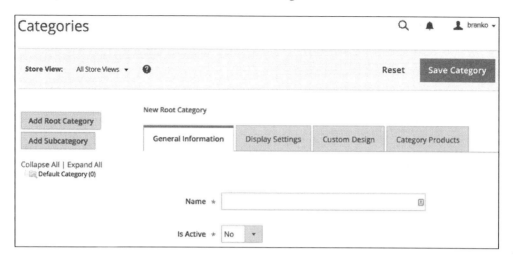

3. On the left-hand side of the screen, click on **Default Category**. Then, when the page reloads, click on the **Add Subcategory** button.

4. Though it may seem that nothing has happened, as the screen content does not change, we should now fill in the required options in the **General Information** tab, setting **Name** to some string value and **Is Active** to Yes.

5. Finally, click on the **Save Category** button.

The new category should now be created. To the left screen area, if you click on the name of the newly created category, you will see its ID value above the **General Information** tab, as shown in the following screenshot:

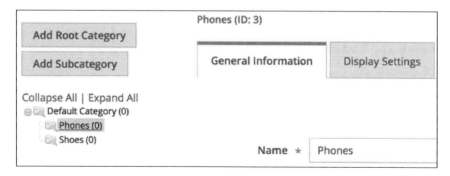

Knowing the category ID enables you to directly test it on a storefront simply by opening a URL such as `http://magento2.ce/index.php/catalog/category/view/id/3` in the browser, where the number 3 is the ID of the category. You will see a loaded category page that probably shows the **We can't find products matching the selection.** message, which is good, as we haven't assigned products to a category.

Though we will not go into its details, it is worth noting that we have simply scratched the surface here, as categories enable us to provide many additional options using the **Display Settings**, **Custom Design** tabs.

Given that categories are EAV entities, their data is stored across several tables in the database, as follows:

- `catalog_category_entity`
- `catalog_category_entity_datetime`
- `catalog_category_entity_decimal`
- `catalog_category_entity_int`
- `catalog_category_entity_text`
- `catalog_category_entity_varchar`

There are a few additional tables that link categories to products:

- `catalog_category_product`
- `catalog_category_product_index`
- `catalog_category_product_index_tmp`
- `catalog_url_rewrite_product_category`

Managing categories via code

Besides the manual creation through the admin interface, we can create categories via code, as shown in the following code snippet:

```
$parentId = \Magento\Catalog\Model\Category::TREE_ROOT_ID;

$parentCategory = $this->_objectManager
                    ->create('Magento\Catalog\Model\Category')
                    ->load($parentId);
```

```
$category = $this->_objectManager
                ->create('Magento\Catalog\Model\Category');

$category->setPath($parentCategory->getPath());
$category->setParentId($parentId);
$category->setName('Test');
$category->setIsActive(true);

$category->save();
```

What is specific here is that when creating a new category, we first created a `$parentCategory` instance, which represents the root category object. We used the `Category` model `TREE_ROOT_ID` constant as the ID value of a parent category ID. Then, we created an instance of the category, set its `path`, `parent_id`, `name`, and `is_active` value.

Managing categories via API

We can further manage category creation through the available APIs method. The following code snippet shows category creation via the console cURL REST API call:

```
curl -X POST "http://magento2.ce/index.php/rest/V1/categories" \
    -H "Content-Type:application/json" \
    -H "Authorization: Bearer lcpnsrk4t6al83lymhfs86jabbi9mmt8" \
    -d '{"category": {"parent_id": "1", "name": "Test API
    Category", "is_active": true}}'
```

The bearer string is just a login token that we obtain by first running the authentication API call, as described in the previous chapter. Once we have the authentication token, we can make a `/V1/categories POST` request, passing a JSON object as data.

We can get the newly created category as a JSON object through an API by executing a snippet of code that looks like the following one:

```
curl -X GET "http://magento2.ce/index.php/rest/V1/categories/9" \
    -H "Content-Type:application/json" \
    -H "Authorization: Bearer lcpnsrk4t6al83lymhfs86jabbi9mmt8"
```

Managing products manually

Now, let's take a look at how to create a new product. We can manually create products by performing the following steps:

1. Log in to the Magento admin area.

2. In the **Products | Inventory | Catalog** menu, click on the **Add Product** button. This opens a screen similar to the one shown in the following screenshot:

3. Now, fill in the required options on the **Product Details** tab.

4. Finally, click on the **Save** button.

If it is successfully saved, the page reloads and shows the **You saved the product.** message.

Like categories, we have barely scratched the surface of products here. Looking at the other available tabs, there are a large number of additional options that can be assigned to a product. Simply assigning the required options should be enough for us to see the product on the store's frontend on a URL such as `http://magento2.ce/index.php/catalog/product/view/id/4`, where the number 4 is the ID value of a product.

Products are also EAV entities, whose data is stored across several tables in a database, as follows:

- `catalog_product_entity`
- `catalog_product_entity_datetime`
- `catalog_product_entity_decimal`
- `catalog_product_entity_gallery`
- `catalog_product_entity_group_price`
- `catalog_product_entity_int`
- `catalog_product_entity_media_gallery`
- `catalog_product_entity_media_gallery_value`
- `catalog_product_entity_text`
- `catalog_product_entity_tier_price`
- `catalog_product_entity_varchar`

There are also a large number of other table referencing products, such as `catalog_product_bundle_selection`, but these are mostly used to link bits of functionalities.

Managing products via code

Besides the manual creation through the admin interface, we can create products via code, as shown in the following code snippet:

```
$catalogConfig = $this->_objectManager
    ->create('Magento\Catalog\Model\Config');

$attributeSetId = $catalogConfig->getAttributeSetId(4, 'Default');

$product = $this->_objectManager
    ->create('Magento\Catalog\Model\Product');

$product
    ->setTypeId(\Magento\Catalog\Model\Product\Type::TYPE_SIMPLE)
    ->setAttributeSetId($attributeSetId)
    ->setWebsiteIds([$this->storeManager->getWebsite()->getId()])
    ->setStatus(\Magento\Catalog\Model\Product\Attribute
      \Source\Status::STATUS_ENABLED)
```

```
    ->setStockData(['is_in_stock' => 1, 'manage_stock' => 0])
    ->setStoreId(\Magento\Store\Model\Store::DEFAULT_STORE_ID)
    ->setVisibility(\Magento\Catalog\Model\Product
      \Visibility::VISIBILITY_BOTH);

$product
    ->setName('Test API')
    ->setSku('tets-api')
    ->setPrice(19.99);

$product->save();
```

Managing products via API

The following example uses the REST API to create a new simple product:

```
curl -X POST "http://magento2.ce/index.php/rest/V1/products" \
    -H "Content-Type:application/json" \
    -H "Authorization: Bearer lcpnsrk4t6al83lymhfs86jabbi9mmt8" \
    -d '{"product":{"sku":"test_api_1","name":"Test API
    #1","attribute_set_id":4,"price":19.99,"status":1,
    "visibility":4,"type_id":"simple","weight":1}}'
```

The `Bearer` token should have been previously obtained by using an authentication request. The response should be a JSON object that contains all the exposed product data.

We can get the existing product as information through an API that executes a snippet of code, as follows:

```
curl -X GET "http://magento2.ce/index.php/rest/V1/products
/product_dynamic_125" \
    -H "Content-Type:application/json"
```

The `product_dynamic_125` part in the preceding URL stands for this specific product SKU value. The response is a JSON object that contains all the exposed product data.

The entire list of the available catalog APIs can be seen in the `vendor/magento/module-catalog/etc/webapi.xml` file.

Customer management

Managing customers is another important aspect of the Magento platform. Most of the time, customer creation is something that is left for a new customer to do. A new customer who visits a store initiates the registration process and finishes up with a customer account being created. Once registered, customers can then further edit their account details on the storefront under the **My Account** page, which is usually available on a link such as `http://magento2.ce/index.php/customer/account/index/`.

As a part of this section, we are interested in the possibility of managing customer accounts by using the admin area, code, and API.

Managing customers manually

The following steps outline the customer account creation process from within the admin interface:

1. Log in to Magento admin area.

2. In the **Customers | All Customers** menu, click on the **Add New Customer** button. This opens a screen that looks similar to the one shown in the following screenshot:

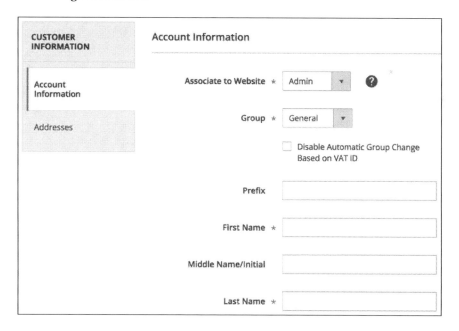

3. Fill in some values for the required fields (**Associate to Website, Group, First Name, Last Name,** and **Email**) and click on the **Save Customer** button.

Once the customer is saved, you will see the **You saved the customer.** success message in the browser.

The **Associate to Website** value is probably the most important value for cases like this one, where customer accounts are being indirectly created by a user who's not a customer.

 Since Magento supports the setting up of multiple websites, customer accounts can be set to either the **Global** or **Per Website** value, depending on the **Stores | Settings | Configuration | Customers | Customer Configuration | Account Sharing Option | Share Customer Accounts** option. Thus, if the **Share Customer Accounts** option has been set to **Per Website**, it is of the utmost important to point the **Associate to Website** value to the proper website. Otherwise, a customer account will be created but the customer won't be able to log in to it on the storefront.

The `Magento_Customer` module uses the EAV structure to store customer data. Thus, there is no single table that stores customer information. Rather, multiple tables exist, depending on the customer property and its data type.

The following list comprises tables that store customer entity:

- `customer_entity`
- `customer_entity_datetime`
- `customer_entity_decimal`
- `customer_entity_int`
- `customer_entity_text`
- `customer_entity_varchar`

Customer accounts will not really be complete without a customer address. The address can be added via the **Addresses** tab under the customer edit screen in the admin area, as shown in the following screenshot:

Note that Magento enables us to set one of the addresses as **Default Shipping Address** and **Default Billing Address**.

Like the customer entity, the customer address entity also uses the EAV structure to store its data.

The following list comprises tables that store the customer address entity:

- `customer_address_entity`
- `customer_address_entity_datetime`
- `customer_address_entity_decimal`
- `customer_address_entity_int`
- `customer_address_entity_text`
- `customer_address_entity_varchar`

Managing customers via code

Besides the manual creation via the admin interface, we can create customers via code, as shown in the following code snippet:

```
$model = $this->_objectManager->
    create('Magento\Customer\Model\Customer');
$model->setWebsiteId(1);
$model->setGroupId(1);
$model->setFirstname('John');
$model->setLastname('Doe');
$model->setEmail('john.doe@mail.com');
$model->save();
```

Here, we are using the instance manager to create a new model instance of the `Magento\Customer\Model\Customer` class. We can then set some properties through the defined methods and finally call the `save` method.

We can load and update an existing customer by using a code snippet that is similar to the following one:

```
$model = $this->_objectManager->
    create('Magento\Customer\Model\Customer');
$model->setWebsiteId(1);
//$model->loadByEmail('john.doe@mail.com');
$model->load(1);
$model->setFirstname('Updated John');
$model->save();
```

We can use either the `load` or `loadByEmail` method call. The `load` method accepts the integer ID value of the existing customer entity, while `loadByEmail` accepts a string e-mail address. It is worth noting that `setWebsiteId` has to be called prior to any of the load methods. Otherwise, we will get an error message that says **A customer website ID must be specified when using the website scope**.

Managing customers via an API

Finally, we can manage the creation and updating of customer information using the available API method. The following code snippet shows how to create a customer via a console cURL REST API call:

```
curl -X POST "http://magento2.ce/index.php/rest/V1/customers" \
    -H "Content-Type:application/json" \
```

```
-H "Authorization: Bearer r9ok12c3wsusrxqomyxiwo0v7etujw9h" \
-d '{"customer": {"website_id": 1, "group_id": 1, "firstname":
"John", "lastname": "Doe", "email": "john.doe@mail.com"},
"password":"abc123"}'
```

Once we have the authentication token, we can make a `V1/customers` POST request, passing a JSON object as data.

We can get the newly created customer via an API by executing a snippet of code that is similar to the following one:

```
curl -X GET "http://magento2.ce/index.php/rest/V1/customers/24" \
    -H "Content-Type:application/json" \
    -H "Authorization: Bearer lcpnsrk4t6al83lymhfs86jabbi9mmt8"
```

We can update an existing customer through an API by executing a snippet of code that is similar to the following one:

```
curl -X PUT "http://magento2.ce/index.php/rest/V1/customers/24" \
    -H "Content-Type:application/json" \
    -H "Authorization: Bearer r9ok12c3wsusrxqomyxiwo0v7etujw9h" \
    -d '{"customer": {"id":24, "website_id": 1, "firstname": "John
    Updated", "lastname": "Doe", "email": "john2@mail.com"},
    "password_hash":"cda57c7995e5f03fe07ad52d99686ba130e0d3e
    fe0d84dd5ee9fe7f6ea632650:cEf8i1f1ZXT1L2NwawTRNEqDWGyru6h3:1"}'
```

Here, we used the HTTP PUT method, passing the integer 24 as a part of the `V1/customers/24` and as part of the body URL. The number 24 represents the ID value of a customer in the database. Also, note the `password_hash` value; without it, the update will fail.

Managing customer address via code

Similar to customers, we can create a customer address using code, as shown in the following code snippet:

```
$model = $this->_objectManager->
    create('Magento\Customer\Model\Address');
//$model->setCustomer($customer);
$model->setCustomerId(24);
$model->setFirstname('John');
$model->setLastname('Doe');
```

```
$model->setCompany('Foggyline');
$model->setStreet('Test street');
$model->setCity('London');
$model->setCountryId('GB');
$model->setPostcode('GU22 7PY');
$model->setTelephone('112233445566');
$model->setIsDefaultBilling(true);
$model->setIsDefaultShipping(true);
$model->save();
```

Here, we used the instance manager to create a new model instance of the `Magento\Customer\Model\Address` class. We then set some properties through the defined methods and finally called the `save` method.

We can load and update the existing customer address by using a code snippet that is similar to the following one:

```
$model = $this->_objectManager->
    create('Magento\Customer\Model\Address');
$model->load(22);
$model->setCity('Update London');
$model->save();
```

Here, we used the `load` method to load an existing address by its ID value. Then, we called the `setCity` method passing it the updated string. After the `save` method is executed, the address should reflect the change.

Managing customers address via an API

Surprisingly, a customer address cannot be created or updated directly via an API call, as there is no POST or PUT REST API defined. However, we can still get the existing customer address information by using an API, as follows:

```
curl -X GET "http://magento2.ce/index.php/rest/V1/customers
/addresses/22" \
    -H "Content-Type:application/json" \
    -H "Authorization: Bearer 1cpnsrk4t6al83lymhfs86jabbi9mmt8"
```

The entire list of available customer APIs can be seen in the `vendor/magento/module-customer/etc/webapi.xml` file.

Products and customers import

Magento provides an out-of-the-box mass import and export functionality via the following modules:

- `AdvancedPricingImportExport`

- `BundleImportExport`

- `CatalogImportExport`

- `ConfigurableImportExport`

- `CustomerImportExport`

- `GroupedImportExport`

- `ImportExport`

- `TaxImportExport`

The heart of the import functionality actually lies in the `ImportExport` module, while other modules provide individual import and export entities through the `vendor/magento/module-{partialModuleName}-import-export/etc/import.xml` and `vendor/magento/module-{partialModuleName}-import-export/etc/export.xml` files.

These functionalities can be accessed from the Magento admin area from the **System | Data Transfer** menu. They enable us to export and import several entity types, such as **Advanced Pricing**, **Products**, **Customers Main File**, and **Customer Addresses**.

The following screenshot shows the **Entity Type** options for the **Import Settings** screen:

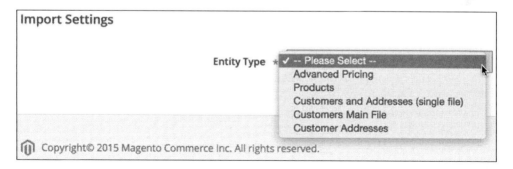

Next to **Import Settings**, when we select **Entity Type** for import, the **Import Behavior** section appears, as shown in the following screenshot:

Most entity types have similar options for **Import Behavior**. Most of the time, we will be interested in the **Add/Update** behavior.

Since importing is a bit more complicated process than exporting, we will focus on importing and the CSV file format. More specifically, our focus is on **Products**, **Customers Main File**, and **Customer Addresses** imports.

When working with a clean Magento installation, the following columns are required during the product import in order to make the product visible on the storefront afterwards:

- `sku` (for example, "test-sku"): This can have almost any value as long as it is unique across Magento.

- `attribute_set_code` (for example, "Default"): This can have any of the values found in a database when the `SELECT DISTINCT attribute_set_name FROM eav_attribute_set;` query is executed.

- `product_type` (for example, "simple"): This can have the values of `simple`, `configurable`, `grouped`, `virtual`, `bundle`, or `downloadable`. Additionally, if we create or install a third-party module that adds a new product type, we can use that one as well.

- `categories` (for example, "Root/Shoes"): Create a full category path using the "Root category name/Child category name/Child child category name" syntax. If there are multiple categories, then a pipe ("|") is used to separate them. An example of this is "Root category name/Child category name/ Child child category name| Root category name/Child_2 category name".

- `product_websites` (for example, "base"): This can have the values found in a database when the `SELECT DISTINCT code FROM store_website;` query is executed.

- `name` (for example, "Test"): This can have almost any value.

- `product_online` (for example, "1"): This can be either 1 for `visible` or 0 for `not visible`

- `visibility` (for example, "Catalog, Search"): This can have the values of "Not Visible Individually", "Catalog", "Search", or "Catalog, Search".

- `price` (for example, "9.99"): This can be an integer or a decimal value.

- `qty` (for example, "100"): This can be an integer or a decimal value.

Though the products will get imported just with the preceding list that comprises a set of columns, we usually would like to assign additional information to them, such as descriptions and images. We can do so with the help of the following columns:

- `description` (for example, "The description"): This can have any string value. HTML and JavaScript are supported.

- `short_description` (for example, "The short description"): This can have any string value. HTML and JavaScript are supported.

- `base_image` (for example, `butterfly.jpg`): This is the final import image name.

- `small_image` (for example, `galaxy.jpg`)

- `thumbnail_image` (for example, `serenity.jpg`)

Regarding the importing of images, we only need to provide the final image name as long as the **Images File Directory** path is set during the import. We can use a relative path for the Magento installation, such as `var/export`, `var/import`, `var/export/some/dir`.

Once the import is finished, it is suggested to run the `php bin/magento indexer:reindex` command via the console. Otherwise, the products won't be visible on the storefront until the indexer is run.

Once the reindexing is done, we can try opening the storefront URL, which looks like `http://magento2.ce/index.php/catalog/product/view/id/1`. The number 1 in this case is a newly imported product ID.

When working with a clean Magento installation, the following columns are required during a customer's main file import in order for our customer to be able to successfully log in to the storefront afterwards:

- `email` (for example, `john.doe@fake.mail`): an e-mail address as a string value

- `_website` (for example, base): This can have any of the values found in the database when the `SELECT DISTINCT code FROM store_website;` query is executed

- `firstname` (for example, John): a string value

- `lastname` (for example, Doe): a string value

- `group_id` (for example, 1): This can have any of the values found in the database when the `SELECT customer_group_id code FROM customer_group WHERE customer_group_id != 0;` query is executed

Though a customer will be able to log in to the storefront with just the previously listed set of columns, we usually would like to assign other relevant pieces of information. We can do so with the help of the following columns:

- `gender` (for example, Male): This can be either Male or Female

- `taxvat` (for example, HR33311122299): any valid VAT number, though an import will accept even the invalid ones

- `dob` (for example, 1983-01-16): date of birth

- `prefix` (for example, Mr): any string value

- `middlename` (for example, the dev guy): any string value

- `suffix` (for example, engineer): any string value

- `password` (for example, 123abc): any string value that has a minimum length of 6 characters, as defined via `\Magento\CustomerImportExport\Model\Import\Customer::MIN_PASSWORD_LENGTH`

We need to pay special attention to the `password` column. This is a clear text password. Therefore, we need to be careful not to distribute a CSV file in a nonsecure manner. Ideally, we can provide the `password_hash` column instead of `password`. However, entries under the `password_hash` column will need to be hashed via the same algorithm as the one that was called within the `hashPassword` method of the `Magento\Customer\Model\Customer` class. This further calls the `getHash` method on an instance of the `Magento\Framework\Encryption\Encryptor` class, which finally resolves to the `md5` or `sha256` algorithm.

When working with a clean Magento installation, the following columns are required during the customer address import in order for our customers to be able to successfully use the addresses on the storefront afterwards:

- _website (for example, base): This can have any of the values found in the database when the SELECT DISTINCT code FROM store_website; query is executed

- _email (for example, john@change.me): an e-mail address as a string value

- _entity_id

- firstname (for example, John): any string value

- lastname (for example, Doe): any string value

- street (for example, Ashton Lane): any string value

- city (for example, Austin): any string value

- telephone (for example, 00 385 91 111 000): any string value

- country_id (for example, GB): the country code in the ISO-2 format

- postcode (for example, TX 78753): any string value

Though a customer will be able to use the addresses on the storefront with just a listed set of columns, we usually would like to assign other relevant pieces of information. We can do so with the help of the following columns:

- region (for example, California): This can be blank, a free form string, or a specific string that matches any of the values found in the database when the SELECT DISTINCT default_name FROM directory_country_region; query is executed. On running SELECT DISTINCT country_id FROM directory_country_region;, 13 different country codes that have entries within the directory_country_region table are shown—AT, BR, CA, CH, DE, EE, ES, FI, FR, LT, LV, RO, US. This means that countries with that code need to have a proper region name assigned.

- company (for example, Foggyline): This can be any string value.

- fax (for example, 00 385 91 111 000): This can be any string value.

- middlename (for example, the developer): This can be any string value.

- prefix (for example, Mr): This can be any string value.

- suffix (for example, engineer): This can be any string value.

- `vat_id` (for example, HR33311122299): This can be any valid VAT number, though import will accept even the non-valid ones.
- `_address_default_billing_` (for example, "1"): This can be either "1" as yes or "0" as no, to flag the address as being the default billing address.
- `_address_default_shipping_` (for example, "1"): This can be either "1" as yes or "0" as no, to flag the address as being default shipping address.

While CSV imports are a great and relatively fast way to mass import products, customers, and their addresses, there are some limitations to it. CSV is simply flat data. We cannot apply any logic to it. Depending on how clean and valid the data is, the CSV import might do just fine. Otherwise, we might want to opt for APIs. We need to keep in mind that a CSV import is much faster than the API creation of products and customers because CSV imports work directly by bulk inserting on the database, while APIs instantiate full models, respect the event observers, and so on.

The custom product types

Magento provides the following six out-of-the-box product types:

- Simple products
- Configurable products
- Grouped products
- Virtual products
- Bundle products
- Downloadable products

Each product has its specifics. For example, the virtual and downloadable products do not have the `weight` attribute. Therefore, they are excluded from the standard shipping calculations. With custom coding around built-in product types, by using observers and plugins we can achieve almost any functionality. However, this is not enough sometimes or there is no solution to the requirement. In cases such as these, we might need to create our own product type that will match the project requirements in a more streamlined way.

Let's create a miniature module called `Foggyline_DailyDeal` that will add a new product type to Magento.

Start by creating a module registration file named app/code/Foggyline/
DailyDeal/registration.php that has the following partial content:

```
\Magento\Framework\Component\ComponentRegistrar::register(
    \Magento\Framework\Component\ComponentRegistrar::MODULE,
    'Foggyline_DailyDeal',
    __DIR__
);
```

Then, create an app/code/Foggyline/DailyDeal/etc/module.xml with the
following content:

```
<config xmlns:xsi="http://www.w3.org/2001/XMLSchema-instance"
  xsi:noNamespaceSchemaLocation="urn:magento:framework:Module
  /etc/module.xsd">
    <module name="Foggyline_DailyDeal" setup_version="1.0.0">
        <sequence>
            <module name="Magento_Catalog"/>
        </sequence>
    </module>
</config>
```

Now, create an app/code/Foggyline/DailyDeal/etc/product_types.xml file that
has the following content:

```
<config xmlns:xsi="http://www.w3.org/2001/XMLSchema-instance"
  xsi:noNamespaceSchemaLocation="urn:magento:module:
  Magento_Catalog:etc/product_types.xsd">
    <type name="foggylinedailydeal"
        label="Daily Deal"
        modelInstance="Foggyline\DailyDeal\Model\Product\Type
          \DailyDeal"
        composite="false"
        isQty="true"
        canUseQtyDecimals="false">
        <priceModel instance="Foggyline\DailyDeal\Model
          \Product\Price"/>
        <indexerModel instance="Foggyline\DailyDeal\Model
          \ResourceModel\Indexer\Price"/>
        <stockIndexerModel instance="Foggyline\DailyDeal\Model
          \ResourceModel\Indexer\Stock"/>
        <!-- customAttributes parsed by
          Magento\Catalog\Model\ProductTypes\Config -->
        <customAttributes>
```

```
            <attribute name="is_real_product" value="true"/>
            <attribute name="refundable" value="false"/>
            <attribute name="taxable" value="true"/>
        </customAttributes>
      </type>
</config>
```

The `customAttributes` **element is parsed by** `vendor/magento/module-catalog/Model/ProductTypes/Config.php`.

Create an `app/code/Foggyline/DailyDeal/Model/Product/Type/DailyDeal.php` **file with partial content, as follows:**

```
namespace Foggyline\DailyDeal\Model\Product\Type;

class DailyDeal extends
  \Magento\Catalog\Model\Product\Type\AbstractType
{
    const TYPE_DAILY_DEAL = 'foggylinedailydeal';

    public function deleteTypeSpecificData
      (\Magento\Catalog\Model\Product $product)
    {
        // TODO: Implement deleteTypeSpecificData() method.
    }
}
```

Now, create an `app/code/Foggyline/DailyDeal/Model/Product/Price.php` **file with partial content, as follows:**

```
namespace Foggyline\DailyDeal\Model\Product;

class Price extends \Magento\Catalog\Model\Product\Type\Price
{

}
```

After this is done, create an `app/code/Foggyline/DailyDeal/Model/ResourceModel/Indexer/Price.php` **file with partial content, as follows:**

```
namespace Foggyline\DailyDeal\Model\ResourceModel\Indexer;

class Price extends \Magento\Catalog\Model\ResourceModel\Product
  \Indexer\Price\DefaultPrice
{
}
```

Then, create an app/code/Foggyline/DailyDeal/Model/ResourceModel/ Indexer/Stock.php file with partial content, as follows:

```
namespace Foggyline\DailyDeal\Model\ResourceModel\Indexer;

class Stock extends \Magento\CatalogInventory\Model\ResourceModel
  \Indexer\Stock\DefaultStock
{

}
```

Finally, create an app/code/Foggyline/DailyDeal/Setup/InstallData.php file with partial content, as follows:

```
namespace Foggyline\DailyDeal\Setup;

class InstallData implements
  \Magento\Framework\Setup\InstallDataInterface
{
    private $eavSetupFactory;

    public function __construct(\Magento\Eav\Setup\EavSetupFactory
      $eavSetupFactory)
    {
        $this->eavSetupFactory = $eavSetupFactory;
    }

    public function install(
        \Magento\Framework\Setup\ModuleDataSetupInterface $setup,
        \Magento\Framework\Setup\ModuleContextInterface $context
    )
    {
        // the "foggylinedailydeal" type specifics
    }
}
```

Extend the install method from within the InstallData class by adding the following foggylinedailydeal type specifics to it:

```
$eavSetup = $this->eavSetupFactory->create(['setup' => $setup]);
$type = \Foggyline\DailyDeal\Model\Product\Type\
  DailyDeal::TYPE_DAILY_DEAL;

$fieldList = [
    'price',
```

```
        'special_price',
        'special_from_date',
        'special_to_date',
        'minimal_price',
        'cost',
        'tier_price',
        'weight',
    ];

    // make these attributes applicable to foggylinedailydeal products
    foreach ($fieldList as $field) {
        $applyTo = explode(
            ',',
            $eavSetup->getAttribute
              (\Magento\Catalog\Model\Product::ENTITY, $field,
              'apply_to')
        );

        if (!in_array($type, $applyTo)) {
            $applyTo[] = $type;
            $eavSetup->updateAttribute(
                \Magento\Catalog\Model\Product::ENTITY,
                $field,
                'apply_to',
                implode(',', $applyTo)
            );
        }
    }
}
```

Now, run `php bin/magento setup:upgrade` from the console.

If you now open the **Products | Inventory | Catalog** menu in the admin area and click on the dropdown icon next to the **Add Product** button, you will see the **Daily Deal** product type on the list, as shown in the following screenshot:

Clicking on the **Daily Deal** product type in the dropdown list should open the product edit page, as shown in the following screenshot:

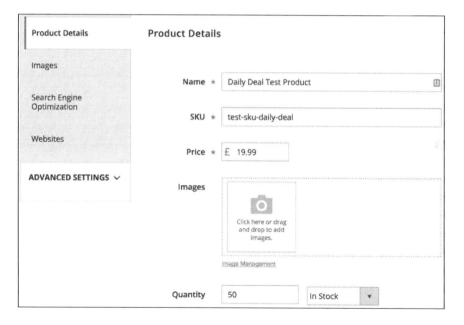

There is no noticeable difference between the custom product type edit screen and one of the built-in product types.

Assuming that we have named the product `Daily Deal Test Product` and saved it, we should be able to see it on the storefront, as shown in the following screenshot:

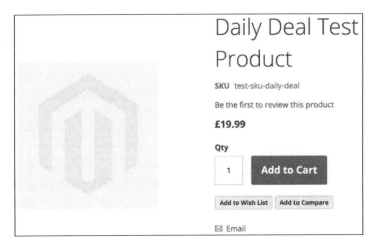

If we add the product to the cart and perform a checkout, an order should be created just as with any other product type. Within the admin area, on the order view page, under **Items Ordered**, we should be able to see the product on the list, as shown in the following screenshot:

Items Ordered

Product	Item Status	Original Price	Price	Qty	Subtotal	Tax Amount	Tax Percent	Discount Amount	Row Total
Daily Deal Test Product	Ordered	£19.99	£19.99	Ordered 1	£19.99	£0.00	0%	£0.00	£19.99
SKU: test-sku-daily-deal									

Again, there is no noticeable difference between the custom product type and the built-in product type that is rendering under the **Items Ordered** section.

Finally, we should run the `php bin/magento indexer:reindex` command on the console. Even though we haven't really implemented any code within the indexers, this is just to ensure that none of the existing indexers broke.

The entire module code can be downloaded from `https://github.com/ajzele/ B05032-Foggyline_DailyDeal`.

Custom offline shipping methods

Magento provides several out-of-the-box offline shipping methods, such as `Flatrate`, `Freeshipping`, `Pickup`, and `Tablerate`. We can see those in the `vendor/magento/module-offline-shipping/Model/Carrier` directory.

However, project requirements quite often are such that we need a custom coded shipping method where a special business logic is applied. Thus, the shipping price calculation can be controlled by us. In such cases, knowing how to code our own offline shipping method might come in handy.

Let's go ahead and create a small module called `Foggyline_Shipbox` that provides Magento an extra offline shipping method.

Start by creating a module registration file named `app/code/Foggyline/Shipbox/registration.php` with partial content, as follows:

```
\Magento\Framework\Component\ComponentRegistrar::register(
    \Magento\Framework\Component\ComponentRegistrar::MODULE,
    'Foggyline_Shipbox',
    __DIR__
);
```

Then, create an `app/code/Foggyline/Shipbox/etc/module.xml` file with the following content:

```
<config xmlns:xsi="http://www.w3.org/2001/XMLSchema-instance"
  xsi:noNamespaceSchemaLocation="urn:magento:framework:Module
  /etc/module.xsd">
    <module name="Foggyline_Shipbox" setup_version="1.0.0">
        <sequence>
            <module name="Magento_OfflineShipping"/>
        </sequence>
    </module>
</config>
```

Now, create an `app/code/Foggyline/Shipbox/etc/config.xml` file with content, as follows:

```
<config xmlns:xsi="http://www.w3.org/2001/XMLSchema-instance"
  xsi:noNamespaceSchemaLocation="urn:magento:module:Magento_Store
  :etc/config.xsd">
    <default>
        <carriers>
            <shipbox>
```

```
            <active>0</active>
            <sallowspecific>0</sallowspecific>
            <model>
              Foggyline\Shipbox\Model\Carrier\Shipbox</model>
            <name>Shipbox</name>
            <price>4.99</price>
            <title>Foggyline Shipbox</title>
            <specificerrmsg>This shipping method is not
              available. To use this shipping method, please
              contact us.</specificerrmsg>
          </shipbox>
        </carriers>
      </default>
  </config>
```

After this is done, create an `app/code/Foggyline/Shipbox/etc/adminhtml/ system.xml` file with content, as follows:

```xml
<config xmlns:xsi="http://www.w3.org/2001/XMLSchema-instance"
  xsi:noNamespaceSchemaLocation="urn:magento:module:
  Magento_Config:etc/system_file.xsd">
    <system>
        <section id="carriers">
            <group id="shipbox" translate="label" type="text"
              sortOrder="99" showInDefault="1" showInWebsite="1"
              showInStore="1">
                <label>Foggyline Shipbox</label>
                <field id="active" translate="label" type="select"
                  sortOrder="1" showInDefault="1"
                  showInWebsite="1" showInStore="0">
                    <label>Enabled</label>
                    <source_model>
                      Magento\Config\Model\Config\Source\Yesno
                      </source_model>
                </field>
                <field id="name" translate="label" type="text"
                 sortOrder="3" showInDefault="1" showInWebsite="1"
                 showInStore="1">
                    <label>Method Name</label>
                </field>
                <field id="price" translate="label" type="text"
                  sortOrder="5" showInDefault="1"
                  showInWebsite="1" showInStore="0">
                    <label>Price</label>
```

```
            <validate>validate-number validate-zero-or-
                greater</validate>
        </field>
        <field id="title" translate="label" type="text"
            sortOrder="2" showInDefault="1"
            showInWebsite="1" showInStore="1">
                <label>Title</label>
        </field>
        <field id="sallowspecific" translate="label"
            type="select" sortOrder="90" showInDefault="1"
            showInWebsite="1" showInStore="0">
                <label>Ship to Applicable Countries</label>
                <frontend_class>shipping-applicable-country
                    </frontend_class>
                <source_model>
                    Magento\Shipping\Model\Config\Source
                    \Allspecificcountries </source_model>
        </field>
        <field id="specificcountry" translate="label"
            type="multiselect" sortOrder="91"
            showInDefault="1" showInWebsite="1"
            showInStore="0">
                <label>Ship to Specific Countries</label>
                <source_model> Magento\Directory\Model
                    \Config\Source\Country </source_model>
                <can_be_empty>1</can_be_empty>
        </field>
    </group>
  </section>
 </system>
</config>
```

Now, create an `app/code/Foggyline/Shipbox/Model/Carrier/Shipbox.php` file
with partial content, as follows:

```
namespace Foggyline\Shipbox\Model\Carrier;

use Magento\Quote\Model\Quote\Address\RateRequest;

class Shipbox extends
  \Magento\Shipping\Model\Carrier\AbstractCarrier
    implements \Magento\Shipping\Model\Carrier\CarrierInterface
{
```

```
    protected $_code = 'shipbox';
    protected $_isFixed = true;
    protected $_rateResultFactory;
    protected $_rateMethodFactory;

    public function __construct(
        \Magento\Framework\App\Config\ScopeConfigInterface
          $scopeConfig,
        \Magento\Quote\Model\Quote\Address\RateResult\ErrorFactory
          $rateErrorFactory,
        \Psr\Log\LoggerInterface $logger,
        \Magento\Shipping\Model\Rate\ResultFactory
          $rateResultFactory,
        \Magento\Quote\Model\Quote\Address\RateResult
          \MethodFactory $rateMethodFactory,
        array $data = []
    )
    {

        $this->_rateResultFactory = $rateResultFactory;
        $this->_rateMethodFactory = $rateMethodFactory;
        parent::__construct($scopeConfig, $rateErrorFactory,
          $logger, $data);
    }

    public function collectRates(RateRequest $request)
    {
        //implement business logic
    }

    public function getAllowedMethods()
    {
        return ['shipbox' => $this->getConfigData('name')];
    }
}
```

Extend the `collectRates` method in the `Carrier\Shipbox` class, as follows:

```
public function collectRates(RateRequest $request)
{
    if (!$this->getConfigFlag('active')) {
        return false;
```

```
    }

    //Do some filtering of items in cart
    if ($request->getAllItems()) {
        foreach ($request->getAllItems() as $item) {
            //$item->getQty();
            //$item->getFreeShipping()
            //$item->isShipSeparately()
            //$item->getHasChildren()
            //$item->getProduct()->isVirtual()
            //...
        }
    }

    //After filtering, start forming final price
    //Final price does not have to be fixed like below
    $shippingPrice = $this->getConfigData('price');
    $result = $this->_rateResultFactory->create();

    $method = $this->_rateMethodFactory->create();

    $method->setCarrier('shipbox');
    $method->setCarrierTitle($this->getConfigData('title'));

    $method->setMethod('shipbox');
    $method->setMethodTitle($this->getConfigData('name'));

    $method->setPrice($shippingPrice);
    $method->setCost($shippingPrice);

    $result->append($method);

    return $result;
}
```

In the Magento admin area, if you now look under **Stores | Settings | Configuration | Sales | Shipping Methods**, you will see **Foggyline Shipbox** on the list, as shown in the following screenshot:

Set the **Enabled** option to **Yes** and click the **Save Config** button.

If you now run the SELECT * FROM core_config_data WHERE path LIKE "%shipbox%"; query on the MySQL server, you will see results that are similar to the ones shown in the following screenshot:

config_id	scope	scope_id	path	value
426	default	0	carriers/shipbox/active	1
427	default	0	carriers/shipbox/title	Foggyline Shipbox
428	default	0	carriers/shipbox/name	Shipbox
429	default	0	carriers/shipbox/price	4.99
430	default	0	carriers/shipbox/sallowspecific	1
431	default	0	carriers/shipbox/specificcountry	HR,GB,US

Note how there is no direct code within the code snippets in the preceding screenshot that is related to the **Ship to Applicable Countries** and **Ship to Specific Countries** options, because the handling of these options is built into the parent `AbstractCarrier` class. Thus, simply by adding the `sallowspecific` option in `config.xml` and `system.xml`, we enabled a feature where the shipping method can be shown or hidden from certain countries.

The crux of the implementation comes down to the `collectRates` method. This is where we implement our own business logic that should calculate the shipping price based on the items in the cart. We can use the `$request->getAllItems()` in the `collectRates` method to fetch the collection of all the cart items, traverse through them, form a final shipping price based on various conditions, and so on.

Now, let's go ahead and jump to the storefront in order to test the checkout. We should be able to see our method on the checkout, as shown in the following screenshot:

Shipping Methods		
● £4.99	Fixed	Foggyline Shipbox
○ £5.00	Fixed	Flat Rate

If we complete one order, we should further see the shipping method details on the order itself. Within the admin area, under **Sales | Operations | Orders**, if we **View** our order in the **Payment & Shipping Method** section, we should see the shipping method, as shown in the following screenshot:

Payment & Shipping Method

Payment Information	Shipping & Handling Information
Check / Money order	**Foggyline Shipbox - Fixed** £4.99
The order was placed using GBP.	

Similarly, in the **Order Totals** section, we should see the shipping amount in **Shipping & Handling**, as shown in the following screenshot:

Order Totals	
Subtotal	£10.00
Shipping & Handling	£4.99
Grand Total	**£14.99**
Total Paid	**£0.00**
Total Refunded	**£0.00**
Total Due	**£14.99**

With this, we conclude our custom offline shipping method module. The full module can be found at `https://github.com/ajzele/B05032-Foggyline_Shipbox`.

Custom offline payment methods

Magento provides several out-of-the-box offline payment methods, such as `Banktransfer`, `Cashondelivery`, `Checkmo`, and `Purchaseorder`. You can see them in the `vendor/magento/module-offline-payments/Model` directory.

When it comes to payment methods, it is more common to use an online payment provider (gateway), such as PayPal or Braintree. Sometimes, project requirements may be such that we may need a custom coded payment method. You will need to think of programmatic product import and order creation script that might specialize in some specifically labeled payment method. Thus, the payment process will be controlled by us.

In such cases, knowing how to code our own offline payment method might come in handy. It is worth noting that while we can make an offline payment that will grab a user's credit card information, it is not really advisable to do so unless our infrastructure is PCI-compliant.

Let's go ahead and create a small module called `Foggyline_Paybox` that provides Magento an extra offline payment method.

Start by creating a module registration file named app/code/Foggyline/Paybox/ registration.php with partial content, as follows:

```
\Magento\Framework\Component\ComponentRegistrar::register(
    \Magento\Framework\Component\ComponentRegistrar::MODULE,
    'Foggyline_Paybox',
    __DIR__
);
```

Then, create an app/code/Foggyline/Paybox/etc/module.xml file with the following content:

```
<config xmlns:xsi="http://www.w3.org/2001/XMLSchema-instance"
  xsi:noNamespaceSchemaLocation="urn:magento:framework:Module
  /etc/module.xsd">
    <module name="Foggyline_Paybox" setup_version="1.0.0">
        <sequence>
            <module name="Magento_OfflinePayments"/>
        </sequence>
    </module>
</config>
```

After this is done, create an app/code/Foggyline/Paybox/etc/config.xml file with the following content:

```
<config xmlns:xsi="http://www.w3.org/2001/XMLSchema-instance"
  xsi:noNamespaceSchemaLocation="urn:magento:module:
  Magento_Store:etc/config.xsd">
    <default>
        <payment>
            <paybox>
                <active>0</active>
                <model>Foggyline\Paybox\Model\Paybox</model>
                <order_status>pending</order_status>
                <title>Foggyline Paybox</title>
                <allowspecific>0</allowspecific>
                <group>offline</group>
            </paybox>
        </payment>
    </default>
</config>
```

Then, create the app/code/Foggyline/Paybox/etc/payment.xml file with the following content:

```
<payment xmlns:xsi="http://www.w3.org/2001/XMLSchema-instance"
  xsi:noNamespaceSchemaLocation="urn:magento:module:
  Magento_Payment:etc/payment.xsd">
    <methods>
        <method name="paybox">
            <allow_multiple_address>1</allow_multiple_address>
        </method>
    </methods>
</payment>
```

Now, create an app/code/Foggyline/Paybox/etc/adminhtml/system.xml file with the following content:

```
<config xmlns:xsi="http://www.w3.org/2001/XMLSchema-instance"
  xsi:noNamespaceSchemaLocation="urn:magento:module:
  Magento_Config:etc/system_file.xsd">
    <system>
        <section id="payment">
            <group id="paybox" translate="label" type="text"
              sortOrder="30" showInDefault="1" showInWebsite="1"
              showInStore="1">
                <label>Paybox</label>
                <field id="active" translate="label" type="select"
                  sortOrder="1" showInDefault="1"
                  showInWebsite="1" showInStore="0">
                    <label>Enabled</label>
                    <source_model>
                      Magento\Config\Model\Config\Source\Yesno
                      </source_model>
                </field>
                <field id="order_status" translate="label"
                  type="select" sortOrder="20" showInDefault="1"
                  showInWebsite="1" showInStore="0">
                    <label>New Order Status</label>
                    <source_model> Magento\Sales\Model\Config
                      \Source\Order\Status\NewStatus
                      </source_model>
                </field>
                <field id="sort_order" translate="label"
                  type="text" sortOrder="100" showInDefault="1"
                  showInWebsite="1" showInStore="0">
                    <label>Sort Order</label>
```

```
        <frontend_class>
            validate-number</frontend_class>
    </field>
    <field id="title" translate="label" type="text"
      sortOrder="10" showInDefault="1"
      showInWebsite="1" showInStore="1">
            <label>Title</label>
    </field>
    <field id="allowspecific" translate="label"
      type="allowspecific" sortOrder="50"
      showInDefault="1" showInWebsite="1"
      showInStore="0">
            <label>Payment from Applicable Countries
              </label>
            <source_model> Magento\Payment\Model\
              Config\Source\Allspecificcountries
              </source_model>
    </field>
    <field id="specificcountry" translate="label"
      type="multiselect" sortOrder="51"
      showInDefault="1" showInWebsite="1"
      showInStore="0">
            <label>Payment from Specific Countries</label>
            <source_model> Magento\Directory\Model
              \Config\Source\Country </source_model>
            <can_be_empty>1</can_be_empty>
    </field>
    <field id="payable_to" translate="label"
      sortOrder="61" showInDefault="1"
      showInWebsite="1" showInStore="1">
            <label>Make Check Payable to</label>
    </field>
    <field id="mailing_address" translate="label"
      type="textarea" sortOrder="62" showInDefault="1"
      showInWebsite="1" showInStore="1">
            <label>Send Check to</label>
    </field>
    <field id="min_order_total" translate="label"
      type="text" sortOrder="98" showInDefault="1"
      showInWebsite="1" showInStore="0">
            <label>Minimum Order Total</label>
    </field>
    <field id="max_order_total" translate="label"
      type="text" sortOrder="99" showInDefault="1"
      showInWebsite="1" showInStore="0">
```

```
                <label>Maximum Order Total</label>
            </field>
            <field id="model"></field>
        </group>
      </section>
    </system>
</config>
```

Create an `app/code/Foggyline/Paybox/etc/frontend/di.xml` file with the following content:

```xml
<config xmlns:xsi="http://www.w3.org/2001/XMLSchema-instance"
  xsi:noNamespaceSchemaLocation="urn:magento:framework:
  ObjectManager/etc/config.xsd">
    <type name="Magento\Checkout\Model\CompositeConfigProvider">
        <arguments>
            <argument name="configProviders" xsi:type="array">
                <item name=
                  "offline_payment_paybox_config_provider"
                  xsi:type="object">
                    Foggyline\Paybox\Model\PayboxConfigProvider
                </item>
            </argument>
        </arguments>
    </type>
</config>
```

After this is done, create an `app/code/Foggyline/Paybox/Model/Paybox.php` file with the following content:

```php
namespace Foggyline\Paybox\Model;

class Paybox extends \Magento\Payment\Model\Method\AbstractMethod
{
    const PAYMENT_METHOD_PAYBOX_CODE = 'paybox';
    protected $_code = self::PAYMENT_METHOD_PAYBOX_CODE;

    protected $_isOffline = true;

    public function getPayableTo()
    {
        return $this->getConfigData('payable_to');
    }
}
```

```
    public function getMailingAddress()
    {
        return $this->getConfigData('mailing_address');
    }
}
```

Now, create an `app/code/Foggyline/Paybox/Model/PayboxConfigProvider.php` file with the following content:

```
namespace Foggyline\Paybox\Model;

class PayboxConfigProvider implements
  \Magento\Checkout\Model\ConfigProviderInterface
{
    protected $methodCode =
      \Foggyline\Paybox\Model\Paybox::PAYMENT_METHOD_PAYBOX_CODE;
    protected $method;
    protected $escaper;

    public function __construct(
        \Magento\Payment\Helper\Data $paymentHelper
    )
    {
        $this->method = $paymentHelper->getMethodInstance($this->
          methodCode);
    }

    public function getConfig()
    {
        return $this->method->isAvailable() ? [
            'payment' => [
                'paybox' => [
                    'mailingAddress' => $this->
                      getMailingAddress(),
                    'payableTo' => $this->getPayableTo(),
                ],
            ],
        ] : [];
    }

    protected function getMailingAddress()
    {
```

```
        $this->method->getMailingAddress();
    }

    protected function getPayableTo()
    {
        return $this->method->getPayableTo();
    }
}
```

Copy the entire `vendor/magento/module-offline-payments/view/frontend/layout/checkout_index_index.xml` Magento core file into the `app/code/Foggyline/Paybox/view/frontend/layout/checkout_index_index.xml` module. Then, edit the module's `checkout_index_index.xml` file by replacing the entire `<item name="offline-payments" xsi:type="array">` element and its children with the following code:

```xml
<item name="foggline-offline-payments" xsi:type="array">
    <item name="component" xsi:type="string">
      Foggyline_Paybox/js/view/payment/foggline-offline-payments
      </item>
    <item name="methods" xsi:type="array">
        <item name="paybox" xsi:type="array">
            <item name="isBillingAddressRequired"
                xsi:type="boolean">true</item>
        </item>
    </item>
</item>
```

Then, create an `app/code/Foggyline/Paybox/view/frontend/web/js/view/payment/offline-payments.js` file with the following content:

```
/*browser:true*/
/*global define*/
define(
    [
        'uiComponent',
        'Magento_Checkout/js/model/payment/renderer-list'
    ],
    function (
        Component,
        rendererList
    ) {
```

```
        'use strict';
        rendererList.push(
            {
                type: 'paybox',
                component:
                  'Foggyline_Paybox/js/view/payment/method-
                  renderer/paybox'
            }
        );
        return Component.extend({});
    }
);
```

After this is done, create an app/code/Foggyline/Paybox/view/frontend/web/
js/view/payment/method-renderer/paybox.js file with the following content:

```
/*browser:true*/
/*global define*/
define(
    [
        'Magento_Checkout/js/view/payment/default'
    ],
    function (Component) {
        'use strict';

        return Component.extend({
            defaults: {
                template: 'Foggyline_Paybox/payment/paybox'
            },

            getMailingAddress: function () {
                return window.checkoutConfig.payment.
                  paybox.mailingAddress;
            },

            getPayableTo: function () {
                return window.checkoutConfig.payment.
                  paybox.payableTo;
            }
        });
    }
);
```

Now, create an `app/code/Foggyline/Paybox/view/frontend/web/template/` `payment/paybox.html` file with the following content:

```html
<div class="payment-method" data-bind="css: {'_active': (getCode()
  == isChecked())}">
    <div class="payment-method-title field choice">
        <input type="radio"
               name="payment[method]"
               class="radio"
               data-bind="attr: {'id': getCode()}, value:
                  getCode(), checked: isChecked, click:
                  selectPaymentMethod, visible:
                  isRadioButtonVisible()"/>
        <label data-bind="attr: {'for': getCode()}"
          class="label"><span data-bind="text:
          getTitle()"></span></label>
    </div>
    <div class="payment-method-content">
        <div class="payment-method-billing-address">
            <!-- ko foreach:
               $parent.getRegion(getBillingAddressFormName()) -->
            <!-- ko template: getTemplate() --><!-- /ko -->
            <!--/ko-->
        </div>
        <!-- ko if: getMailingAddress() || getPayableTo() -->
        <dl class="items check payable">
            <!-- ko if: getPayableTo() -->
            <dt class="title"><!-- ko i18n: 'Make Check payable
               tooooooo:' --><!-- /ko --></dt>
            <dd class="content"><!-- ko i18n: getPayableTo() -->
              <!-- /ko --></dd>
            <!-- /ko -->
            <!-- ko if: getMailingAddress() -->
            <dt class="title"><!-- ko i18n: 'Send Check toxyz:' --
               ><!-- /ko --></dt>
            <dd class="content">
                <address class="paybox mailing address" data-bind
                  ="html: $t(getMailingAddress())"></address>
            </dd>
            <!-- /ko -->
        </dl>
        <!-- /ko -->
        <div class="checkout-agreements-block">
```

```
        <!-- ko foreach: $parent.getRegion('before-place-
          order') -->
        <!-- ko template: getTemplate() --><!-- /ko -->
        <!--/ko-->
    </div>
    <div class="actions-toolbar">
        <div class="primary">
            <button class="action primary checkout"
                    type="submit"
                    data-bind="
                    click: placeOrder,
                    attr: {title: $t('Place Order')},
                    css: {disabled:
                       !isPlaceOrderActionAllowed()},
                    enable: (getCode() == isChecked())
                    "
                    disabled>
                <span data-bind="i18n: 'Place Order'"></span>
            </button>
        </div>
    </div>
  </div>
</div>
```

With this, we conclude our custom offline payment method module. The entire module can be found at `https://github.com/ajzele/B05032-Foggyline_Paybox`.

Summary

In this chapter, we touched upon some of the most common bits of functionality that developers come in contact with. We learned where to look in the admin area and how to programmatically manage the entities behind these functionalities. Thus, we were effectively able to manually and programmatically create and fetch CMS pages, blocks, categories, and products. We also learned how to create product and customer import scripts. Finally, we studied how to create our own custom product type, simple payment, and shipment module.

The following chapter will guide us through Magento's in-built tests and how we can use them to effectively QA an application to keep it healthy.

11
Testing

Software testing can be defined as a critical step in the development life cycle. This step is often silently overlooked by a number of developers because a certain amount of time need to be invested into writing a decent test suite for a code base. Rather than being a single one-time activity, writing tests is a process that follows our code as it grows and changes. Test results should, at any given time, validate and verify that our software works as expected, thus meeting the business and technical requirements. Writing tests should follow writing the actual application code early on in the life cycle. This helps prevent defects from being introduced in the code.

On a high level, we can divide tests into the following categories:

- **Static**: Application code is not executed during testing. Possible errors are found by inspecting the application code files and not on their execution.

- **Dynamic**: Application code is executed during testing. Possible errors are found while checking for functional behavior of an application.

In this chapter, we will take a look at the testing options that Magento offers. Along the way, we will build a basic module with some testing features in it.

Types of tests

Magento provides several types of tests out of the box. We can see a list of these tests on running the following command on the console in the Magento root folder:

```
php bin/magento dev:tests:run -help
```

The result of the command is an output that looks like this:

```
Usage:
 dev:tests:run [type]
Arguments:
 type Type of test to run. Available types: all, unit, integration,
 integration-all, static, static-all, integrity, legacy, default
 (default: "default")
```

This output originates from the `Console/Command/DevTestsRunCommand.php` file in the core `Magento_Developer` module. Looking at the output, we might say that there are actually nine types of tests, which are as follows:

- all
- unit
- integration
- integration-all
- static
- static-all
- integrity
- legacy
- default

However, these are not unique types of tests; these are combinations, as we will soon see.

Let's take a closer look at the code in the `DevTestsRunCommand` class and its `setupTestInfo` method.

The `setupTestInfo` method defines the internal `commands` property, as follows:

```
$this->commands = [
    'unit'                  => ['../tests/unit', ''],
    'unit-performance'      => ['../tests/performance/
                                framework/tests/unit', ''],
    'unit-static'           => ['../tests/static/
                                framework/tests/unit', ''],
    'unit-integration'      => ['../tests/integration/
                                framework/tests/unit', ''],
    'integration'           => ['../tests/integration', ''],
    'integration-integrity' => ['../tests/integration', '
                                testsuite/Magento/
                                Test/Integrity'],
```

```
    'static-default'          => ['../tests/static', ''],
    'static-legacy'           => ['../tests/static', '
                                 testsuite/Magento/Test/Legacy'],
    'static-integration-js'   => ['../tests/static', '
                                 testsuite/Magento/Test/
                                 Js/Exemplar'],
];
```

Furthermore, we can see the types property in the `setupTestInfo` method defined in the following way:

```
$this->types = [
    'all'                => array_keys($this->commands),
    'unit'               => ['unit', 'unit-performance', 'unit-
                             static', 'unit-integration'],
    'integration'        => ['integration'],
    'integration-all'    => ['integration', 'integration-integrity'],
    'static'             => ['static-default'],
    'static-all'         => ['static-default', 'static-legacy',
                             'static-integration-js'],
    'integrity'          => ['static-default', 'static-legacy',
                             'integration-integrity'],
    'legacy'             => ['static-legacy'],
    'default'            => [
        'unit',
        'unit-performance',
        'unit-static',
        'unit-integration',
        'integration',
        'static-default',
    ],
];
```

The types property logically groups one or more tests into a single name that is found under the commands property. We can see how like unit single type encompasses the unit, unit-performance, unit-static, and unit-integration tests in it. The commands property points to the disk location of the actual test library. Relative to the Magento root installation folder, tests can be found in the dev/tests/ directory.

Unit testing

Unit tests are designed to test individual class methods in isolation, asserting all possible combinations and taking care of the smallest testable part of an application. Magento uses the **PHPUnit** testing framework for its unit tests. Being highly focused, unit tests make it easy to identify the root cause of issues if a certain test fails.

We can specifically trigger the unit tests from the root of the Magento installation by using the following command:

```
php bin/magento dev:tests:run unit
```

Once triggered, Magento will run the `execute` command in the `vendor/magento/module-developer/Console/Command/DevTestsRunCommand.php` file. Since the unit type is mapped to several commands, what will happen internally is that Magento will change the directories from one directory to another, as follows:

- `dev/tests/unit`
- `dev/tests/performance/framework/tests/unit`
- `dev/tests/static/framework/tests/unit`
- `dev/tests/integration/framework/tests/unit`

We can say that all of these directories are considered unit test directories.

Within each of those directories, Magento internally runs the `passthru($command, $returnVal)` method, where the `$command` parameter gets resolved to a string similar to the following one:

```
php /www/magento2/./vendor/phpunit/phpunit/phpunit
```

The PHPUnit will then look for the `phpunit.xml` configuration file accordingly in each of these directories. If `phpunit.xml` does not exist, we need to copy the contents of `phpunit.xml.dist` into `phpunit.xml`.

Let's take a closer look at the `dev/tests/unit/phpunit.xml` file for `testsuite`, `filter`, `whitelist`, and other configuration elements.

The following default `testsuite` directory list is found in the `dev/tests/unit/phpunit.xml file`, which lists the directories in which you need to look for `tests` files prefixed with `Test.php`:

```
../../../app/code/*/*/Test/Unit
../../../dev/tools/*/*/Test/Unit
../../../dev/tools/*/*/*/Test/Unit
../../../lib/internal/*/*/Test/Unit
../../../lib/internal/*/*/*/Test/Unit
```

```
../../../setup/src/*/*/Test/Unit
../../../update/app/code/*/*/Test/Unit
../../../vendor/*/module-*/Test/Unit
../../../vendor/*/framework/Test/Unit
../../../vendor/*/framework/*/Test/Unit
```

The list is relative to the `dev/tests/unit/` directory. For example, if we take a look at the first line in the preceding code and then look at the `Magento_Catalog` module, it is clear that the `Test` files are found under the `app/code/<vendorName>/<moduleName>/Test/` directory and its subdirectories. Everything suffixed with `Test.php` in these folders will get executed as a part of a unit test.

> If we were building our own module, we could easily make a copy of `dev/tests/unit/phpunit.xml.dist`, properly edit `testsuite` and `filter > whitelist` to quickly execute only our module's unit tests, thus saving some time on avoiding frequent execution of entire Magento unit tests.

Integration testing

Integration tests test the interaction between individual components, layers, and an environment. They can be found in the `dev/tests/integration` directory. Like unit tests, Magento also uses PHPUnit for integration tests. Thus, the difference between a unit and an integration test is not that much of a technical nature; rather, it's of a logical nature.

To specifically trigger integration tests only, we can execute the following command on the console:

```
php bin/magento dev:tests:run integration
```

When executed, Magento internally changes the directory to `dev/tests/integration` and executes a command that is similar to the following one:

```
php /Users/branko/www/magento2/./vendor/phpunit/phpunit/phpunit
```

The integration directory has its own `phpunit.xml.dist` file. Looking at its `testsuite` definition, we can see that it is pointing to all the `Test.php` suffixed files that are found in the `dev/tests/integration/testsuite` directory.

Static testing

Static tests do not really run the code; they analyze it. They are used to verify that the code conforms to certain coding standards, such as PSR-1. We can find them under the `dev/tests/static` directory.

To specifically trigger static tests only, we can execute the following command on the console:

```
php bin/magento dev:tests:run static
```

When executed, Magento internally changes the directory to `dev/tests/static` and executes a command that is similar to the following one:

```
php /Users/branko/www/magento2/./vendor/phpunit/phpunit/phpunit
```

The static directory has its own `phpunit.xml.dist` file. Looking at its `testsuite` definition, you will see the following four test suites defined:

- JavaScript static code analysis
- PHP coding standard verification
- Code integrity tests
- XSS unsafe output test

`JSHint`, a JavaScript code quality tool, is used for JavaScript static code analysis. For PHP code standard verification, the elements of `PHP_CodeSniffer` libraries are used. `PHP_CodeSniffer` tokenizes PHP, JavaScript, and CSS files and detects violations of a defined set of coding standards.

Integrity testing

Integrity tests check how an application is linked. They check for things such as merged configuration validation. Basically, they tell us if your application should be able to run.

We can specifically trigger the integrity tests from the root of the Magento installation by using the following command:

```
php bin/magento dev:tests:run integrity
```

When this is executed, Magento first internally changes the directory to `dev/tests/static` and then executes two commands that are similar to the following ones:

```
php /Users/branko/www/magento2/./vendor/phpunit/phpunit/phpunit
```

```
php /Users/branko/www/magento2/./vendor/phpunit/phpunit/phpunit
testsuite/Magento/Test/Legacy
```

Then, Magento internally changes the directory to `dev/tests/integration` and executes a command that is similar to the following one:

```
php /Users/branko/www/magento2/./vendor/phpunit/phpunit/phpunit
testsuite/Magento/Test/Integrity
```

Integration tests also utilize the PHPUnit to write the actual tests.

Legacy testing

Legacy tests comprise fragments of libraries that help developers port their modules to a new version of Magento.

We can trigger legacy tests specifically from the root of the Magento installation by using the following command:

```
php bin/magento dev:tests:run legacy
```

When this is executed, Magento first internally changes the directory to `/dev/tests/static` and then executes a command, which is similar to the following one:

```
php /Users/branko/www/magento2/./vendor/phpunit/phpunit/phpunit
testsuite/Magento/Test/Legacy
```

Once this is triggered, the code runs a check for obsolete access lists, connections, menus, responses, system configuration, and a few other things.

Performance testing

Performance tests can be found under the `setup/performance-toolkit/` directory. These tests require Apache JMeter to be installed and are available on the console via the `jmeter` command. Apache JMeter can be downloaded and installed by following the instructions at `http://jmeter.apache.org`.

The crux of the performance test is defined in the `benchmark.jmx` file, which can be opened in the JMeter GUI tool, as shown in the following screenshot:

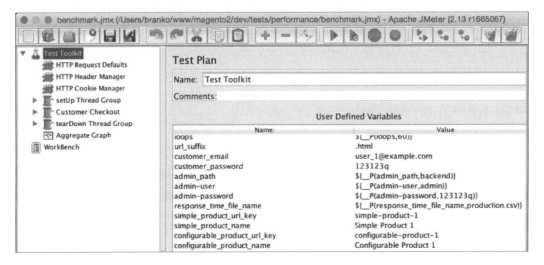

As shown in the preceding screenshot, the default `benchmark.jmx` tests are sectioned into three thread groups that are named **setUp Thread Group**, **Customer Checkout**, and **tearDown Thread Group**. We might want to additionally click on each group and configure it with some extra parameters, thus possibly changing **Number of Threads (users)**, as shown in the following screenshot. We can then simply save the changes as modifications to the `benchmark.jmx` file or a file with new name:

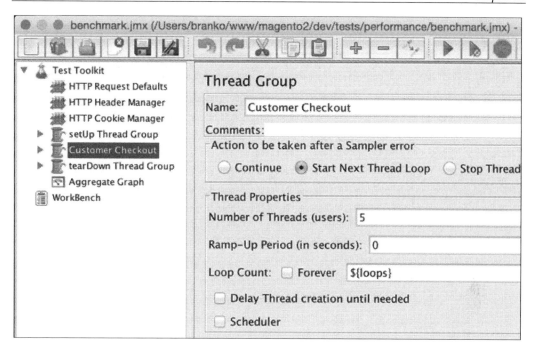

We can manually trigger a performance test from the console without using a GUI interface by running the following command:

```
jmeter -n \
-t /Users/branko/www/magento2/setup/performance-toolkit/benchmark.jmx \
-l /Users/branko/Desktop/jmeter-tmp/results.jtl \
-Jhost="magento2.ce" \
-Jbase_path="/" \
-Jreport_save_path="/Users/branko/report" \
-Jloops=2 \
-Jurl_suffix=".html" \
-Jcustomer_email="john.doe@email.loc" \
-Jcustomer_password="abc123" \
-Jadmin_path="/admin_nwb0bx" \
-Jadmin-user="john" \
-Jadmin-password="abc123" \
```

```
-Jresponse_time_file_name="/Users/branko/report/AggregateGraph.csv" \
-Jsimple_product_url_key="simple-product-1" \
-Jsimple_product_name="Simple Product 1" \
-Jconfigurable_product_url_key="configurable-product-1" \
-Jconfigurable_product_name="Configurable Product 1" \
-Jcategory_url_key="category-1" \
-Jcategory_name="Category 1" \
-Jsleep_between_steps=50
```

The console parameters that are listed here and which start with -J also match the names of the **Used Defined Variables** test toolkit, as shown in the preceding screenshot. We need to be careful and set them according to the Magento installation. The -n parameter instructs jmeter to run in the run *nongui* mode. The -t parameter is where we set the path of the test (.jmx) file to run. The -l parameter sets the file where we need to log samples to.

Functional testing

Functional tests mimic the user interaction with our application. They literally mean testing in the form of browser interaction, which involves clicking on the page, adding products to the cart, and so on. For this purpose, Magento uses **Magento Testing Framework (MTF)**. It's a PHP wrapper around **Selenium**, which is a portable software testing framework for web applications. MTF is not available out of the box via the console. It can be downloaded at https://github.com/magento/mtf.

The following requirements need to be met before installing MTF:

- Git must be installed.
- The Firefox browser must be installed.
- The PHP openssl extension must be installed and enabled.
- Java version 1.6 or later is required and it's JAR executable must be in the system PATH.
- The Selenium standalone server, which is available at http://www.seleniumhq.org/, needs to be downloaded. The download should provide a JAR file that we will later need to refer to.
- Magento must be installed and configured to not use the secret URL key. We can set the secret URL key option by navigating to **Stores** | **Configuration** | **Advanced** | **Admin** | **Security** | **Add Secret Key to URLs** [Yes/No] and setting it to **No**.

Once the minimal requirements are met, we can install MTF, as follows:

1. Run the `composer install` command from the `dev/tests/functional/` directory. This creates a new directory named `vendor`; MTF is pulled from the Git repository at `https://github.com/magento/mtf`. We should see a new directory named `vendor` that is created with the checked off MTF. The `vendor` directory contains the content that is shown in the following screenshot:

2. Run the `generate.php` file from the `dev/tests/functional/utils/` directory. This should give us a console output that is similar to the following one:

```
|| Item              || Count || Time ||
|| Page Classes      || 152   || 0    ||
|| Fixture Classes   || 46    || 0    ||
|| Repository Classes || 67   || 0    ||
|| Block             || 475   || 0    ||
|| Fixture           || 100   || 0    ||
|| Handler           || 3     || 0    ||
|| Page              || 165   || 0    ||
|| Repository        || 67    || 0    ||
```

The generator tool creates factories for fixtures, handlers, repositories, page objects, and block objects. When MTF is initialized, the factories are pregenerated to facilitate the creation and running of tests.

Before we can actually run the tests, there are a few more things that we need to configure, as follows:

1. Edit the `dev/tests/functional/phpunit.xml` file. Under the `php` element, for `name="app_frontend_url"`, set the value of the actual URL for the Magento storefront under test. For `name="app_backend_url"`, set the value of the actual URL for the Magento admin URL under test. For `name="credentials_file_path"`, set the value of `./credentials.xml`.

 If `phpunit.xml` does not exist, we need to create it and copy the contents of `dev/tests/functional/phpunit.xml.dist` into it and then edit it afterwards.

2. Edit the `dev/tests/functional/etc/config.xml` file. Under the `application` element, find and edit the information about `backendLogin`, `backendPassword`, and `appBackendUrl` so that it matches that of our store.

 If `config.xml` does not exist, we need to create it and copy the contents of `dev/tests/functional/etc/config.xml.dist` into it and then edit it afterwards.

3. Edit the `dev/tests/functional/credentials.xml` file. Chances are that we will not need this on a blank Magento installation, as we can see by default the entries for the `fedex`, `ups`, `dhl US`, and `dhl EU` carriers, which haven't been set on the freshly installed Magento.

 If `credentials.xml` does not exist, we need to create it and copy the contents of `dev/tests/functional/credentials.xml.dist` into it and then edit it afterwards.

4. Run the `java -jar {selenium_directory}/selenium-server.jar` command via the console. This is to ensure that the Selenium server is running.

5. Open a new console or a console tab and execute the `phpunit` command in the `dev/tests/functional/` directory. This command should open the Firefox browser and start running test cases in it, simulating a user clicking on the browser window and filling in the form inputs.

While a test is running, Magento will log all the failed tests under the `dev/tests/functional/var/log` directory in a structure that is similar to the one shown in the following screenshot:

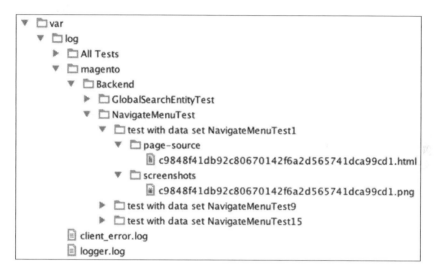

The `log` path can be configured in the `dev/tests/functional/phpunit.xml` file under the `php` element with `name="basedir"`.

If we want to target a specific test within the entire test suite, we can simply trigger a command like the following one in the `dev/tests/functional/` directory:

```
phpunit tests/app/Magento/Customer/Test/TestCase
/RegisterCustomerFrontendEntityTest.php
```

The preceding command will run a single test called `RegisterCustomerFrontendEntityTest.php`. We can also use a shorter form expression for the same thing, as follows:

```
phpunit --filter RegisterCustomerFrontendEntityTest
```

Once this is executed, the browser should open and simulate the customer registration process on the storefront.

Writing a simple unit test

Now that we took a quick look at all the type of tests that Magento offers, let's take a step back and look at unit tests again. In practice, unit tests are probably the ones that we will be writing most of the time. With this in mind, let's grab the `Foggyline_Unitly` module from `https://github.com/ajzele/B05032-Foggyline_Unitly` and start writing unit tests for it.

If you do not already have the `Foggyline_Unitly` module in the code base that was a part of the previous chapters, then you need to place its content under `app/code/Foggyline/Unitly` and execute the following commands on the console from the root of the Magento directory:

```
php bin/magento module:enable Foggyline_Unitly

php bin/magento setup:upgrade
```

The tests that we will write reside in the module's `Test/Unit` directory. This makes the entire path of the test directory look like `app/code/Foggyline/Unitly/Test/Unit/`. Magento knows that it needs to look inside this folder simply because of the test suite directory definitions found in the `dev/tests/unit/phpunit.xml` file, as shown in the following piece of code:

```
<directory suffix="Test.php">
    ../../../app/code/*/*/Test/Unit
</directory>
```

The structure of files and the folder within the individual module `Test/Unit` directory also follows the structure of that module's files and folders. The following screenshot shows a structure of the `Test/Unit` directory for the `Magento_Catalog` module:

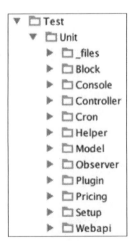

This shows that almost any PHP class can be unit tested irrespective of the fact that it is a controller, block, helper, module, observer, or something else. To keep things simple, we will focus on the controller and block unit tests in relation to the `Foggyline_Unitly` module, which is structured as follows:

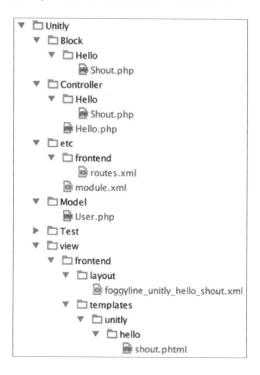

Let's start by first writing a test for the `Foggyline\Unitly\Controller\Hello\Shout` controller class. The `Shout` class, ignoring the `__construct`, has only one method called `execute`.

We will write a test for it under the same directory structure, relative to the module's `Test\Unit` directory, placing the test under the `app/code/Foggyline/Unitly/Test/Unit/Controller/Hello/ShoutTest.php` file with (partial), as follows:

```php
namespace Foggyline\Unitly\Test\Unit\Controller\Hello;

class ShoutTest extends \PHPUnit_Framework_TestCase
{
    protected $resultPageFactory;
    protected $controller;

    public function setUp()
    {
```

```
        /* setUp() code here */
    }

    public function testExecute()
    {
        /* testExecute() code here */
    }
}
```

Every unit test in the Magento module directory extends from the \PHPUnit_ Framework_TestCase class. The setUp method is called before the test is executed; we can think of it as PHP's __construct. Here, we would usually set up the fixtures, open a network connection, or perform similar actions.

The testExecute method name is actually formed from test + the method name from the class that we are testing. Since the Shout class has an execute method, the test method formed becomes test + execute. By capitalizing the first letter of the class method name, the final name is testExecute.

Now, let's go ahead and replace /* setUp() code here */ with content. as follows:

```
$request = $this->getMock(
    'Magento\Framework\App\Request\Http',
    [],
    [],
    '',
    false
);

$context = $this->getMock(
    '\Magento\Framework\App\Action\Context',
    ['getRequest'],
    [],
    '',
    false
);

$context->expects($this->once())
    ->method('getRequest')
    ->willReturn($request);

$this->resultPageFactory = $this-> getMockBuilder
    ('Magento\Framework\View\Result\PageFactory')
    ->disableOriginalConstructor()
    ->setMethods(['create'])
```

```
    ->getMock();

$this->controller = new \Foggyline\Unitly\Controller\Hello\Shout(
    $context,
    $this->resultPageFactory
);
```

The whole concept of tests is based on mocking the objects that we need to work with. We use the getMock method that returns a mock object for a specified class. Besides the class name, the getMock method accepts quite a bit of other arguments. The second $methods parameter marks the names of the methods that are replaced with a test double. Providing null for the $methods parameter means that no methods will be replaced. The third parameter for the getMock method stands for $arguments, which are parameters that are passed to the original class constructor.

We can see from the preceding code that the $request mock object does not provide any $methods or $arguments parameters to its getMock method. On the other hand, the $context object passes on the array with a single getRequest element in it. Once the $context object is initialized, it then calls the expects method, which registers a new expectation in the mock object and returns InvocationMocker on which we call method and willReturn. In this case, the instance on the previously initiated $request object is passed to willReturn. We used getMockBuilder to create a Result\PageFactory mock object and instantiated the Shout controller action class, passing the context and result page mocks to it.

All the code in this setUp method served a purpose in getting out the controller instance, which will be used in the testExecute method.

 The final, private, and static methods cannot be mocked. They are ignored by PHPUnit's test functionality because they retain their original behavior.

Let's go ahead and replace the /* testExecute() code here */ with content, as follows:

```
$title = $this->
  getMockBuilder('Magento\Framework\View\Page\Title')
    ->disableOriginalConstructor()
    ->getMock();
$title->expects($this->once())
    ->method('set')
    ->with('Unitly');
```

```
$config = $this->
  getMockBuilder('Magento\Framework\View\Page\Config')
    ->disableOriginalConstructor()
    ->getMock();
$config->expects($this->once())
    ->method('getTitle')
    ->willReturn($title);

$page = $this->
  getMockBuilder('Magento\Framework\View\Result\Page')
    ->disableOriginalConstructor()
    ->getMock();
$page->expects($this->once())
    ->method('getConfig')
    ->willReturn($config);

$this->resultPageFactory->expects($this->once())
    ->method('create')
    ->willReturn($page);

$result = $this->controller->execute();

$this->assertInstanceOf('Magento\Framework\View\Result\Page',
  $result);
```

In the preceding code, we checked into the page title, page, and result page object. To get to the page title from within the controller code, we would normally use an expression such as `$resultPage->getConfig()->getTitle()`. This expression involves three objects. The `$resultPage` object calls the `getConfig()` method, which returns the instance of the `Page\Config` object. This object calls for the `getTitle` method, which returns the instance of the `Page\Title` object. Thus, we are mocking and testing all the three objects.

Now that we took a look at the controller test case, let's see how we can make one for the block class. Create an `app/code/Foggyline/Unitly/Test/Unit/Block/Hello/ShoutTest.php` file with partial content, as follows:

```
namespace Foggyline\Unitly\Test\Unit\Block\Hello;

class ShoutTest extends \PHPUnit_Framework_TestCase
{
    /**
     * @var \Foggyline\Unitly\Block\Hello\Shout
     */
```

```
    protected $block;

    protected function setUp()
    {
        $objectManager = new \Magento\Framework\TestFramework\Unit
          \Helper\ObjectManager($this);
        $this->block = $objectManager->
          getObject('Foggyline\Unitly\Block\Hello\Shout');
    }

    public function testGreeting()
    {
        $name = 'Foggyline';

        $this->assertEquals(
            'Hello '.$this->block->escapeHtml($name),
            $this->block->greeting($name)
        );
    }
}
```

Here, we have also defined the setUp method and testGreeting. The
testGreeting method is used as a test for the greeting method on the Shout
block class.

Conceptually, there is no difference between unit testing a controller, block, or model
class. Therefore, we will omit the model unit test in this example. What's important
for you to realize is that the test is what we make of it. Technically speaking, we
can test a single method for various cases or just the most obvious one. However,
to serve the purpose of the tests in a better way, we should test it for any possible
number of result combinations.

Let's go ahead and create a dev/tests/unit/foggyline-unitly-phpunit.xml file
with content, as follows:

```
<phpunit xmlns:xsi="http://www.w3.org/2001/XMLSchema-instance"
  xsi:noNamespaceSchemaLocation="http://schema.phpunit.de
  /4.1/phpunit.xsd"
        colors="true"
        bootstrap="./framework/bootstrap.php"
      >
    <testsuite name="Foggyline_Unitly - Unit Tests">
        <directory suffix="Test.php">
            ../../../app/code/Foggyline/Unitly/Test/Unit
        </directory>
    </testsuite>
```

```xml
<php>
    <ini name="date.timezone" value="Europe/Zagreb"/>
    <ini name="xdebug.max_nesting_level" value="200"/>
</php>
<filter>
    <whitelist addUncoveredFilesFromWhiteList="true">
        <directory suffix=".php">
            ../../../app/code/Foggyline/Unitly/*
        </directory>
    </whitelist>
</filter>
<logging>
    <log type="coverage-html"
        target="coverage_dir/Foggyline_Unitly/test-
        reports/coverage" charset="UTF-8" yui="true"
        highlight="true"/>
</logging>
</phpunit>
```

Finally, we can execute only our own module unit tests by running a command such as `phpunit -c foggyline-unitly-phpunit.xml`.

Once tests are executed, we should be able to see the entire code coverage report in the `dev/tests/unit/coverage_dir/Foggyline_Unitly/test-reports/coverage/index.html` file, as shown in the following screenshot:

/Users/branko/www/magento2/app/code/Foggyline/Unitly / (Dashboard)

	Code Coverage								
	Lines			**Functions and Methods**			**Classes and Traits**		
Total		90.28%	65 / 72		80.00%	8 / 10		83.33%	5 / 6
Block		100.00%	1 / 1		100.00%	1 / 1		100.00%	1 / 1
Controller		100.00%	7 / 7		100.00%	3 / 3		100.00%	2 / 2
Model		0.00%	0 / 7		0.00%	0 / 2		0.00%	0 / 1
Test		100.00%	57 / 57		100.00%	4 / 4		100.00%	2 / 2

Legend

Low: 0% to 50%   **Medium:** 50% to 90%   **High:** 90% to 100%

Generated by PHP_CodeCoverage 2.1.7 using PHP 5.5.22 and PHPUnit 4.7.6 at Tue Sep 15 13:03:36 CEST 2015.

The preceding screenshot demonstrates how detailed the code coverage is, which shows even the percentages and lines of code covered with test.

Summary

In this chapter, we took a look at the testing facility embedded in Magento through the libraries in the root `dev/tests/` directory and the `Magento_Developer` module. We learned how to run all of its test types and studied a simple example of writing our own unit tests. The examples that are given here do not do justice to PHPUnit, given its robustness. More information on PHPUnit can be found at `https://phpunit.de/`.

We will now move on to the final chapter of this book, where we will reiterate the things that we learned so far and develop a functional miniature module that involves some basic testing.

12
Building a Module
from Scratch

Based on the knowledge acquired from previous chapters, we will now build a miniature `Helpdesk` module. Though miniature, the module will showcase the usage of several important Magento platform features as we go through the following sections:

- Registering a module (`registration.php` and `module.xml`)
- Creating a configuration file (`config.xml`)
- Creating e-mail templates (`email_templates.xml`)
- Creating a system configuration file (`system.xml`)
- Creating access control lists (`acl.xml`)
- Creating an installation script (`InstallSchema.php`)
- Managing entity persistence (model, resource, collection)
- Building a frontend interface
- Building a backend interface
- Creating unit tests

Module requirements

Module requirements are defined as follows:

- Name used, `Foggyline/Helpdesk`
- Data to be stored in table is called `foggyline_helpdesk_ticket`

- Tickets entity will contain `ticket_id`, `customer_id`, `title`, `severity`, `created_at`, and `status` properties

- The `customer_id` property is to be foreign key on the `customer_entity` table

- There will be three available ticket severity values: `low`, `medium`, and `high`

- If not specified, the default severity value for new tickets is `low`

- There will be two available ticket statuses: `opened` and `closed`

- If not specified, the default status value for new tickets is `opened`

- Two e-mails templates: `store_owner_to_customer_email_template` and `customer_to_store_owner_email_template` are to be defined for pushing e-mail updates upon ticket creation and status change

- Customers will be able to submit a ticket through their **My Account** section

- Customers will be able to see all of their previously submitted tickets under their **My Account** section

- Customers will not be able to edit any existing tickets

- Once a customer submits a new ticket, transactional e-mail (let's call it **Foggyline – Helpdesk – Customer | Store Owner**) is sent to the store owner

- Configurable option is required for possibly overriding **Foggyline – Helpdesk – Customer | Store Owner** e-mail

- Admin users will be able to access a list of all tickets under **Customers | Helpdesk Tickets**

- Admin users will be able to change ticket status from **Opened** to **Closed** and other way round

- Once an admin user changes the ticket status, transactional e-mail (let's call it **Foggyline – Helpdesk – Store Owner | Customer**) is sent to the customer

- Configurable option is required for possibly overriding **Foggyline – Helpdesk – Store Owner | Customer** e-mail

With the requirements outlined, we are ready to begin our module development.

Registering a module

We first start by defining the `app/code/Foggyline/Helpdesk/registration.php` file with the following content:

```php
<?php
\Magento\Framework\Component\ComponentRegistrar::register(
    \Magento\Framework\Component\ComponentRegistrar::MODULE,
    'Foggyline_Helpdesk',
    __DIR__
);
```

We then define the `app/code/Foggyline/Helpdesk/etc/module.xml` file with the following content:

```xml
<?xml version="1.0"?>
<config xmlns:xsi="http://www.w3.org/2001/XMLSchema-instance"
  xsi:noNamespaceSchemaLocation="urn:magento:framework:Module
  /etc/module.xsd">
    <module name="Foggyline_Helpdesk" setup_version="1.0.0">
        <sequence>
            <module name="Magento_Store"/>
            <module name="Magento_Customer"/>
        </sequence>
    </module>
</config>
```

Looking at the preceding file, if we strip away the boilerplate that repeats itself across all modules, we are left with three important things here:

- The module name attribute, defined as `Foggyline_Helpdesk`. We need to be sure to follow a certain pattern when naming our modules, like `Vendor` + `_` + `Module` name. The module name attribute can contain only letters and numbers [A-Z, a-z, 0-9, _].

- The schema `setup_version` attribute that defines our module version. Its value can contain only numbers [0-9]. Our example sets the value of `1.0.0` for the `setup_version` attribute.

- The sequence module name attribute, which defines module dependencies. Our module basically says it requires `Magento_Store` and `Magento_Customer` modules to be enabled.

Once this file is in place, we need to go to the command line, change the directory to that of Magento installation, and simply execute the following command:

```
php bin/magento module:enable Foggyline_Helpdesk
```

However, if we now open either the admin of the frontend area in our browser, we might get an error page, which generates the following error under the `var/reports/` folder:

```
Please upgrade your database: Run "bin/magento setup:upgrade" from
the Magento root directory.
```

Luckily, the error is pretty self-descriptive so we simply move back to the console, change the directory to the Magento root folder, and execute the following command:

```
php bin/magento setup:upgrade
```

Executed commands will activate our module.

We can confirm that by looking under the `app/etc/config.php` file, as shown in the following screenshot (on line 33):

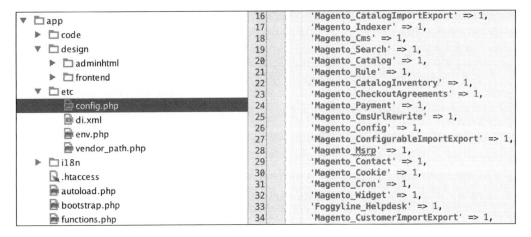

Further if we log in to the admin area, and go to **Stores | Configuration | Advanced | Advanced**, we should see our module listed there, as shown in the following screenshot:

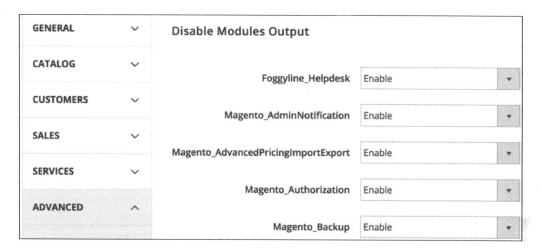

Creating a configuration file (config.xml)

Now we will create an app/code/Foggyline/Helpdesk/etc/config.xml file with the content, as follows:

```xml
<?xml version="1.0"?>
<config xmlns:xsi="http://www.w3.org/2001/XMLSchema-instance"
  xsi:noNamespaceSchemaLocation="urn:magento:module:Magento_Store:
  etc/config.xsd">
    <default>
        <foggyline_helpdesk>
            <email_template>
                <customer>
                    foggyline_helpdesk_email_template_customer
                </customer>
                <store_owner>
                    foggyline_helpdesk_email_template_store_owner
                </store_owner>
            </email_template>
        </foggyline_helpdesk>
    </default>
</config>
```

This might look confusing at first as to where the `default` | `foggyline_helpdesk` | `email_template` structure comes from. The structure itself denotes the position of our configuration values that we will map to the administrative interface visible in our browser under the **Stores | Configuration** section. Given that all things visual regarding the **Stores | Configuration** section originate from `system.xml` files, this structure we have now in `config.xml` will then map to another `system.xml` file we will define soon.

Right now, just remember the structure and the values contained within the `customer` and `store_owner` attributes. These values will further map to another `email_templates.xml` file, which we will soon create.

There is one more important thing regarding the `config.xml` file. We need to be very careful of the `xsi:noNamespaceSchemaLocation` attribute value. This value needs to be set to `urn:magento:module:Magento_Store:etc/config.xsd`. It's an alias that actually points to the `vendor/magento/module-store/etc/config.xsd` file.

Creating e-mail templates (email_templates.xml)

Our module requirements specify that two e-mail templates need to be defined. Hints to this have already been given in the `app/code/Foggyline/Helpdesk/etc/config.xml` file previously defined. The actual definition of e-mail templates available to our modules is done through the `app/code/Foggyline/Helpdesk/etc/email_templates.xml file`, with the content as follows:

```xml
<?xml version="1.0"?>
<config xmlns:xsi="http://www.w3.org/2001/XMLSchema-instance"
  xsi:noNamespaceSchemaLocation="urn:magento:module:
  Magento_Email:etc/email_templates.xsd">
    <template id="foggyline_helpdesk_email_template_customer"
      label="Foggyline Helpdesk - Customer Email"
            file="store_owner_to_customer.html" type="html"
              module="Foggyline_Helpdesk" area="frontend"/>
    <template id="foggyline_helpdesk_email_template_store_owner"
      label="Foggyline Helpdesk - Store Owner Email"
            file="customer_to_store_owner.html" type="html"
              module="Foggyline_Helpdesk" area="frontend"/>
</config>
```

Looking into `email_templates.xsd`, we can conclude that the values for `id`, `label`, `file`, `type`, and `module` are all required. `id` should be defined unique to our module, giving some sensible and reasonable code name to our e-mail templates, as this code name is going to be used further in other XML files or in code.

What we defined as ID values here, can be found under `app/code/Foggyline/Helpdesk/etc/config.xml`, as the value of `default` | `foggyline_helpdesk` | `email_template` | `customer` and `default` | `foggyline_helpdesk` | `email_template` | `store_owner` elements.

If it is not yet fully clear what the connection between the two is; we will get to it when we start building our `system.xml` file soon.

The value of the `label` attribute is something that is visible later on, within the Magento admin area under **Marketing | Communications | Email Templates**, so be sure to put something user friendly and easily recognizable here.

Further, the values of the `file` attribute point to the location of the following files:

- `app/code/Foggyline/Helpdesk/view/frontend/email/customer_to_store_owner.html`
- `app/code/Foggyline/Helpdesk/view/frontend/email/store_owner_to_customer.html`

The content of the files will be set such that later on, in the code, we will need to pass it on certain variables in order to fill in the variable placeholders.

The `customer_to_store_owner.html` e-mail template, with content as follows, will be triggered later on in the code when a customer creates a new ticket:

```
<!--@subject New Ticket Created @-->
<h1>Ticket #{{var ticket.ticket_id}} created</h1>

<ul>
    <li>Id: {{var ticket.ticket_id}}</li>
    <li>Title: {{var ticket.title}}</li>
    <li>Created_at: {{var ticket.created_at}}</li>
    <li>Severity: {{var ticket.severity}}</li>
</ul>
```

Later on, we will see how to pass the `ticket` object as a variable into the template, in order to enable calls like `{{var ticket.title}}` within the HTML template.

The `store_owner_to_customer.html` e-mail template, with content as follows, will be triggered later on in the code when the store owner changes the status of a ticket:

```
<!--@subject Ticket Updated @-->
<h1>Ticket #{{var ticket.ticket_id}} updated</h1>

<p>Hi {{var customer_name}}.</p>

<p>Status of your ticket #{{var ticket.ticket_id}} has been updated</p>

<ul>
    <li>Title: {{var ticket.title}}</li>
    <li>Created_at: {{var ticket.created_at}}</li>
    <li>Severity: {{var ticket.severity}}</li>
</ul>
```

If we now log in to the Magento admin area, go under **Marketing | Communications | Email Templates**, click on the **Add New Template** button, and we should be able to see our two e-mail templates under the **Template** drop-down, as shown in the following screenshot:

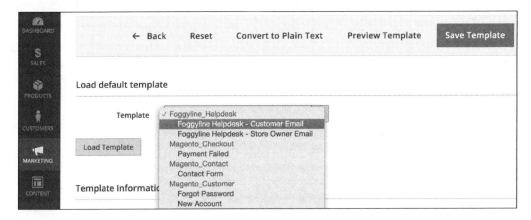

If we look back at our `config.xml` and `email_templates.xml`, there is still no clear connection as to what `default | foggyline_helpdesk | email_template | customer` and `default | foggyline_helpdesk | email_template | store_owner` under `config.xml` actually do. That is because we still lack two more ingredients that will link them together: the `app/code/Foggyline/Helpdesk/etc/adminhtml/system.xml` and `app/code/Foggyline/Helpdesk/etc/acl.xml` files.

Creating a system configuration file (system.xml)

The system.xml file is essentially the **Stores | Configuration** interface builder. Entries we define in our module's system.xml file will render certain parts of the **Stores | Configuration** interface under the Magento admin area.

Unlike the previous two XML files, this configuration file is located under an additional subfolder, so its full path goes like app/code/Foggyline/Helpdesk/etc/adminhtml/system.xml, with content as follows:

```
<?xml version="1.0"?>
<config xmlns:xsi="http://www.w3.org/2001/XMLSchema-instance"
  xsi:noNamespaceSchemaLocation="urn:magento:module:
  Magento_Config:etc/system_file.xsd">
    <system>
        <tab id="foggyline" translate="label" sortOrder="200">
            <label>Foggyline</label>
        </tab>
        <section id="foggyline_helpdesk" translate="label"
          type="text" sortOrder="110" showInDefault="1"
                showInWebsite="1" showInStore="1">
            <label>Helpdesk</label>
            <tab>foggyline</tab>
            <resource>Foggyline_Helpdesk::helpdesk</resource>
            <group id="email_template" translate="label"
              type="text" sortOrder="1" showInDefault="1"
              showInWebsite="1" showInStore="1">
                <label>Email Template Options</label>
                <field id="customer" translate="label"
                  type="select" sortOrder="1" showInDefault="1"
                  showInWebsite="1" showInStore="1">
                    <label>
                        Store Owner to Customer Email Template
                    </label>
                    <source_model>
                        Magento\Config\Model\Config\Source\
                            Email\Template
                    </source_model>
                </field>
                <field id="store_owner" translate="label"
                  type="select" sortOrder="1" showInDefault="1"
                  showInWebsite="1" showInStore="1">
```

```
                                    <label>
                                        Customer to Store Owner Email Template
                                    </label>
                                    <source_model>
                                        Magento\Config\Model\Config\Source\
                                            Email\Template
                                    </source_model>
                                </field>
                            </group>
                        </section>
                    </system>
                </config>
```

Even though we have a lot going on in this file, it can all be summed up in a few important bits.

 Determining where we want to show our module configuration options is a matter of choice. Either we define and use our own tab or we use an existing tab from one of the core modules. It really comes down to where we decide to put our configuration options.

system.xml defines one tab, as noted by the tab element assigned id attribute value of foggyline. We can have multiple tabs defined under a single system.xml file. The tab element attribute id needs to be unique under all tabs, not just those defined within our module. Within the tab element, we have a label element with the value of Foggyline. This value is what shows up under the Magento admin **Stores | Configuration** area.

The final results should be as shown in the following image:

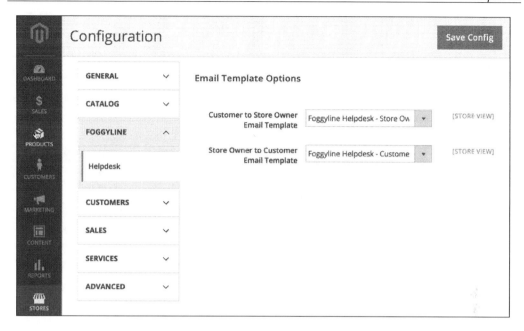

Magento has six pre-existing tabs defined (**General**, **Service**, **Advanced**, **Catalog**, **Customer**, **Sales**) across its core modules. We can easily get a list of all defined tabs in Magento just by doing a search for the `tab` string, filtering only on files named `system.xml`.

Next to the `tab` element, we have the `config | system | section` element. This is the element within which we further define what are to become HTML input fields for accepting configuration options, as visible on the previous image.

We can have multiple sections defined within a single `system.xml` file. The actual `section` element attributes require us to specify the `id` attribute value, which in our example is set to `foggyline_helpdesk`. Other important `section` element attributes are `showInWebsite` and `showInStore`. These can have either `0` or `1` as a value. Depending on our module business logic, we might find a good reason for choosing one value over the other.

Looking further, the elements contained within our `section` element are:

- `label`: This specifies the label we will see under the Magento admin **Store | Configuration** area.

- `tab`: This specifies the ID value of a tab under which we want this section to appear, which in our case equals to `foggyline`.

- `resource`: This specifies the ACL resource ID value.

- `group`: This specifies the group of fields. Similar to the `section` element, it also has `id`, `sortOrder`, `showInWebsite`, and `showInStore` attributes. Further, the group element has child field elements, which translate to HTML input fields under the Magento admin **Store | Configuration** area.

We defined two fields, `customer` and `store_owner`. Similar to `section` and `group`, `field` elements also have `id`, `sortOrder`, `showInWebsite`, and `showInStore` attributes.

Notice how `field` further contains child elements that define its options. Given that our `field` element type attribute was set to `select` with both fields, we needed to define the `source_model` element within each `field`. Both fields have the same `source_model` value which points to the Magento core class, `Magento\Config\Model\Config\Source\Email\Template`. Looking into that class, we can see it implements `\Magento\Framework\Option\ArrayInterface` and defines the `toOptionArray` method. During rendering the admin **Stores | Configuration** area, Magento will call this method to fill in the values for the select HTML element.

> Understanding what we can do with `system.xml` comes down to understanding what is defined under `vendor/magento/module-config/etc/system_file.xsd` and studying existing Magento core module `system.xml` files to get some examples.

As noted previously, our `system.xml` has a resource element that points to the `app/code/Foggyline/Helpdesk/etc/acl.xml` file, which we will now look into.

Creating access control lists (acl.xml)

The `app/code/Foggyline/Helpdesk/etc/acl.xml` file is where we define our module access control list resources. Access control list resources are visible under the Magento admin **System | Permissions | User Roles** area, when we click on the **Add New Role** button, as shown in the following screenshot:

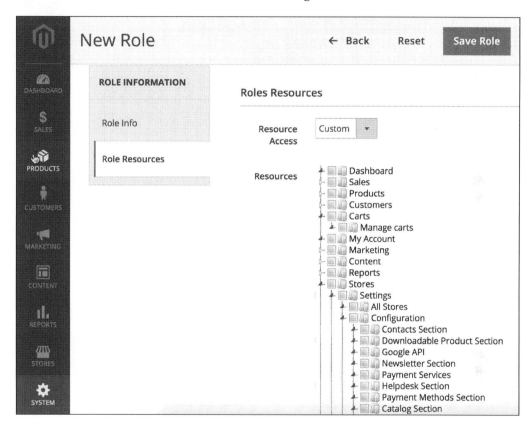

Looking at the preceding screenshot, we can see our **Helpdesk Section** under **Stores | Settings | Configuration**. How did we put it there? We have defined it in our `app/code/Foggyline/Helpdesk/etc/acl.xml` file with content as follows:

```xml
<?xml version="1.0"?>
<config xmlns:xsi="http://www.w3.org/2001/XMLSchema-instance"
  xsi:noNamespaceSchemaLocation="urn:magento:framework:Acl/
  etc/acl.xsd">
    <acl>
        <resources>
            <resource id="Magento_Backend::admin">
                <resource id="Magento_Customer::customer">
                    <resource id="Foggyline_Helpdesk::
                      ticket_manage" title="Manage Helpdesk
                      Tickets" />
                </resource>
                <resource id="Magento_Backend::stores">
                    <resource id="Magento_Backend::
                      stores_settings">
                        <resource id="Magento_Config::config">
                            <resource id=
                              "Foggyline_Helpdesk::helpdesk"
                              title="Helpdesk Section" />
                        </resource>
                    </resource>
                </resource>
            </resource>
        </resources>
    </acl>
</config>
```

Looking at the provided code, the immediate conclusion is that resources can be nested into each other. It is unclear how we should know where to nest our custom-defined resource with an ID value of `Foggyline_Helpdesk::helpdesk`. The simple answer is we followed the Magento structure. By looking into a few of the Magento core modules `system.xml` files and their `acl.xml` files, a pattern emerged where modules nest their resource under `Magento_Backend::admin` | `Magento_Backend::stores` | `Magento_Backend::stores_settings` | `Magento_Config::config`. These are all existing resources defined in core Magento, so we are merely referencing them, not defining them. The only resource we are defining in our `acl.xml` file is our own, which we are then referencing from our `system.xml` file. We can define other resources within `acl.xml` and not all would be nested into the same structure as `Foggyline_Helpdesk::helpdesk`.

The value of the `title` attribute we assign to a resource element is shown in the admin area, as in the previous screenshot.

 Be sure to use a descriptive label so that our module resource is easily recognizable.

Creating an installation script (InstallSchema.php)

`InstallSchema`, or install script, is a way for us to set up tables in the database that will be used to persist our models later on.

If we look back at the module requirements, the following fields need to be created in the `foggyline_helpdesk_ticket` table:

- `ticket_id`
- `customer_id`
- `title`
- `severity`
- `created_at`
- `status`

Our `InstallSchema` is defined under the `app/code/Foggyline/Helpdesk/Setup/InstallSchema.php` file with (partial) content as follows:

```php
<?php

namespace Foggyline\Helpdesk\Setup;

use Magento\Framework\Setup\InstallSchemaInterface;
use Magento\Framework\Setup\ModuleContextInterface;
use Magento\Framework\Setup\SchemaSetupInterface;

/**
 * @codeCoverageIgnore
 */
```

```
class InstallSchema implements InstallSchemaInterface
{
    public function install(SchemaSetupInterface $setup,
      ModuleContextInterface $context)
    {
        $installer = $setup;

        $installer->startSetup();

        $table = $installer->getConnection()
            ->newTable($installer->
              getTable('foggyline_helpdesk_ticket'))
            /* ->addColumn ...   */
            /* ->addIndex ...   */
            /* ->addForeignKey ...   */
            ->setComment('Foggyline Helpdesk Ticket');
        $installer->getConnection()->createTable($table);

        $installer->endSetup();
    }
}
```

The InstallSchema class conforms to InstallSchemaInterface by implementing a single install method. Within this method, we start the installer, create new tables, create new fields, add indexes and foreign keys to the table, and finally end the installer, as shown in the following (partial) code:

```
->addColumn(
    'ticket_id',
    \Magento\Framework\DB\Ddl\Table::TYPE_INTEGER,
    null,
    ['identity' => true, 'unsigned' => true, 'nullable' => false,
      'primary' => true],
    'Ticket Id'
)
->addColumn(
    'customer_id',
    \Magento\Framework\DB\Ddl\Table::TYPE_INTEGER,
    null,
    ['unsigned' => true],
    'Customer Id'
)
```

```
->addColumn(
    'title',
    \Magento\Framework\DB\Ddl\Table::TYPE_TEXT,
    null,
    ['nullable' => false],
    'Title'
)
->addColumn(
    'severity',
    \Magento\Framework\DB\Ddl\Table::TYPE_SMALLINT,
    null,
    ['nullable' => false],
    'Severity'
)
->addColumn(
    'created_at',
    \Magento\Framework\DB\Ddl\Table::TYPE_TIMESTAMP,
    null,
    ['nullable' => false],
    'Created At'
)
->addColumn(
    'status',
    \Magento\Framework\DB\Ddl\Table::TYPE_SMALLINT,
    null,
    ['nullable' => false],
    'Status'
)
->addIndex(
    $installer->getIdxName('foggyline_helpdesk_ticket',
        ['customer_id']),
    ['customer_id']
)
->addForeignKey(
    $installer->getFkName('foggyline_helpdesk_ticket',
        'customer_id', 'customer_entity', 'entity_id'),
    'customer_id',
    $installer->getTable('customer_entity'),
    'entity_id',
    \Magento\Framework\DB\Ddl\Table::ACTION_SET_NULL
)
```

The provided code shows each of the fields from the module requirement being added to the database using the addColumn method call and passing it certain parameters such as the field type and nullable state. It is worth getting familiar with the addColumn, addIndex, and addForeignKey methods as these are most commonly used when specifying new tables for our modules.

> We could further deepen our understanding of the installation script by studying how other core modules handle the InstallSchema.php file. Following a good database design practice, we should always create indexes and foreign keys on our table when referencing data from other tables.

Managing entity persistence (model, resource, collection)

With InstallSchema in place, we now have conditions for entity persistence. Our next step is to define model, resource, and collection classes for the Ticket entity.

The Ticket entity model class is defined under the app/code/Foggyline/Helpdesk/Model/Ticket.php file with content as follows:

```php
<?php

namespace Foggyline\Helpdesk\Model;

class Ticket extends \Magento\Framework\Model\AbstractModel
{
    const STATUS_OPENED = 1;
    const STATUS_CLOSED = 2;

    const SEVERITY_LOW = 1;
    const SEVERITY_MEDIUM = 2;
    const SEVERITY_HIGH = 3;

    protected static $statusesOptions = [
        self::STATUS_OPENED => 'Opened',
        self::STATUS_CLOSED => 'Closed',
    ];
```

```
    protected static $severitiesOptions = [
        self::SEVERITY_LOW => 'Low',
        self::SEVERITY_MEDIUM => 'Medium',
        self::SEVERITY_HIGH => 'High',
    ];

    /**
     * Initialize resource model
     * @return void
     */
    protected function _construct()
    {
        $this->_init('Foggyline\Helpdesk\Model\
          ResourceModel\Ticket');
    }

    public static function getSeveritiesOptionArray()
    {
        return self::$severitiesOptions;
    }

    public function getStatusAsLabel()
    {
        return self::$statusesOptions[$this->getStatus()];
    }

    public function getSeverityAsLabel()
    {
        return self::$severitiesOptions[$this->getSeverity()];
    }
}
```

Reading the preceding code, we see it extends the `\Magento\Framework\Model\`
`AbstractModel` class, which further extends the `\Magento\Framework\Object` class.
This brings a lot of extra methods into our `Ticket` model class, such as `load`, `delete`,
`save`, `toArray`, `toJson`, `toString`, `toXml`, and so on.

The only actual requirement for us is to define the `_construct` method that,
through the `_init` function call, specifies the resource class the model will be using
when persisting data. We have set this value to `Foggyline\Helpdesk\Model\`
`ResourceModel\Ticket`, which will be the next class we will define, the so-called
resource class.

We have further defined several constants, STATUS_* and SEVERITY_*, as a sign of good programming practice and not to hardcode values that we will use across the code, which we can centralize into a class constant. These constants, in a way, map to our module requirements.

Additionally, we have three additional methods (getSeveritiesOptionArray, getStatusAsLabel, and getSeverityAsLabel) that we will use later on in our block class and template file.

The Ticket entity resource class is defined under app/code/Foggyline/Helpdesk/ Model/ResourceModel/Ticket.php with content as follows:

```php
<?php

namespace Foggyline\Helpdesk\Model\ResourceModel;

class Ticket extends
  \Magento\Framework\Model\ResourceModel\Db\AbstractDb
{
    /**
     * Initialize resource model
     * Get table name from config
     *
     * @return void
     */
    protected function _construct()
    {
        $this->_init('foggyline_helpdesk_ticket', 'ticket_id');
    }
}
```

We can see the code extends the \Magento\Framework\Model\ResourceModel\ Db\AbstractDb class, which further extends the \Magento\Framework\Model\ ResourceModel\AbstractResource class. This brings a lot of extra methods into our Ticket resource class, such as load, delete, save, commit, rollback, and so on.

The only actual requirement for us is to define the _construct method, through which we call the _init function that accepts two parameters. The first parameter of the _ init function specifies the table name foggyline_helpdesk_ticket and the second parameter specifies identifying the ticket_id column within that table where we will be persisting data.

Finally, we define the `Ticket` entity collection class under `app/code/Foggyline/Helpdesk/Model/ResourceModel/Ticket/Collection.php` with content as follows:

```php
<?php

namespace Foggyline\Helpdesk\Model\ResourceModel\Ticket;

class Collection extends \Magento\Framework\Model\
  ResourceModel\Db\Collection\AbstractCollection
{
    /**
     * Constructor
     * Configures collection
     *
     * @return void
     */
    protected function _construct()
    {
        $this->_init('Foggyline\Helpdesk\Model\Ticket',
            'Foggyline\Helpdesk\Model\ResourceModel\Ticket');
    }
}
```

The collection class code extends the `\Magento\Framework\Model\ResourceModel\Db\Collection\AbstractCollection` class, which further extends the `\Magento\Framework\Data\Collection\AbstractDb` class, which further extends `\Magento\Framework\Data\Collection`. The final parent collection class then implements the following interfaces: `\IteratorAggregate`, `\Countable`, `Magento\Framework\Option\ArrayInterface`, and `Magento\Framework\Data\CollectionDataSourceInterface`. Through this deep inheritance, a large number of methods become available to our collection class, such as `count`, `getAllIds`, `getColumnValues`, `getFirstItem`, `getLastItem`, and so on.

With regard to our newly defined collection class, the only actual requirement for us is to define the `_construct` method. Within the `_construct` method, we call the `_init` function to which we pass two parameters. The first parameter specifies the `Ticket` model class `Foggyline\Helpdesk\Model\Ticket` and the second parameter specifies the `Ticket` resource class `Foggyline\Helpdesk\Model\ResourceModel\Ticket`.

The three classes we just defined (`model`, `resource`, `collection`) act as an overall single entity persistence mechanism. With the currently defined code, we are able to save, delete, update, lookup with filtering, and list our `Ticket` entities, which we demonstrate in the upcoming sections.

Building a frontend interface

Now that we have defined the necessary minimum for data persistence functionality, we can move forward to building a frontend interface. The module requirement says that customers should be able to submit a ticket through their **My Account** section. We will therefore add a link called **Helpdesk Tickets** under the customer's **My Account** section.

The following are needed for a fully functional frontend:

- A route that will map to our controller
- A controller that will catch requests from a mapped route
- A controller action that will load the layout
- Layout XMLs that will update the view making it look as if we are on the **My Account** section while providing content of our own
- A block class to power our template file
- A template file that we will render into the content area of a page
- A controller action that will save the **New Ticket** form once it is posted

Creating routes, controllers, and layout handles

We start by defining a route within the app/code/Foggyline/Helpdesk/etc/frontend/routes.xml file with content as follows:

```xml
<?xml version="1.0"?>
<config xmlns:xsi="http://www.w3.org/2001/XMLSchema-instance"
  xsi:noNamespaceSchemaLocation="urn:magento:framework:App/
  etc/routes.xsd">
    <router id="standard">
        <route id="foggyline_helpdesk"
          frontName="foggyline_helpdesk">
            <module name="Foggyline_Helpdesk"/>
        </route>
    </router>
</config>
```

Note that the route element id and frontName attributes have the same value, but they do not serve the same purpose, as we will see soon.

Now we define our controller app/code/Foggyline/Helpdesk/Controller/
Ticket.php file with content as follows:

```php
<?php

namespace Foggyline\Helpdesk\Controller;

abstract class Ticket extends \Magento\Framework\App\Action\Action
{
    protected $customerSession;

    public function __construct(
        \Magento\Framework\App\Action\Context $context,
        \Magento\Customer\Model\Session $customerSession
    )
    {
        $this->customerSession = $customerSession;
        parent::__construct($context);
    }

    public function dispatch(\Magento\Framework\App
      \RequestInterface $request)
    {
        if (!$this->customerSession->authenticate()) {
            $this->_actionFlag->set('', 'no-dispatch', true);
            if (!$this->customerSession->getBeforeUrl()) {
                $this->customerSession->setBeforeUrl($this->
                  _redirect->getRefererUrl());
            }
        }
        return parent::dispatch($request);
    }
}
```

Our controller loads the customer session object through its constructor. The
customer session object is then used within the dispatch method to check if the
customer is authenticated or not. If the customer is not authenticated, all frontend
actions in the Internet browser that lead to this controller will result in the customer
being redirected to the login screen.

Once the controller is in place, we can then define the actions that extend from it. Each action is a class file on its own, extending from the parent class. We will now define our index action, the one that will render the view under **My Account | Helpdesk Tickets**, within the app/code/Foggyline/Helpdesk/Controller/ Ticket/Index.php file with content as follows:

```php
<?php

namespace Foggyline\Helpdesk\Controller\Ticket;

class Index extends \Foggyline\Helpdesk\Controller\Ticket
{
    public function execute()
    {
        $resultPage = $this->resultFactory->create(\Magento
          \Framework\Controller\ResultFactory::TYPE_PAGE);
        return $resultPage;
    }
}
```

Controller action code lives within the execute method of its class. We simply extend from the \Foggyline\Helpdesk\Controller\Ticket controller class and define the necessary logic within the execute method. Simply calling loadLayout and renderLayout is enough to render the page on the frontend.

The frontend XML layout handles reside under the app/code/Foggyline/ Helpdesk/view/frontend/layout folder. Having the route ID, controller, and controller action is enough for us to determine the handle name, which goes by formula *{route id}_{controller name}_{controller action name}.xml*. Thus, we define an index action layout within the app/code/Foggyline/Helpdesk/view/frontend/ layout/foggyline_helpdesk_ticket_index.xml file with content as follows:

```xml
<?xml version="1.0"?>

<page xmlns:xsi="http://www.w3.org/2001/XMLSchema-instance"
  xsi:noNamespaceSchemaLocation="urn:magento:framework:View/Layout
  /etc/page_configuration.xsd">
    <update handle="customer_account"/>
    <body>
        <referenceContainer name="content">
            <block class="Foggyline\Helpdesk\Block\Ticket\Index"
                name="foggyline.helpdesk.ticket.index" template=
                "Foggyline_Helpdesk::ticket/index.phtml"
                cacheable="false"/>
        </referenceContainer>
    </body>
</page>
```

Notice how we immediately call the update directive, passing it the `customer_account` handle attribute value. This is like saying, "Include everything from the `customer_account` handle into our handle here." We are further referencing the content block, within which we define our own custom block type `Foggyline\Helpdesk\Block\Ticket\Index`. Though a block class can specify its own template, we are using a template attribute with a module-specific path, `Foggyline_Helpdesk::ticket/index.phtml`, to assign a template to a block.

Simply including the `customer_acount` handle is not enough; we need something extra to define our link under the **My Account** section. We define this extra something under the `app/code/Foggyline/Helpdesk/view/frontend/layout/customer_account.xml` file with content as follows:

```xml
<?xml version="1.0"?>

<page xmlns:xsi="http://www.w3.org/2001/XMLSchema-instance"
    xsi:noNamespaceSchemaLocation="urn:magento:framework:View/
    Layout/etc/page_configuration.xsd">
    <head>
        <title>Helpdesk Tickets</title>
    </head>
    <body>
        <referenceBlock name="customer_account_navigation">
            <block class="Magento\Framework\View\Element\Html
                \Link\Current" name="foggyline-helpdesk-ticket">
                <arguments>
                    <argument name="path" xsi:type="string">
                    foggyline_helpdesk/ticket/index
                    </argument>
                    <argument name="label" xsi:type="string">
                    Helpdesk Tickets
                    </argument>
                </arguments>
            </block>
        </referenceBlock>
    </body>
</page>
```

What is happening here is that we are referencing an existing block called `customer_account_navigation` and defining a new block within it of class `Magento\Framework\View\Element\Html\Link\Current`. This block accepts two parameters: the path that is set to our controller action and the label that is set to **Helpdesk Tickets**.

Creating blocks and templates

The `Foggyline\Helpdesk\Block\Ticket\Index` block class we pointed to from `foggyline_helpdesk_ticket_index.xml` is defined under the `app/code/Foggyline/Helpdesk/Block/Ticket/Index.php` file with content as follows:

```php
<?php

namespace Foggyline\Helpdesk\Block\Ticket;

class Index extends \Magento\Framework\View\Element\Template
{
    /**
     * @var \Magento\Framework\Stdlib\DateTime
     */
    protected $dateTime;

    /**
     * @var \Magento\Customer\Model\Session
     */
    protected $customerSession;

    /**
     * @var \Foggyline\Helpdesk\Model\TicketFactory
     */
    protected $ticketFactory;

    /**
     * @param \Magento\Framework\View\Element\Template\Context
       $context
     * @param array $data
     */
    public function __construct(
        \Magento\Framework\View\Element\Template\Context $context,
        \Magento\Framework\Stdlib\DateTime $dateTime,
        \Magento\Customer\Model\Session $customerSession,
        \Foggyline\Helpdesk\Model\TicketFactory $ticketFactory,
        array $data = []
    )
    {
        $this->dateTime = $dateTime;
        $this->customerSession = $customerSession;
        $this->ticketFactory = $ticketFactory;
```

```
            parent::__construct($context, $data);
    }


    /**
     * @return \Foggyline\Helpdesk\Model\ResourceModel
       \Ticket\Collection
     */
    public function getTickets()
    {
        return $this->ticketFactory
            ->create()
            ->getCollection()
            ->addFieldToFilter('customer_id', $this->
              customerSession->getCustomerId());
    }


    public function getSeverities()
    {
        return \Foggyline\Helpdesk\Model\
          Ticket::getSeveritiesOptionArray();
    }
}
```

The reason why we defined the `Foggyline\Helpdesk\Block\Ticket` block class
instead of using just `\Magento\Framework\View\Element\Template` is because
we wanted to define some helper methods we could then use in our `index.phtml`
template. These methods are `getTickets` (which we will use for listing all customer
tickets) and `getSeverities` (which we will use for creating a dropdown of possible
severities to choose from when creating a new ticket).

The template is further defined under the `app/code/Foggyline/Helpdesk/view/`
`frontend/templates/ticket/index.phtml` file with content as follows:

```
<?php $tickets = $block->getTickets() ?>

<form
    id="form-validate"
    action="<?php echo $block->
      getUrl('foggyline_helpdesk/ticket/save') ?>"
    method="post">
    <?php echo $block->getBlockHtml('formkey') ?>

    <div class="field title required">
```

```
    <label class="label" for="title"><span>
      <?php echo __('Title') ?></span></label>

    <div class="control">
        <input
            id="title"
            type="text"
            name="title"
            data-validate="{required:true}"
            value=""
            placeholder="<?php echo __('Something
              descriptive') ?>"/>
    </div>
</div>
<div class="field severity">
    <label class="label" for="severity"><span><?php echo
      __('Severity') ?></span></label>

    <div class="control">
        <select name="severity">
            <?php foreach ($block->getSeverities() as $value
              => $name): ?>
                <option value="<?php echo $value ?>"><?php
                  echo $this->escapeHtml($name) ?></option>
            <?php endforeach; ?>
        </select>
    </div>
</div>

<button type="submit" class="action save primary">
    <span><?php echo __('Submit Ticket') ?></span>
</button>
</form>

<script>
    require([
        'jquery',
        'mage/mage'
    ], function ($) {
        var dataForm = $('#form-validate');
        dataForm.mage('validation', {});
    });
```

```
        </script>

    <?php if ($tickets->count()): ?>
        <table class="data-grid">
            <?php foreach ($tickets as $ticket): ?>
                <tr>
                    <td><?php echo $ticket->getId() ?></td>
                    <td><?php echo $block->escapeHtml($ticket->
                        getTitle()) ?></td>
                    <td><?php echo $ticket->getCreatedAt() ?></td>
                    <td><?php echo $ticket->getSeverityAsLabel() ?>
                        </td>
                    <td><?php echo $ticket->getStatusAsLabel() ?></td>
                </tr>
            <?php endforeach; ?>
        </table>
    <?php endif; ?>
```

Though this is a big chunk of code, it is easily readable as it is divided into a few very different role-playing chunks.

The $block variable is actually the same as if we wrote $this, which is a reference to the instance of the Foggyline\Helpdesk\Block\Ticket class where we defined the actual getTickets method. Thus, the $tickets variable is first defined as a collection of tickets that belong to the currently logged-in customer.

We then specified a form with a POST method type and an action URL that points to our Save controller action. Within the form, we have a $block->getBlockHtml('formkey') call, which basically returns a hidden input field named form_key whose value is a random string. Form keys in Magento are a means of preventing against **Cross-Site Request Forgery (CSRF)**, so we need to be sure to use them on any form we define. As part of the form, we have also defined a title input field, severity select field, and submit button. Notice the CSS classes tossed around, which guarantee that our form's look will match those of other Magento forms.

Right after the closing form tag, we have a RequireJS type of JavaScript inclusion for validation. Given that our form ID value is set to **form-validate**, the JavaScript dataForm variable binds to it and triggers a validation check when we press the **Submit** button.

We then have a count check and a foreach loop that renders all possibly existing customer tickets.

The final result of the template code can be seen in the following image:

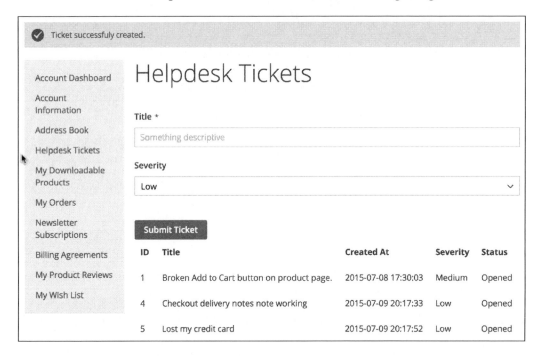

Handling form submissions

There is one more piece we are missing in order to complete our frontend functionality – a controller action that will save the **New Ticket** form once it is posted. We define this action within the app/code/Foggyline/Helpdesk/ Controller/Ticket/Save.php file with content as follows:

```php
<?php

namespace Foggyline\Helpdesk\Controller\Ticket;

class Save extends \Foggyline\Helpdesk\Controller\Ticket
{
    protected $transportBuilder;
    protected $inlineTranslation;
    protected $scopeConfig;
    protected $storeManager;
    protected $formKeyValidator;
```

```
protected $dateTime;
protected $ticketFactory;

public function __construct(
    \Magento\Framework\App\Action\Context $context,
    \Magento\Customer\Model\Session $customerSession,
    \Magento\Framework\Mail\Template\TransportBuilder
      $transportBuilder,
    \Magento\Framework\Translate\Inline\StateInterface
      $inlineTranslation,
    \Magento\Framework\App\Config\ScopeConfigInterface
      $scopeConfig,
    \Magento\Store\Model\StoreManagerInterface $storeManager,
    \Magento\Framework\Data\Form\FormKey\Validator
      $formKeyValidator,
    \Magento\Framework\Stdlib\DateTime $dateTime,
    \Foggyline\Helpdesk\Model\TicketFactory $ticketFactory
)
{

    $this->transportBuilder = $transportBuilder;
    $this->inlineTranslation = $inlineTranslation;
    $this->scopeConfig = $scopeConfig;
    $this->storeManager = $storeManager;
    $this->formKeyValidator = $formKeyValidator;
    $this->dateTime = $dateTime;
    $this->ticketFactory = $ticketFactory;
    $this->messageManager = $context->getMessageManager();
    parent::__construct($context, $customerSession);
}

public function execute()
{
    $resultRedirect = $this->resultRedirectFactory->create();

    if (!$this->formKeyValidator->validate($this->
      getRequest())) {
        return $resultRedirect->setRefererUrl();
    }

    $title = $this->getRequest()->getParam('title');
    $severity = $this->getRequest()->getParam('severity');
```

```
try {
    /* Save ticket */
    $ticket = $this->ticketFactory->create();
    $ticket->setCustomerId($this->customerSession->
        getCustomerId());
    $ticket->setTitle($title);
    $ticket->setSeverity($severity);
    $ticket->setCreatedAt($this->dateTime->
        formatDate(true));
    $ticket->setStatus(\Foggyline\Helpdesk\Model\
        Ticket::STATUS_OPENED);
    $ticket->save();

    $customer = $this->customerSession->getCustomerData();

    /* Send email to store owner */
    $storeScope =
        \Magento\Store\Model\ScopeInterface::SCOPE_STORE;
    $transport = $this->transportBuilder
        ->setTemplateIdentifier($this->scopeConfig->
            getValue('foggyline_helpdesk/email_template/
            store_owner', $storeScope))
        ->setTemplateOptions(
            [
                'area' => \Magento\Framework\App\
                    Area::AREA_FRONTEND,
                'store' => $this->storeManager->
                    getStore()->getId(),
            ]
        )
        ->setTemplateVars(['ticket' => $ticket])
        ->setFrom([
            'name' => $customer->getFirstname() . ' ' .
                $customer->getLastname(),
            'email' => $customer->getEmail()
        ])
        ->addTo($this->scopeConfig->getValue(
            'trans_email/ident_general/email', $storeScope))
        ->getTransport();
```

```
        $transport->sendMessage();
        $this->inlineTranslation->resume();

        $this->messageManager->addSuccess(__('Ticket
            successfully created.'));
    } catch (Exception $e) {
        $this->messageManager->addError(__('Error occurred
            during ticket creation.'));
    }

    return $resultRedirect->setRefererUrl();
    }
}
```

First, we look at `__construct` to see what parameters are passed to it. Given that the code we run in the `execute` method needs to check if the form key is valid, create a ticket in the database, pass on the ticket and some customer info to the e-mail that is being sent to the store owner; then, we get an idea of what kind of objects are being passed around.

The `execute` method starts by checking the validity of the form key. If the form key is invalid, we return with a redirection to the referring URL.

Passing the form key check, we grab the title and severity variables as passed by the form. We then instantiate the ticket entity by the ticket factory create method and simply set the `ticket` entity values one by one. Note that the `Ticket` entity model `Foggyline\Helpdesk\Model\Ticket` does not really have methods like `setSeverity` on its own. This is the inherited property of its `\Magento\Framework\Object` parent class.

Once the ticket entity is saved, we initiate the `transport builder` object, passing along all of the required parameters for successful e-mail sending. Notice how `setTemplateIdentifier` uses our `system.xml` configuration option `foggyline_helpdesk/email_template/store_owner`. This, if not specifically set under the admin **Store | Configuration | Foggyline | Helpdesk** area, has a default value defined under `config.xml` that points to the e-mail template ID in the `email_templates.xml` file.

`setTemplateVars` expects the array or instance of `\Magento\Framework\Object` to be passed to it. We pass the entire `$ticket` object to it, just nesting it under the ticket key, thus making the properties of a `Ticket` entity, like a title, become available in the e-mail HTML template as `{{var ticket.title}}`.

When a customer now submits the **New Ticket** form from **My Account | Helpdesk Tickets**, the HTTP POST request will hit the save controller action class. If the preceding code is successfully executed, the ticket is saved to the database and redirection back to **My Account | Helpdesk Tickets** will occur showing a **Ticket successfully created** message in the browser.

Building a backend interface

Until now, we have been dealing with setting up general module configuration, e-mail templates, frontend route, frontend layout, block, and template. What remains to complete the module requirements is the admin interface, where the store owner can see submitted tickets and change statuses from open to closed.

The following are needed for a fully functional admin interface as per the requirements:

- ACL resource used to allow or disallow access to the ticket listing
- Menu item linking to tickets listing the controller action
- Route that maps to our admin controller
- Layout XMLs that map to the ticket listing the controller action
- Controller action for listing tickets
- Full XML layout grid definition within layout XMLs defining grid, custom column renderers, and custom dropdown filter values
- Controller action for closing tickets and sending e-mails to customers

Linking the access control list and menu

We start by adding a new ACL resource entry to the previously defined app/code/Foggyline/Helpdesk/etc/acl.xml file, as a child of the Magento_Backend::admin resource as follows:

```
<resource id="Magento_Customer::customer">
    <resource id="Foggyline_Helpdesk::ticket_manage" title="Manage
    Helpdesk Tickets"/>
</resource>
```

On its own, the defined resource entry does not do anything. This resource will later be used within the menu and controller.

The menu item linking to the tickets listing the controller action is defined under the `app/code/Foggyline/Helpdesk/etc/adminhtml/menu.xml` file as follows:

```xml
<?xml version="1.0"?>

<config xmlns:xsi="http://www.w3.org/2001/XMLSchema-instance"
  xsi:noNamespaceSchemaLocation="urn:magento:module:
  Magento_Backend:etc/menu.xsd">
    <menu>
        <add id="Foggyline_Helpdesk::ticket_manage"
          title="Helpdesk Tickets" module="Foggyline_Helpdesk"
            parent="Magento_Customer::customer"
              action="foggyline_helpdesk/ticket/index"
              resource="Foggyline_Helpdesk::ticket_manage"/>
    </menu>
</config>
```

We are using the `menu | add` element to add a new menu item under the Magento admin area. The position of an item within the admin area is defined by the attribute parent, which in our case means under the existing **Customer** menu. If the parent is omitted, our item would appear as a new item on a menu. The `title` attribute value is the label we will see in the menu. The `id` attribute has to uniquely differentiate our menu item from others. The `resource` attribute references the ACL resource defined in the `app/code/Foggyline/Helpdesk/etc/acl.xml` file. If a role of a logged-in user does not allow him to use the `Foggyline_Helpdesk::ticket_manage` resource, the user would not be able to see the menu item.

Creating routes, controllers, and layout handles

Now we add a route that maps to our admin controller, by defining the `app/code/Foggyline/Helpdesk/etc/adminhtml/routes.xml` file as follows:

```xml
<?xml version="1.0"?>

<config xmlns:xsi="http://www.w3.org/2001/XMLSchema-instance"
  xsi:noNamespaceSchemaLocation="urn:magento:framework:App/etc
  /routes.xsd">
    <router id="admin">
        <route id="foggyline_helpdesk"
          frontName="foggyline_helpdesk">
            <module name="Foggyline_Helpdesk"/>
        </route>
    </router>
</config>
```

The admin route definition is almost identical to the frontend router definition, where the difference primarily lies in the router ID value, which equals to the admin here.

With the router definition in place, we can now define our three layout XMLs, under the `app/code/Foggyline/Helpdesk/view/adminhtml/layout` directory, which map to the ticket listing the controller action:

- `foggyline_helpdesk_ticket_grid.xml`
- `foggyline_helpdesk_ticket_grid_block.xml`
- `foggyline_helpdesk_ticket_index.xml`

The reason we define three layout files for a single action controller and not one is because of the way we use the listing in control in the Magento admin area.

The content of the `foggyline_helpdesk_ticket_index.xml` file is defined as follows:

```xml
<?xml version="1.0" encoding="UTF-8"?>

<page xmlns:xsi="http://www.w3.org/2001/XMLSchema-instance"
  xsi:noNamespaceSchemaLocation="urn:magento:framework:View/Layout
  /etc/page_configuration.xsd">
    <update handle="formkey"/>
    <update handle="foggyline_helpdesk_ticket_grid_block"/>
    <body>
        <referenceContainer name="content">
            <block class="Foggyline\Helpdesk\Block
                \Adminhtml\Ticket"
                name="admin.block.helpdesk.ticket.grid.container">
            </block>
        </referenceContainer>
    </body>
</page>
```

Two update handles are specified, one pulling in `formkey` and the other pulling in `foggyline_helpdesk_ticket_grid_block`. We then reference the content container and define a new block of the `Foggyline\Helpdesk\Block\Adminhtml\Ticket` class with it.

Utilizing the grid widget

We could have used `Magento\Backend\Block\Widget\Grid\Container` as a block class name. However, given that we needed some extra logic, like removing the **Add New** button, we opted for a custom class that then extends `\Magento\Backend\Block\Widget\Grid\Container` and adds the required logic.

The `Foggyline\Helpdesk\Block\Adminhtml\Ticket` class is defined under the `app/code/Foggyline/Helpdesk/Block/Adminhtml/Ticket.php` file as follows:

```php
<?php

namespace Foggyline\Helpdesk\Block\Adminhtml;

class Ticket extends \Magento\Backend\Block\Widget\Grid\Container
{
    protected function _construct()
    {
        $this->_controller = 'adminhtml';
        $this->_blockGroup = 'Foggyline_Helpdesk';
        $this->_headerText = __('Tickets');

        parent::_construct();

        $this->removeButton('add');
    }
}
```

Not much is happening in the `Ticket` block class here. Most importantly, we extend from `\Magento\Backend\Block\Widget\Grid\Container` and define `_controller` and `_blockGroup`, as these serve as a sort of glue for telling our grid where to find other possible block classes. Since we won't have an **Add New** ticket feature in admin, we are calling the `removeButton` method to remove the default **Add New** button from the grid container.

Back to our second XML layout file, the `foggyline_helpdesk_ticket_grid.xml` file, which we define as follows:

```xml
<?xml version="1.0"?>

<layout xmlns:xsi="http://www.w3.org/2001/XMLSchema-instance"
  xsi:noNamespaceSchemaLocation="urn:magento:framework:View/Layout
  /etc/layout_generic.xsd">
```

```
        <update handle="formkey"/>
        <update handle="foggyline_helpdesk_ticket_grid_block"/>
        <container name="root">
            <block class="Magento\Backend\Block\Widget\Grid\Container"
                name="admin.block.helpdesk.ticket.grid.container"
                template="Magento_Backend::widget/grid/container
                /empty.phtml"/>
        </container>
    </layout>
```

Notice how the content of `foggyline_helpdesk_ticket_grid.xml` is nearly identical to that of `foggyline_helpdesk_ticket_index.xml`. The only difference between the two is the value of the `block` class and the template attribute. The `block` class is defined as `Magento\Backend\Block\Widget\Grid\Container`, where we previously defined it as `Foggyline\Helpdesk\Block\Adminhtml\Ticket`.

If we look at the content of the `\Magento\Backend\Block\Widget\Grid\Container` class, we can see the following property defined:

```
protected $_template =
    'Magento_Backend::widget/grid/container.phtml';
```

If we look at the content of the `vendor/magento/module-backend/view/adminhtml/templates/widget/grid/container.phtml` and `vendor/magento/module-backend/view/adminhtml/templates/widget/grid/container/empty.phtml` files, the difference can be easily spotted. `container/empty.phtml` only returns grid HTML, whereas `container.phtml` returns buttons and grid HTML.

Given that `foggyline_helpdesk_ticket_grid.xml` will be a handle for the AJAX loading grid listing during sorting and filtering, we need it to return only grid HTML upon reload.

We now move on to the third and largest of XML's layout files, the `app/code/Foggyline/Helpdesk/view/adminhtml/layout/foggyline_helpdesk_ticket_grid_block.xml` file. Given the size of it, we will split it into two code chunks as we explain them one by one.

The first part, or initial content of the `foggyline_helpdesk_ticket_grid_block.xml` file, is defined as follows:

```
<?xml version="1.0" encoding="UTF-8"?>

<page xmlns:xsi="http://www.w3.org/2001/XMLSchema-instance"
    xsi:noNamespaceSchemaLocation="urn:magento:framework:View/Layout
    /etc/page_configuration.xsd">
```

```
<body>
    <referenceBlock name=
      "admin.block.helpdesk.ticket.grid.container">
        <block class="Magento\Backend\Block\Widget\Grid"
          name="admin.block.helpdesk.ticket.grid" as="grid">
            <arguments>
                <argument name="id" xsi:type="string">
                  ticketGrid</argument>
                <argument name="dataSource" xsi:type="object">
                  Foggyline\Helpdesk\Model\ResourceModel
                  \Ticket\Collection
                </argument>
                <argument name="default_sort"
                  xsi:type="string">ticket_id</argument>
                <argument name="default_dir"
                  xsi:type="string">desc</argument>
                <argument name="save_parameters_in_session"
                  xsi:type="boolean">true</argument>
                <argument name="use_ajax"
                  xsi:type="boolean">true</argument>
            </arguments>
            <block class="Magento\Backend\Block
              \Widget\Grid\ColumnSet" name=
              "admin.block.helpdesk.ticket.grid.columnSet"
              as="grid.columnSet">
                <!-- Column definitions here -->
            </block>
        </block>
    </referenceBlock>
</body>
</page>
```

Notice `<!-- Column definitions here -->`; we will come back to that soon.
For now, let's analyze what is happening here. Right after a body element, we
have a reference to `admin.block.helpdesk.ticket.grid.container`, which is a
content block child defined under the `foggyline_helpdesk_ticket_grid.xml` and
`foggyline_helpdesk_ticket_index.xml` files. Within this reference, we are defining
another block of class `Magento\Backend\Block\Widget\Grid`, passing it a name of
our choosing and an alias. Further, this block has an arguments list and another block
of class `Magento\Backend\Block\Widget\Grid\ColumnSet` as child elements.

Through the arguments list we specify the:

- id: Set to the value of ticketGrid, we can set any value we want here, ideally sticking to formula *{entity name}*.

- dataSource: Set to the value of Foggyline\Helpdesk\Model\ ResourceModel\Ticket\Collection, which is the name of our Ticket entity resource class.

- default_sort: Set to the value of ticket_id, which is the property of the Ticket entity by which we want to sort.

- default_dir: Set to the value of desc, to denote a descending order of sorting. This value functions together with default_sort as a single unit.

- save_parameters_in_session: Set to true, this is easiest to explain using the following example: if we do some sorting and filtering on the Ticket grid and then move on to another part of the admin area, then come back to Ticket grid, if this value is set to **yes**, the grid we see will have those filters and sorting set.

- use_ajax: Set to true, when grid filtering and sorting is triggered, an AJAX loader kicks in and reloads only the grid area and not the whole page.

Right after the grid blocks argument list, we have the grid column set. This brings us to the second part of foggyline_helpdesk_ticket_grid_block.xml content. We simply replace the <!-- Columns here --> comment with the following:

```xml
<block class="Magento\Backend\Block\Widget\Grid\Column"
  as="ticket_id">
    <arguments>
        <argument name="header" xsi:type="string"
          translate="true">ID</argument>
        <argument name="type" xsi:type="string">number</argument>
        <argument name="id" xsi:type="string">ticket_id</argument>
        <argument name="index"
          xsi:type="string">ticket_id</argument>
    </arguments>
</block>
<block class="Magento\Backend\Block\Widget\Grid\Column"
  as="title">
    <arguments>
        <argument name="header" xsi:type="string"
      translate="true">Title</argument>
        <argument name="type" xsi:type="string">string</argument>
```

```
            <argument name="id" xsi:type="string">title</argument>
            <argument name="index" xsi:type="string">title</argument>
        </arguments>
</block>
<block class="Magento\Backend\Block\Widget\Grid\Column"
|   as="severity">
    <arguments>
        <argument name="header" xsi:type="string"
          translate="true">Severity</argument>
        <argument name="index"
          xsi:type="string">severity</argument>
        <argument name="type" xsi:type="string">options</argument>
        <argument name="options" xsi:type="options"
          model="Foggyline\Helpdesk\Model\Ticket\Grid\Severity"/>
        <argument name="renderer" xsi:type="string">
          Foggyline\Helpdesk\Block\Adminhtml\Ticket\Grid\Renderer
          \Severity
        </argument>
        <argument name="header_css_class" xsi:type="string">
          col-form_id</argument>
        <argument name="column_css_class" xsi:type="string">
          col-form_id</argument>
    </arguments>
</block>
<block class="Magento\Backend\Block\Widget\Grid\Column"
  as="status">
    <arguments>
        <argument name="header" xsi:type="string"
          translate="true">Status</argument>
        <argument name="index" xsi:type="string">status</argument>
        <argument name="type" xsi:type="string">options</argument>
        <argument name="options" xsi:type="options"
                  model="Foggyline\Helpdesk\Model\Ticket
                    \Grid\Status"/>
        <argument name="renderer" xsi:type="string">
          Foggyline\Helpdesk\Block\Adminhtml\Ticket\Grid
          \Renderer\Status
        </argument>
        <argument name="header_css_class" xsi:type="string">
          col-form_id</argument>
        <argument name="column_css_class" xsi:type="string">
          col-form_id</argument>
    </arguments>
```

```
</block>
<block class="Magento\Backend\Block\Widget\Grid\Column"
  as="action">
    <arguments>
        <argument name="id" xsi:type="string">action</argument>
        <argument name="header" xsi:type="string"
          translate="true">Action</argument>
        <argument name="type" xsi:type="string">action</argument>
        <argument name="getter" xsi:type="string">getId</argument>
        <argument name="filter"
          xsi:type="boolean">false</argument>
        <argument name="sortable"
          xsi:type="boolean">false</argument>
        <argument name="actions" xsi:type="array">
            <item name="view_action" xsi:type="array">
                <item name="caption" xsi:type="string"
                  translate="true">Close</item>
                <item name="url" xsi:type="array">
                    <item name="base"
                      xsi:type="string">*/*/close</item>
                </item>
                <item name="field" xsi:type="string">id</item>
            </item>
        </argument>
        <argument name="header_css_class" xsi:type="string">
          col-actions</argument>
        <argument name="column_css_class" xsi:type="string">
          col-actions</argument>
    </arguments>
</block>
```

Similar to grid, column definitions also have arguments that define its look and behavior:

- `header`: Mandatory, the value we want to see as a label on top of the column.
- `type`: Mandatory, can be anything from: `date`, `datetime`, `text`, `longtext`, `options`, `store`, `number`, `currency`, `skip-list`, `wrapline`, and `country`.
- `id`: Mandatory, a unique value that identifies our column, preferably matching the name of the entity property.
- `index`: Mandatory, the database column name.

- `options`: Optional, if we are using a type like options, then for the options argument we need to specify the class like `Foggyline\Helpdesk\Model\Ticket\Grid\Severity` that implements `\Magento\Framework\Option\ArrayInterface`, meaning it provides the `toOptionArray` method that then fills the values of options during grid rendering.

- `renderer`: Optional, as our `Ticket` entities store severity and status as integer values in the database, columns would render those integer values into columns, which is not really useful. We want to turn those integer values into labels. In order to do so, we need to rewrite the rendering bit of a single table cell, which we do with the help of the renderer argument. The value we pass to it, `Foggyline\Helpdesk\Block\Adminhtml\Ticket\Grid\Renderer\Severity`, needs to be a class that extends `\Magento\Backend\Block\Widget\Grid\Column\Renderer\AbstractRenderer` and does its own implementation of the render method.

- `header_css_class`: Optional, if we prefer to specify a custom header class.

- `column_css_class`: Optional, if we prefer to specify a custom column class.

Creating a grid column renderer

The `Foggyline\Helpdesk\Block\Adminhtml\Ticket\Grid\Renderer\Severity` class, defined in the `app/code/Foggyline/Helpdesk/Block/Adminhtml/Ticket/Grid/Renderer/Severity.php` file, is as follows:

```php
<?php

namespace Foggyline\Helpdesk\Block\Adminhtml\Ticket\Grid\Renderer;

class Severity extends \Magento\Backend\Block\Widget\Grid
  \Column\Renderer\AbstractRenderer
{
    protected $ticketFactory;

    public function __construct(
        \Magento\Backend\Block\Context $context,
        \Foggyline\Helpdesk\Model\TicketFactory $ticketFactory,
        array $data = []
    )
    {
        parent::__construct($context, $data);
        $this->ticketFactory = $ticketFactory;
```

```
        }

        public function render(\Magento\Framework\DataObject $row)
        {
            $ticket = $this->ticketFactory->create()->load($row->
              getId());

            if ($ticket && $ticket->getId()) {
                return $ticket->getSeverityAsLabel();
            }

            return '';

        }

    }
```

Here, we are passing the instance of the ticket factory to the constructor and then using that instance within the render method to load a ticket based on the ID value fetched from the current row. Given that `$row->getId()` returns the ID of the ticket, this is a nice way to reload the entire ticket entity and then fetch the full label from the ticket model by using `$ticket->getSeverityAsLabel()`. Whatever string we return from this method is what will be shown under the grid row.

Another renderer class that is referenced within the `foggyline_helpdesk_ticket_grid_block.xml` file is `Foggyline\Helpdesk\Block\Adminhtml\Ticket\Grid\Renderer\Status`, and we define its content under the `app/code/Foggyline/Helpdesk/Block/Adminhtml/Ticket/Grid/Renderer/Status.php` file as follows:

```php
<?php

namespace Foggyline\Helpdesk\Block\Adminhtml\Ticket\Grid\Renderer;

class Status extends \Magento\Backend\Block\Widget\Grid\Column
  \Renderer\AbstractRenderer
{
    protected $ticketFactory;

    public function __construct(
        \Magento\Backend\Block\Context $context,
        \Foggyline\Helpdesk\Model\TicketFactory $ticketFactory,
        array $data = []
    )
    {
```

```
        parent::__construct($context, $data);
        $this->ticketFactory = $ticketFactory;
    }

    public function render(\Magento\Framework\DataObject $row)
    {
        $ticket = $this->ticketFactory->create()->load($row->
          getId());

        if ($ticket && $ticket->getId()) {
            return $ticket->getStatusAsLabel();
        }

        return '';
    }
}
```

Given that it too is used for a renderer, the content of the Status class is nearly identical to the content of the Severity class. We pass on the ticket factory object via the constructor, so we have it internally for usage within the render method. Then we load the Ticket entity using the ticket factory and ID value fetched from a $row object. As a result, the column will contain the label value of a status and not its integer value.

Creating grid column options

Besides referencing renderer classes, our foggyline_helpdesk_ticket_grid_block.xml file also references the options class for the Severity field.

We define the Foggyline\Helpdesk\Model\Ticket\Grid\Severity options class under the app/code/Foggyline/Helpdesk/Model/Ticket/Grid/Severity.php file as follows:

```php
<?php

namespace Foggyline\Helpdesk\Model\Ticket\Grid;

class Severity implements \Magento\Framework\Option\ArrayInterface
{
    public function toOptionArray()
    {
        return \Foggyline\Helpdesk\Model
            \Ticket::getSeveritiesOptionArray();
    }
}
```

The `options` value from XML layouts refers to a class that has to implement the `toOptionArray` method, which returns an array of arrays, such as the following example:

```
return [
    ['value'=>'theValue1', 'theLabel1'],
    ['value'=>'theValue2', 'theLabel2'],
];
```

Our `Severity` class simply calls the static method we have defined on the `Ticket` class, the `getSeveritiesOptionArray`, and passes along those values.

Creating controller actions

Up to this point, we have defined the menu item, ACL resource, XML layouts, block, `options` class, and `renderer` classes. What remains to connect it all are controllers. We will need three controller actions (`Index`, `Grid`, and `Close`), all extending from the same admin `Ticket` controller.

We define the admin `Ticket` controller under the app/code/Foggyline/Helpdesk/ Controller/Adminhtml/Ticket.php file as follows:

```php
<?php

namespace Foggyline\Helpdesk\Controller\Adminhtml;

class Ticket extends \Magento\Backend\App\Action
{
    protected $resultPageFactory;
    protected $resultForwardFactory;
    protected $resultRedirectFactory;

    public function __construct(
        \Magento\Backend\App\Action\Context $context,
        \Magento\Framework\View\Result\PageFactory
          $resultPageFactory,
        \Magento\Backend\Model\View\Result\ForwardFactory
          $resultForwardFactory
    )
    {
        $this->resultPageFactory = $resultPageFactory;
        $this->resultForwardFactory = $resultForwardFactory;
        $this->resultRedirectFactory = $context->
          getResultRedirectFactory();
```

```
        parent::__construct($context);
    }

    protected function _isAllowed()
    {
        return $this->_authorization->
            isAllowed('Foggyline_Helpdesk::ticket_manage');
    }

    protected function _initAction()
    {
        $this->_view->loadLayout();
        $this->_setActiveMenu(
            'Foggyline_Helpdesk::ticket_manage'
        )->_addBreadcrumb(
            __('Helpdesk'),
            __('Tickets')
        );
        return $this;
    }
}
```

There are a few things to note here. `$this->resultPageFactory`, `$this->resultForwardFactory` and `$this->resultRedirectFactory` are objects to be used on the child (`Index`, `Grid`, and `Close`), so we do not have to initiate them in each child class separately.

The `_isAllowed()` method is extremely important every time we have a custom-defined controller or controller action that we want to check against our custom ACL resource. Here, we are the `isAllowed` method call on the `\Magento\Framework\AuthorizationInterface` type of object (`$this->_authorization`). The parameter passed to the `isAllowed` method call should be the ID value of our custom ACL resource.

We then have the `_initAction` method, which is used for setting up logic shared across child classes, usually things like loading the entire layout, setting up the active menu flag, and adding breadcrumbs.

Moving forward, we define the `Index` controller action within the app/code/Foggyline/Helpdesk/Controller/Adminhtml/Ticket/Index.php file as follows:

```php
<?php

namespace Foggyline\Helpdesk\Controller\Adminhtml\Ticket;
```

```
class Index extends
  \Foggyline\Helpdesk\Controller\Adminhtml\Ticket
{
    public function execute()
    {
        if ($this->getRequest()->getQuery('ajax')) {
            $resultForward = $this->resultForwardFactory->
              create();
            $resultForward->forward('grid');
            return $resultForward;
        }
        $resultPage = $this->resultPageFactory->create();

        $resultPage->
          setActiveMenu('Foggyline_Helpdesk::ticket_manage');
        $resultPage->getConfig()->getTitle()->
          prepend(__('Tickets'));

        $resultPage->addBreadcrumb(__('Tickets'), __('Tickets'));
        $resultPage->addBreadcrumb(__('Manage Tickets'),
          __('Manage Tickets'));

        return $resultPage;
    }
}
```

Controller actions execute within their own class, within the `execute` method. Our `execute` method first checks if the coming request is the AJAX parameter within it. If there is an AJAX parameter, the request is forwarded to the `Grid` action of the same controller.

If there is no AJAX controller, we simply create the instance of the `\Magento\Framework\View\Result\PageFactory` object, and set title, active menu item, and breadcrumbs in it.

A logical question at this point would be how does all of this work and where can we see it. If we log in to the Magento admin area, under the **Customers** menu we should be able to see the **Helpdesk Tickets** menu item. This item, defined previously within `app/code/Foggyline/Helpdesk/etc/adminhtml/menu.xml`, says the menu `action` attribute equals to `foggyline_helpdesk/ticket/index`, which basically translates to the `Index` action of our `Ticket` controller.

Once we click on the **Helpdesk Tickets** link, Magento will hit the Index action within its Ticket controller and try to find the XML file that has the matching route *{id}+{controller name }+{controller action name }+{xml file extension }*, which in our case translates to *{foggyline_helpdesk}+{ticket}+{index}+{.xml}*.

At this point, we should be able to see the screen, as shown in the following screenshot:

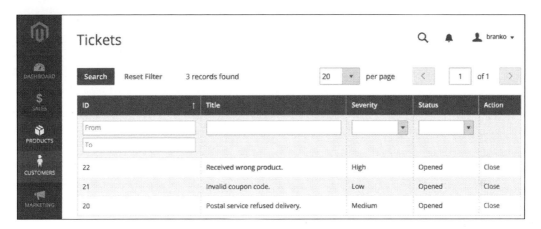

However, if we now try to use sorting or filtering, we would get a broken layout. This is because based on arguments defined under the foggyline_helpdesk_ticket_grid_block.xml file, we are missing the controller Grid action. When we use sorting or filtering, the AJAX request hits the Index controller and asks to be forwarded to the Grid action, which we haven't defined yet.

We now define the Grid action within the app/code/Foggyline/Helpdesk/ Controller/Adminhtml/Ticket/Grid.php file as follows:

```php
<?php

namespace Foggyline\Helpdesk\Controller\Adminhtml\Ticket;

class Grid extends \Foggyline\Helpdesk\Controller\Adminhtml\Ticket
{
    public function execute()
    {
        $this->_view->loadLayout(false);
        $this->_view->renderLayout();
    }
}
```

There is only one execute method with the Grid controller action class, which is expected. The code within the execute method simply calls the loadLayout(false) method to prevent the entire layout loading, making it load only the bits defined under the foggyline_helpdesk_ticket_grid.xml file. This effectively returns the grid HTML to the AJAX, which refreshes the grid on the page.

Finally, we need to handle the Close action link we see on the grid. This link was defined as part of the column definition within the foggyline_helpdesk_ticket_ grid_block.xml file and points to */*/close, which translates to "router as relative from current URL / controller as relative from current URL / close action", which further equals to our Ticket controller Close action.

We define the Close controller action under the app/code/Foggyline/Helpdesk/ Controller/Adminhtml/Ticket/Close.php file as follows:

```php
<?php

namespace Foggyline\Helpdesk\Controller\Adminhtml\Ticket;

class Close extends
  \Foggyline\Helpdesk\Controller\Adminhtml\Ticket
{
    protected $ticketFactory;
    protected $customerRepository;
    protected $transportBuilder;
    protected $inlineTranslation;
    protected $scopeConfig;
    protected $storeManager;

    public function __construct(
        \Magento\Backend\App\Action\Context $context,
        \Magento\Framework\View\Result\PageFactory
          $resultPageFactory,
        \Magento\Backend\Model\View\Result\ForwardFactory
          $resultForwardFactory,
        \Foggyline\Helpdesk\Model\TicketFactory $ticketFactory,
        \Magento\Customer\Api\CustomerRepositoryInterface
          $customerRepository,
        \Magento\Framework\Mail\Template\TransportBuilder
          $transportBuilder,
        \Magento\Framework\Translate\Inline\StateInterface
          $inlineTranslation,
        \Magento\Framework\App\Config\ScopeConfigInterface
          $scopeConfig,
```

```
        \Magento\Store\Model\StoreManagerInterface $storeManager
    )
    {

        $this->ticketFactory = $ticketFactory;
        $this->customerRepository = $customerRepository;
        $this->transportBuilder = $transportBuilder;
        $this->inlineTranslation = $inlineTranslation;
        $this->scopeConfig = $scopeConfig;
        $this->storeManager = $storeManager;
        parent::__construct($context, $resultPageFactory,
            $resultForwardFactory);
    }


    public function execute()
    {
        $ticketId = $this->getRequest()->getParam('id');
        $ticket = $this->ticketFactory->create()->load($ticketId);

        if ($ticket && $ticket->getId()) {
            try {
                $ticket->setStatus(\Foggyline
                    \Helpdesk\Model\Ticket::STATUS_CLOSED);
                $ticket->save();
                $this->messageManager->addSuccess(__('Ticket
                    successfully closed.'));

                /* Send email to customer */
                $customer = $this->customerRepository->
                    getById($ticket->getCustomerId());
                $storeScope = \Magento\Store\Model\
                    ScopeInterface::SCOPE_STORE;
                $transport = $this->transportBuilder
                    ->setTemplateIdentifier($this->scopeConfig->
                        getValue('foggyline_helpdesk/email_template
                        /customer', $storeScope))
                    ->setTemplateOptions(
                        [
                            'area' => \Magento\Framework\App\
Area::AREA_ADMINHTML,
                            'store' => $this->storeManager-
                                >getStore()->getId(),
                        ]
                    )
```

```
                ->setTemplateVars([
                    'ticket' => $ticket,
                    'customer_name' => $customer->
                        getFirstname()
                ])
                ->setFrom([
                    'name' => $this->scopeConfig->
                        getValue('trans_email/ident_general
                        /name', $storeScope),
                    'email' => $this->scopeConfig->
                        getValue('trans_email/ident_general
                        /email', $storeScope)
                ])
                ->addTo($customer->getEmail())
                ->getTransport();
            $transport->sendMessage();
            $this->inlineTranslation->resume();
            $this->messageManager->addSuccess(__('Customer
                notified via email.'));

        } catch (Exception $e) {
            $this->messageManager->addError(__('Error with
                closing ticket action.'));
        }
    }

    $resultRedirect = $this->resultRedirectFactory->create();
    $resultRedirect->setPath('*/*/index');

    return $resultRedirect;
    }
}
```

The Close action controller has two separate roles to fulfill. One is to change the ticket status; the other is to send an e-mail to the customer using the proper e-mail template. The class constructor is being passed a lot of parameters that all instantiate the objects we will be juggling around.

Within the execute action, we first check for the existence of the id parameter and then try to load a Ticket entity through the ticket factory, based on the provided ID value. If the ticket exists, we set its status label to \Foggyline\Helpdesk\Model\ Ticket::STATUS_CLOSED and save it.

Following the ticket save is the e-mail-sending code, which is very similar to the one that we already saw in the customer **New Ticket** save action. The difference is that the e-mail goes out from the admin user to the customer this time. We are setting the template ID to the configuration value at path `foggyline_helpdesk/ email_template/customer`. The `setTemplateVars` method is passed to the member array this time, both `ticket` and `customer_name`, as they are both used in the e-mail template. The `setFrom` method is passed the general store username and e-mail, and the `sendMessage` method is called on the `transport` object.

Finally, using the `resultRedirectFactory` object, the user is redirected back to the tickets grid.

With this, we finalize our module functional requirement.

Though we are done with the functional requirement of a module, what remains for us as developers is to write tests. There are several types of tests, such as unit, functional, integration, and so on. To keep things simple, within this chapter we will cover only unit tests across a single model class.

Creating unit tests

This chapter assumes that we have PHPUnit configured and available on the command line. If this is not the case, PHPUnit can be installed using instructions from the `https://phpunit.de/` website.

To build and run tests using the PHPUnit testing framework, we need to define test locations and other configuration options via an XML file. Magento defines this XML configuration file under `dev/tests/unit/phpunit.xml.dist`. Let's make a copy of that file under `dev/tests/unit/phpunit-foggyline-helpdesk.xml`, with adjustments as follows:

```xml
<?xml version="1.0" encoding="UTF-8"?>

<phpunit xmlns:xsi="http://www.w3.org/2001/XMLSchema-instance"
  xsi:noNamespaceSchemaLocation="http://schema.phpunit.de/4.1
  /phpunit.xsd"
        colors="true"
        bootstrap="./framework/bootstrap.php"
      >
    <testsuite name="Foggyline_Helpdesk - Unit Tests">
        <directory suffix="Test.php">
          ../../../app/code/Foggyline/Helpdesk/Test/Unit
        </directory>
```

```
    </testsuite>
    <php>
        <ini name="date.timezone" value="Europe/Zagreb"/>
        <ini name="xdebug.max_nesting_level" value="200"/>
    </php>
    <filter>
        <whitelist addUncoveredFilesFromWhiteList="true">
            <directory suffix=".php">
             ../../../app/code/Foggyline/Helpdesk/*</directory>
            <exclude>
                <directory>
                 ../../../app/code/Foggyline/Form/Helpdesk
                </directory>
            </exclude>
        </whitelist>
    </filter>
    <logging>
        <log type="coverage-html"
         target="coverage_dir/Foggyline_Helpdesk/test-
         reports/coverage" charset="UTF-8"
         yui="true" highlight="true"/>
    </logging>
</phpunit>
```

 We are making a special XML configuration file for our module alone because we want to quickly run a few of the tests contained within our module alone and not the entire Magento app/code folder.

Given that the actual art of writing unit tests is beyond the scope of this book and writing the full unit test with 100 percent code coverage for this simple module would require at least a dozen more pages, we will only write a single test, one that covers the Ticket entity model class.

We define our Ticket entity model class test under the app/code/Foggyline/ Helpdesk/Test/Unit/Model/TicketTest.php file as follows:

```php
<?php

namespace Foggyline\Helpdesk\Test\Unit\Model;

class TicketTest extends \PHPUnit_Framework_TestCase
{
    protected $objectManager;
    protected $ticket;
```

```
    public function setUp()
    {
        $this->objectManager = new
          \Magento\Framework\TestFramework\Unit\Helper
          \ObjectManager($this);
        $this->ticket = $this->objectManager->
          getObject('Foggyline\Helpdesk\Model\Ticket');
    }


    public function testGetSeveritiesOptionArray()
    {
        $this-> assertNotEmpty(\Foggyline
          \Helpdesk\Model\Ticket::getSeveritiesOptionArray());
    }


    public function testGetStatusesOptionArray()
    {
        $this->assertNotEmpty(\Foggyline
          \Helpdesk\Model\Ticket::getStatusesOptionArray());
    }


    public function testGetStatusAsLabel()
    {
        $this->ticket->setStatus(\Foggyline\Helpdesk
          \Model\Ticket::STATUS_CLOSED);

        $this->assertEquals(
            \Foggyline\Helpdesk\Model\Ticket::$statusesOptions
              [\Foggyline\Helpdesk\Model\Ticket::STATUS_CLOSED],
            $this->ticket->getStatusAsLabel()
        );
    }


    public function testGetSeverityAsLabel()
    {
        $this->ticket->setSeverity(\Foggyline
          \Helpdesk\Model\Ticket::SEVERITY_MEDIUM);

        $this->assertEquals(
            \Foggyline\Helpdesk\Model\Ticket::$severitiesOptions
              [\Foggyline\Helpdesk\Model\Ticket::SEVERITY_MEDIUM],
            $this->ticket->getSeverityAsLabel()
        );
    }
}
```

The location of test files should map those of the files being tested. The naming of the test file should also follow the naming of the file being tested with the suffix `Test` attached to it. This means that if our `Ticket` model is located under the modules `Model/Ticket.php` file, then our test should be located under `Test/Unit/TicketTest.php`.

Our `Foggyline\Helpdesk\Test\Unit\Model\TicketTest` extends the `\PHPUnit_Framework_TestCase` class. There is a `setUp` method we need to define, which acts like a constructor, where we set up the variables and everything that requires initializing.

Using Magento `ObjectManager`, we instantiate the `Ticket` model, which is then used within the test methods. The actual test methods follow a simple naming pattern, where the name of the method from the `Ticket` model matches the *{test}+{method name}* from the `TicketTest` class.

We defined four test methods: `testGetSeveritiesOptionArray`, `testGetStatusesOptionArray`, `testGetStatusAsLabel`, and `testGetSeverityAsLabel`. Within the test methods, we are using only `assertEquals` and `assertNotEmpty` methods from the PHPUnit testing framework library to do basic checks.

We can now open a console, change the directory to our Magento installation directory, and execute the following command:

```
phpunit -c dev/tests/unit/phpunit-foggyline-helpdesk.xml
```

After the command executes, the console should show an output as shown:

```
PHPUnit 4.7.6 by Sebastian Bergmann and contributors.

. . . .


Time: 528 ms, Memory: 11.50Mb


OK (4 tests, 4 assertions)


Generating code coverage report in HTML format ... done
```

Looking back at our `dev/tests/unit/phpunit-foggyline-helpdesk.xml` file, under the `target` attribute of the `phpunit > logging > log` element, we can see that the test report is dumped into the `coverage_dir/Foggyline_Helpdesk/test-reports/coverage` folder relative to the XML file.

If we open the `dev/tests/unit/coverage_dir/Foggyline_Helpdesk/test-reports/coverage/` folder, we should see a whole lot of files generated there, as shown in the following screenshot:

Opening the `index.html` file in the browser should give us a page as shown in the following screenshot:

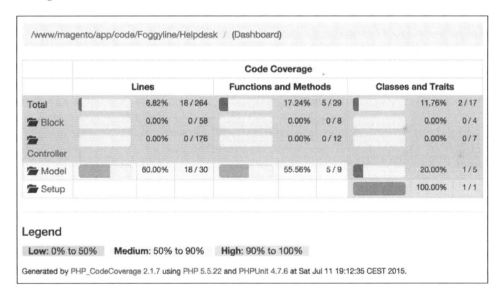

We can see the code coverage report showing 60% on lines and methods for our `Model` folder and 0% for the rest. This is because we only wrote the test for the `Ticket` entity model class, whereas the rest remain untested.

Summary

This chapter gave a full step-by-step guide to writing a simple yet functional Magento module. Seemingly simple in terms of functionality, we can see that the module code is significantly scattered across multiple PHP, XML, and PHMTL files.

With this simple module, we covered quite a lot of various Magento platform parts, from routes, ACLs, controllers, blocks, XML layouts, grids, controller actions, models, resources, collections, install scripts, interactions with session, e-mail templates, e-mail transport, and layout objects.

At the end, we wrote a few simple unit tests for our models. Although the practice is to write unit tests for all of our PHP code, we opted for a shorter version or else we would need more pages to cover everything.

The full module code is available here: `https://github.com/ajzele/B05032-Foggyline_Helpdesk`.

With this being the last chapter, let us look at a short overview of the things we learned throughout the whole book. Our journey started by grasping the Magento platform architecture, where we gained significant insight into the technology stack behind it. We then progressed to environment management. Although it might seem like a wrong order of things, we opted for this next step in order to quickly get us set for development. We then looked into programming concepts and conventions, which served as a precursor to actual hands-on development bits. Details of entity persistence were shown through model, resource, collection classes, and indexers. We further covered the importance and practical details of dependency injection and interception. Backend and frontend-related development was covered in their own two chapters, outlining the most common bits and pieces for making customizations to our Magento platform. We then dug into details of the web API, showing how to make authenticated API calls and even define our own APIs. Along the way, we covered a few major functional areas as well, such as customers, reports, import export, cart, and so on. The testing and QA took up a significant chunk as we briefly covered all forms of available tests. Finally, we used what we learned to build a fully functional module.

Although we have covered a significant path on our journey, this is merely a first step. Given its massive code base, diverse technology stacks, and feature list, Magento is not an easy platform to master. Hopefully, this book will give enough incentive to take further steps into profiling ourselves as true Magento experts.

Index

module filesystem structure 8, 9
persistence layer 4
presentation layer 3
service layer 3
top-level filesystem structure 4-7
Magento Testing Framework (MTF)
about 2, 314
requirements 314
URL 3
miniature module
creating 62, 63
EAV model, creating 66-68
simple model, creating 64-66
modernizr
URL 190
module
registering 329-331
module requirements
defining 327, 328
moment.js
URL 191

N

NetBeans PHP 184
new entities
creating 88, 89
notification messages
defining 124-127

O

OAuth 1.0a handshake process 202
OAuth-based authentication
defining 207-213
OAuth-based Web API calls
defining 213-217
OAuth client
URL 209
object manager 102, 103
Object Relational Mapping (ORM) 61
observers
defining 138-142

P

performance testing
defining 312-314
PHP
URL 58
PHP coding standard 58
PHP OOP 2
PhpStorm 184
PHPUnit
URL 379
PHPUnit testing framework 308
plugin
about 113
creating 114-116
plugin sort order 119
production environment
access, setting up for S3 usage 22
Amazon Web Services (AWS) 20, 22
bash script, for automated EC2 setup 30-34
S3, setting up for database and media files
    backup 28-30
setting up 20
products and customers Import
defining 275-279
profiler
about 136-138
defining 137, 138
enabling 136
Prototype
URL 190

R

relational database management system
    (RDBMS) 2
Representational State Transfer. *See* **REST**
RequireJS
URL 190
REST
versus SOAP 202, 203

S

schema flow
  defining 69, 70
Search Criteria Interface
  used, for list filtering 250-254
service contract 3, 52-54
session 127-132
session-based authentication
  defining 217, 218
Slide Repository Interface 225
SOAP
  versus REST 202, 203
SoapClient 203
software testing 305
standards
  URL 59
static testing
  defining 310
Symfony 2
system configuration file (system.xml)
  creating 335-338

T

templates 181, 182
tests
  dynamic 305
  static 305
test types
  defining 305-307
themes, view elements
  about 186
  new theme, creating 187-190
token-based authentication
  defining 203-206

U

Ui component 192
Underscore.js
  URL 191
unit testing
  creating 379-383
  defining 308, 309
  writing 318-325

upgrade data script (UpgradeData.php)
  creating 83-85
upgrade schema script
    (UpgradeSchema.php)
  creating 78, 79
user types
  about 198-201
  administrator or integration 198
  customer 198
  guest user 198

V

Vagrant
  about 12
  URL 12
Vagrant project
  about 13-16
  Apache, provisioning 17
  Magento installation, provisioning 18, 19
  MySQL, provisioning 17
  PHP, provisioning 16
var directory 57
view elements
  about 167
  block architecture 174-180
  blocks 172-174
  containers 169, 170
  CSS 194, 195
  JavaScript 190-192
  layouts 183-186
  life cycle 174-180
  templates 181, 182
  themes 186
  Ui components 167, 168
VirtualBox
  about 12
  URL 12
virtual types
  about 110
  using 110
VMware 12

W

Web Service Definition
        Language (WSDL) 203
widgets
  defining 146-149

Y

Yum 47

Z

Zend Framework 2

Thank you for buying
Magento 2 Developer's Guide

About Packt Publishing

Packt, pronounced 'packed', published its first book, *Mastering phpMyAdmin for Effective MySQL Management*, in April 2004, and subsequently continued to specialize in publishing highly focused books on specific technologies and solutions.

Our books and publications share the experiences of your fellow IT professionals in adapting and customizing today's systems, applications, and frameworks. Our solution-based books give you the knowledge and power to customize the software and technologies you're using to get the job done. Packt books are more specific and less general than the IT books you have seen in the past. Our unique business model allows us to bring you more focused information, giving you more of what you need to know, and less of what you don't.

Packt is a modern yet unique publishing company that focuses on producing quality, cutting-edge books for communities of developers, administrators, and newbies alike. For more information, please visit our website at www.packtpub.com.

About Packt Open Source

In 2010, Packt launched two new brands, Packt Open Source and Packt Enterprise, in order to continue its focus on specialization. This book is part of the Packt Open Source brand, home to books published on software built around open source licenses, and offering information to anybody from advanced developers to budding web designers. The Open Source brand also runs Packt's Open Source Royalty Scheme, by which Packt gives a royalty to each open source project about whose software a book is sold.

Writing for Packt

We welcome all inquiries from people who are interested in authoring. Book proposals should be sent to author@packtpub.com. If your book idea is still at an early stage and you would like to discuss it first before writing a formal book proposal, then please contact us; one of our commissioning editors will get in touch with you.

We're not just looking for published authors; if you have strong technical skills but no writing experience, our experienced editors can help you develop a writing career, or simply get some additional reward for your expertise.

Mastering Magento

ISBN: 978-1-84951-694-5   Paperback: 300 pages

Maximize the power of Magento: for developers, designers, and store owners

1. Learn how to customize your Magento store for maximum performance.

2. Exploit little known techniques for extending and tuning your Magento installation.

3. Step-by-step guides for making your store run faster, better, and more productively.

Magento Beginner's Guide

Second Edition

ISBN: 978-1-78216-270-4   Paperback: 320 pages

Learn how to create a fully featured, attractive online store with the most powerful open source solution for e-commerce

1. Install, configure, and manage your own e-commerce store.

2. Extend and customize your store to reflect your brand and personality.

3. Handle tax, shipping, and custom orders.

Please check **www.PacktPub.com** for information on our titles

15771775R00228

Printed in Great Britain
by Amazon